THE NIGHT BATTLES

Also by Carlo Ginzburg

The Cheese and the Worms
The Cosmos of a Sixteenth-Century Miller

Clues, Myths, and the Historical Method

Both translated by John and Anne Tedeschi

The Night Battles

Witchcraft & Agrarian Cults in the Sixteenth & Seventeenth Centuries

Carlo Ginzburg

Translated by John & Anne Tedeschi

The Johns Hopkins University Press
Baltimore, Maryland

Originally published in Italy as *I Benandanti: Stregoneria e culti agrari tra Cinquecento e Seicento,* copyright © 1966 Giulio Einaudi editore

Printed in the United States of America on acid-free paper

First published in the United States of America in 1983 by
The Johns Hopkins University Press
2715 North Charles Street
Baltimore, Maryland 21218-4363
www.press.jhu.edu

Johns Hopkins Paperbacks edition, 1992
9 8 7

LIBRARY OF CONGRESS CATALOGING-IN-PUBLICATION DATA

Ginsburg, Carlo.
The night battles.
Translation of: I benandanti.
Includes bibliographical references and index.
1. Friuli (Italy : Province)—Religious life and customs. 2. Witchcraft—Italy—Friuli (Province)
I. Title.
BL′980.I8G5613 1983 398′.41′094539 83-48061
ISBN 0-8018-4386-3 ISBN 0-8018-2605-5

C'est l'auberge fameuse inscrite sur le livre,
Où l'on pourra manger, et dormir, et s'asseoir.

BAUDELAIRE, *La mort des pauvres*

CONTENTS

Foreword by Eric Hobsbawm *ix*
Translators' note *xi*
Preface to the English edition *xiii*
Preface to the Italian edition *xvii*

I The night battles *1*
II The processions of the dead *33*
III The benandanti between inquisitors and witches *69*
IV The benandanti at the sabbat *99*

Appendix *147*
Notes *173*
Index of names *205*

FOREWORD

Some time in the late sixteenth century the attention of a perplexed Church was drawn to the prevalence of a curious practice in the region of the Friuli, where German, Italian and Slav customs meet. This was the ritual association of the 'good walkers', a body of men chosen from those born with the caul, who fell into a trance or deep sleep on certain nights of the year while their souls (sometimes in the form of small animals) left their bodies so that they could do battle, armed with stalks of fennel, against analogous companies of male witches for the fate of the season's crops. They also performed cures and other kinds of benevolent magic. Carlo Ginzburg argues that theirs was a fertility ritual once widespread throughout central Europe, but by this period perhaps flourishing mainly in marginal regions such as the Friuli (and Lithuania, whence a strictly similar institution of benevolent werewolves is recorded from the late seventeenth century), and suggests Slav or even Ural-Altaic influences, which must be left to the judgment of experts in popular religion.

However, the real interest of his extremely lucidly written book lies elsewhere. The Holy Inquisition (not unhampered both by its representatives' ignorance of the Friulian dialect and the suspicions of the Venetian Republic) did not quite know what to make of the 'good walkers'. It therefore attempted to assimilate them to the well-classified and heretical practice of witchcraft, and to press its victims to admit their participation in the diabolist sabbaths. What is more, it succeeded. A series of inquisitions and trials stretching from the 1570s to the 1640s, details of which Signor Ginzburg has extracted from a variety of archives, show the 'good walkers' gradually assimilating themselves to witches (though attempting to maintain their benevolent functions) under the pressure of the now alerted Church. It was no doubt fortunate for them that their conversion into witches came too late for serious persecution. The main effect of the Church's intervention in traditional peasant practices appears in this instance to have been to lead to their decadence.

The story is local, but its relevance to the general study of the 'witch-cult' is obvious. For here we have not Margaret Murray's subterranean old religion hostile to Christianity but ritual practices which had long established a symbiosis with the dominant religion – the *benandanti* originally regarded themselves as champions of Christ against the devil – but which are forced into opposition (one of the accused thought their practices were similar to those of the 'Turks, Jews and Heretics') by Church policy.

Yet the interest of Carlo Ginzburg's book lies not merely in the light it throws on religion, magic and witchcraft in the sixteenth and seventeenth centuries, a subject much written about since 1966, but still a rather specialized one. His primary concern is to 'reconstruct the peasant mentality of the period'. Writing the history of those whose opinions are rarely documented has become an extremely popular practice in recent years. Justifiably so, since they constitute the great majority of humanity. It is Ginzburg's merit to have recognized, long before Le Roy Ladurie's *Montaillou*, that – contrary to what has often been assumed – the documents of the Inquisition allow us to catch the voices of its victims and to reconstruct their intellectual universe, public and private. It takes a highly skilled and, above all, an imaginative historian to do so. But those who have read Ginzburg's later book *The Cheese and the Worms* will not need to be told that he is both. In this early work he has written a study which will fascinate and stimulate all historians of the popular mind. Fortunately it will find many more of them to stimulate in 1983 than in the pioneer days of 1966.

E.J. Hobsbawm

TRANSLATORS' NOTE

We are very pleased to have been offered the opportunity, with *The Night Battles*, of presenting to the English reader a second work by the innovative Italian social historian, Carlo Ginzburg. Actually, the present book, which quickly became a classic in the historiography of witchcraft after it first appeared with its original Italian title *I Benandanti* in 1966, preceded by more than a decade *The Cheese and the Worms*, Ginzburg's pioneering study in popular culture. These two works represent only a small part of the best of the new social, cultural and religious history being written today by a host of distinguished Italian scholars. The agenda of future translations should be a long one.

A few words of explanation about our English version may be helpful. There are a number of seeming inconsistencies among name forms but these occurred in the original documents, written in an age before orthography had become standardized, and we simply retained them. Unless it was clear that a name was a family name (and the instances of this were few), rather than a Christian name with the addition of a place for identification, we have used the form, 'Agnabella of San Lorenzo', etc. The exception to this is for ecclesiastics whose places of origin often became a permanent name by which they were henceforth known: thus, Bernardino da Siena.

We have appropriated from the Italian the words benandante/benandanti, the singular and plural forms, to designate the members of the fertility cult who are the subject of this book. A literal translation of the word would be 'those who go well' or 'good-doers'. We have also typically used 'witch' in the broader sense for both males and females, unless the Italian text mentioned together both *strega* and *stregone* which we then rendered as 'witch' and 'warlock'.

As we noted in detail in our preface to Ginzburg's *The Cheese and the Worms*, the wording in the inquisitorial trial records was transposed by the notary of the court from direct testimony to speech in the third person, and questions and answers were transformed into an indirect form of discourse. Nevertheless the author was obliged to put these passages within quotation marks, even though in this indirect form, because they are taken directly from the original documents.

Our translation, with the exception of one deleted paragraph (pp. 46–7) reproduces the Einaudi 1974 second edition of *I Benandanti*. In addition to Ginzburg's new preface for the English edition, only a handful of new bibliographical references have been added by the translators. No attempt has been made, otherwise, to update the apparatus. In the Index we have used full names for historical personages and writers, and initials for the first names of modern authors.

J.T.
A.C.T.

PREFACE TO THE ENGLISH EDITION

Several years after it first appeared, *I Benandanti* is being made available to English readers as *The night battles*. In the period since the book was originally published, studies on European witchcraft have proliferated, many of which have made important contributions. What was at first considered little more than a curiosity, today is a fashionably current theme of research, and new works on the subject are appearing in a steady stream. Nevertheless, all modesty aside, I believe that the present book is still of interest and perhaps more so today than fifteen years ago, capable of appealing to a wider public, and one not confined to specialists.

It was E.W. Monter who, in 1969, drew attention in very generous terms to the *I Benandanti*,[1] thereby introducing into international scholarly discussion this monograph dealing with a peripheral area (the Friuli) written in a language which today is also peripheral (Italian). In his review Monter observed that the documents which I had collected and studied furnished unexpected support for the old (and discredited) thesis of M. Murray which regarded witchcraft as a fertility cult. Elsewhere, Monter explained that what had been confirmed was only part of Murray's thesis.[2] This was an important qualification: Murray, in fact, had asserted: (a) that witchcraft had its roots in an ancient fertility cult, and (b) that the sabbat described in the witchcraft trials referred to gatherings which had actually taken place.[3] What my work really demonstrated, even if unintentionally, was simply the first point. While there is an indisputable connection between benandanti and fertility cults (in this respect, I think, we should acknowledge the 'kernel of truth' in Murray's thesis), no document allows us to conclude with certainty that the benandanti actually met on set occasions to perform the rites described in their confessions.[4] Certain scholars, to be sure, have claimed for the benandanti that 'no firmer bit of evidence has ever been presented that witchcraft existed', (J.B. Russell) or that 'they remain to date the only authenticated witch cult in early modern Europe', (H.C. Erik Midelfort).[5] I consider this interpretation unfounded if it infers from the link between benandanti and fertility cults the physical existence of an organized sect of witches. Equally unjustified on the other hand, in my opinion, is the assurance with which N. Cohn, in a polemic with Russell (and also because of a misinterpretation of my book) concluded that 'the experiences of the benandanti . . . were all trance experiences.'[6] On the basis of the available documents, the existence or non-existence of an organized sect of witches in fifteenth- to seventeenth-century Europe seems to be indeterminate. It is a dilemma, however, which to my eyes at least has only relative importance. Those who believe the contrary (and they are still the vast majority of scholars dealing with this subject) remain unconsciously bound to the view taken by those long-ago judges, ecclesiastical or secular, who asked themselves before all else whether the accused had participated *physically* in the diabolical gatherings. Even if the sabbat had been a purely mental phenomenon (and this cannot be proved) its importance for the historian would not be diminished.

This point should be stressed because the benandanti have been discussed too often in witchcraft studies for the wrong reasons. No one has cast doubt on the unprecedented richness of the materials gathered and analysed here. But the exceptional nature of the documents has no bearing on the question of the physical reality of the witches' congregations. This has to be searched for in a totally different direction: the gap between the questions of the judges and the confessions of the accused which was gradually reduced only in the course of decades. To his credit, P. Burke has seen in the use I have made of this gap a device by which, through broader application, the student of popular culture may circumvent the limitations inherent in judicial sources.[7] In the present case it was possible to achieve an in-depth analysis (which if I am not mistaken seems to have remained a somewhat isolated effort in the study of European witchcraft) of a stratum of popular beliefs which the inquisitors could only slowly make coincide with their own preconceived ideas. The extraordinary characteristics of the group of documents collected here make possible this reconstruction from within (from the point of view of the benandanti) and demonstrates that the history of witchcraft need not be limited to the study of its repression. Popular beliefs relative to witchcraft – 'mental rubbish of peasant credulity and feminine hysteria' as Trevor-Roper scornfully defined them – are neither 'universal' (and therefore lacking specificity) nor unworthy of study.[8] Today, the emergence of the feminist movement, the interest in popular culture and the vogue of the occult make this quite obvious. For this reason, a review of some of the difficulties which research of this type encounters may serve a useful purpose.

We can try then to extend the type of analysis adopted for the benandanti: but with what results? If the phenomenon of the benandanti had been an episode with totally anomalous characteristics, strictly circumscribed in time and space, the unusual nature of the documentation would also have to be accepted in a diminished sense. Its importance for the history of European witchcraft would be, all in all, quite negligible.

Here too it is essential to make distinctions. The process of acculturation through which diabolical witchcraft was superimposed on beliefs, such as those of the benandanti, was not a phenomenon restricted to the Friuli. There are obvious parallels with the cult of Diana in Modena which unfortunately cannot be pursued systematically because adequate sources are lacking. Consequently, the story of the benandanti sheds a great deal of light on the ways in which the image of diabolical witchcraft as envisioned by demonologists, judges and inquisitors gained ascendancy in Europe. (Beginning from what? we ask ourselves at this point. This is a question I would like to pursue in another work.)

It is difficult, however, to find analogies outside the Friuli with the complex of ideas which emerges with such a wealth of details in the accounts of the benandanti. Nevertheless, many more parallels could be added to those which are already noted in the following pages. In particular, the connection between the benandanti and shamans alluded to in the original preface, and confirmed by M. Eliade, could be developed further.[9] I intend to attempt this in the book mentioned above. In some respects, it will integrate, and in others continue, on a vaster chronological and spatial scale, the research which began with *The night battles*.

C.G.
Bologna, 1982

PREFACE TO THE ITALIAN EDITION

In this book I have studied the religious attitudes and, in a broad sense, the mentality of a peasant society – the Friulian – between the end of the sixteenth century and the first half of the seventeenth, but from an extremely limited point of view: the history of a nucleus of popular beliefs, which little by little, as a result of specific forces, became assimilated by witchcraft. It is an episode in history that has been unknown until now, but one which casts a great deal of light on the general problem of witchcraft and its persecution.

A rich variety of individual attitudes and behaviour emerges from the sources analysed. In dwelling on them, one risks plunging into an excess of the picturesque. Nevertheless, I've preferred to run this risk rather than make use at every step of such general and vague terms as 'collective mentality', or 'collective psychology'. This Friulian testimony reveals a continuous criss-crossing of trends enduring for decades and even centuries, and of individual, private, and frequently wholly unconscious, reactions. It is apparently impossible to make history from such reactions, and yet without them, the history of 'collective mentalities' becomes nothing more than a series of disembodied and abstract tendencies and forces.

The principal characteristic of this documentation is its immediacy. Except for the fact that the notaries of the Holy Office translated the testimony from Friulian into Italian, it is fair to say that the voices of these peasants reach us directly, without barriers, not by way, as usually happens, of fragmentary and indirect testimony, filtered through a different and inevitably distorting mentality.

Such a statement may seem paradoxical, and this leads to the specific interest of the research. We have become accustomed to accepting the confessions of those accused of witchcraft as the consequences of torture and of suggestive questioning by the judges, and thus denying that they possess any element of spontaneity. The fundamental investigations of J. Hansen,[1] more precisely, have demonstrated how the image of diabolical witchcraft, with all its appendages – the pact with the devil, the sabbat, the profanation of the sacraments – was developed between the mid-thirteenth and mid-fifteenth centuries largely through the efforts of theologians and inquisitors, and gradually spread by means of treatises, sermons, depictions, throughout Europe and, eventually, even across the Atlantic.[2] This transformation, or rather, closer to the truth, superimposition of the inquisitorial schema on a pre-existent stratum of generic superstitions, occurred in a particularly dramatic form during the trials themselves, through the moulding of the confessions of the accused by means of the two devices mentioned above: torture and 'suggestive' questioning. All this, as we have said, has been documented exhaustively, but almost always at the educated level in the elaboration of doctrine. F. Byloff's attempt[3] to demonstrate, in a well-defined geographical area, the penetration into the popular mentality of diabolical witchcraft as formed by inquisitors and demonologists, achieved meagre results. The exceptional richness of the Friulian sources permits us to reconstruct this process with much greater precision and clarity. It reveals how a cult with such obviously popular characteristics as that of the benandanti gradually was transformed under inquisitorial pressure, ending up with the distinctive features of traditional witchcraft. But this discrepancy, this gap between the image underlying the interrogations of the judges and the actual testimony of the accused, permits us to reach a genuinely popular stratum of beliefs which was later deformed, and then expunged by the superimposition of the schema of the educated classes. Because of this discrepancy, which endured over several decades, the benandanti trials constitute a precious source for the reconstruction of the peasant mentality of this period.

Thus, the goal of the present research is to document and build upon the approach to the question originally developed by Hansen. What is new about this effort, even if limited in scope, is the contribution that it can make to our understanding of the significance and nature of popular witchcraft, as distinguished from the learned conceptions of inquisitorial origin. The debates of the Enlightenment (exemplified in Italy by a Tartarotti[4]) obviously, and understandably, were not interested in the confessions of the witches: what really counted was to be able to disclose the barbarity and irrationality of the persecutions. The accounts of the witches were passed over as absurd fantasies or confessions extorted by the cruelty and superstition of the judges. A first attempt at serious interpretation came with the erudite researches of the second half of the nineteenth century, which generally viewed the witches' confessions as the results of hallucinations caused by the use of drug-containing ointments, or from pathological states, especially hysteria. But the most well-researched and best documented studies endeavoured principally – often in a more or less explicit spirit of anti-Catholic or anti-clerical polemic – to explain the events and the mechanism of the persecution.

A real interest in the beliefs of the witches, or presumed witches, themselves is not encountered (if we exclude Michelet's romantic admiration for the 'rebellious' witch[5]) until the researches of the English Egyptologist, M. Murray.[6] A follower of J. Frazer, and therefore interested in questions of magic and the mentality of 'primitives', Murray did not limit herself to underscoring the importance of the confessions of the witchcraft suspects from an ethnological or folkloristic point of view. Paradoxically overthrowing the accepted approach – which was actually more an instinctive attitude than a reasoned approach – she re-evaluated the trustworthiness of those confessions (in the positivistic sense of the *external* reliability of a source). According to Murray, the conventicles described by the accused were real, and witchcraft was a very ancient religion, a pre-Christian fertility cult, in which the judges, more or less deliberately, chose to see only a diabolical perversion. Although this thesis contained a kernel of truth, it was formulated in a wholly uncritical way;[7] moreover, the reconstruction of the general characteristics of this supposed fertility cult was based on very late trials in which the assimilation of the inquisitorial schema (sabbat, nuptials with the devil, etc.) was by now complete. And yet, despite these serious defects, Murray's 'thesis', which was rejected by anthropologists and folklorists when it first appeared, ended by prevailing. What had been lacking then, and the need persists today if I'm not mistaken, was an all-encompassing explanation of popular witchcraft: and the thesis of the English scholar, purified of its most daring affirmations, seemed plausible where it discerned in the orgies of the sabbat the deformation of an ancient fertility rite. In this mitigated form it was reformulated by W.E. Peuckert, among others.[8]

And yet it is not easy to demonstrate that popular witchcraft (as distinct from generic superstitions, such as love potions, spells, etc., which are not traceable to a precise cult) actually went back to an ancient agricultural and fertility cult. One primary objection has already been raised about Murray's work: we cannot rely uncritically on the confessions of the witches without attempting to distinguish in them between what is of inquisitorial provenance and what is of genuinely popular origin. But this is not a fatal objection. J. Marx had already noted the existence of a cluster of beliefs which, while of unequivocally popular origin, nevertheless resembled, to some extent, the witches' sabbat pictured by theologians and inquisitors.[9] More recently, L. Weiser-Aall has placed great weight on the existence of this point of contact between popular and learned witchcraft,[10] in regard to beliefs first recorded for the tenth century, but unquestionably of much earlier origin.[11] These involve mysterious nocturnal flights, especially by women, to gatherings where there is no trace of the devil, of the profanation of sacraments or of apostasy from the faith – conventicles over which a feminine divinity presided, called, in turn, Diana, Herodias, Holda or Perchta. Does the presence of goddesses linked to vegetation, such as Perchta or Diana, mean that the beliefs underlying later diabolical witchcraft lead back to fertility cults? It is a plausible hypothesis, but one that has not yet been satisfactorily demonstrated, despite the efforts of a German scholar, A. Mayer,[12] who, in my opinion, has come closer than anyone else to formulating the question correctly. Nevertheless, even his attempt, founded as it was on thin and insufficient evidence, basically failed. Moreover, a second objection can be raised against it, and this one is not so easy to answer. Like Murray, Mayer did not explain why witches, priestesses in this presumed fertility cult, appeared from the beginning (and not only in the later manifestations of witchcraft which had been deformed by the judges) portrayed as enemies of the harvests, deliverers of hail and storms, carriers of sterility to humans and beasts alike.[13]

The present research now establishes, in an area such as the Friuli, where Germanic and Slavic traditions came together, the positive existence at a relatively late date (from *c.* 1570) of a fertility cult whose participants, the benandanti, represented themselves as defenders of harvests and the fertility of fields. On the one hand, this belief is tied to a larger complex of traditions (connected, in turn, with the myth of nocturnal gatherings over which female deities named Perchta, Holda, Diana presided) in an area that extends from Alsace to Hesse and from Bavaria to Switzerland. On the other hand, it is found in an almost identical form in the lands which once comprised Livonia (present day Latvia and Estonia). Given this geographic spread it may not be too daring to suggest that in antiquity these beliefs must once have covered much of central Europe. In the span of a century, as we shall see, the benandanti were transformed into witches and their nocturnal gatherings, intended to induce fertility, became the devil's sabbat, with the resulting storms and destruction. We can thus state for a fact that for the Friuli diabolical witchcraft grew out of the deformation of a preceding agrarian cult. Of course, it is impossible to extend this conclusion by simple analogy to other parts of Europe; nevertheless, though limited and circumscribed, it may serve as a working hypothesis for future research. At any rate the existence of this complex of beliefs over a large, key area implies, in my opinion, a new approach to the problem of the popular origins of witchcraft.

Folklorists and historians of religion will be able to draw much larger inferences from this documentary material, while correcting my errors, filling in lacunae and making greater use of the comparative method. As we will see, I have made only very cautious use of the latter; or, to be more precise, I have availed myself of only one of the two comparative methods identified by M. Bloch: the more strictly historical one. Thus, I have not dealt with the question of the relationship which undoubtedly must exist between benandanti and shamans.[14] This sums up the basic characteristics and limitations of the present plan of research.

There are no studies of any kind on the benandanti. Investigations which have been concerned with Friulian popular traditions, either for scholarly or antiquarian reasons – by G. Marcotti, E. Fabris Bellavitis, V. Ostermann, A. Lazzarini, G. Vidossi and others – have treated the term 'benandante' as synonymous with 'witch', without perceiving the underlying historical problem.[15] This was due neither to neglect nor to faulty analysis. Rather, it was because these studies were limited (for perfectly valid reasons, such as the difficulty of access to the sources in the archive of the Curia Arcivescovile in Udine) to testimony that was oral, or at least not older than the end of the last century or beginning of the present one. In reality, the identification of 'benandante' with 'witch' constitutes, as will be seen, only the final crystallized stage in a complex, contradictory process which can be reconstructed quite precisely in its various phases.

The present work was made possible, in a sense, by a methodology that differed from the traditional one of folklore, a departure that has been deliberately accentuated in the course of the research. In fact, I have attempted to penetrate behind the apparent uniformity of these beliefs and grasp the various attitudes of the men and women who lived by them, and how they were altered under influences of several kinds, both of popular and inquisitorial provenance. The specifically folkloristic aspects of the problem have thus been strictly subordinated to an emphatically historical approach.

I have been helped by many people in the course of this study: it is impossible to thank them all. I shall mention those who directly or indirectly have facilitated my access to the sources: first of all Monsignor Pio Paschini (deceased); Monsignor Guglielmo Biasutti (in a very particular way) and Monsignor Garlatti, respectively librarian and chancellor of the Curia Arcivescovile in Udine; Monsignor Romeo De Maio of the Vatican Library; Father Massimiliano Peloza; Vinko Foretić, former director of the Archive of State in Dubrovnik; Angelo Tamborra, Paolo Sambin and Marino Berengo. I should also like to thank the Fondazione Luigi Einaudi which provided me with a fellowship in 1962, and Norberto Bobbio, Luigi Firpo, Aldo Garosci and Franco Venturi who followed my work in that period. The Warburg Institute in London, at the suggestion of the former and highly esteemed Gertrud Bing, gave me in the summer of 1964 the possibility of using its library, an unparalleled instrument of research: I should like to thank its director, E.H. Gombrich, for unforgettable hospitality, and O. Kurz and A.A. Barb for their advice and suggestions. Encouragement to pursue this investigation came from a meeting with the now deceased Ernesto De Martino. An early version of this work was presented and discussed as a thesis at the Scuola Normale Superiore in Pisa in the spring of 1964: I am grateful for their criticisms and suggestions to Armando Saitta, and the other examiners, Arsenio Frugoni and Cinzio Violante. Other assistance and advice is acknowledged in the course of the volume.

Delio Cantimori read the first draft of this book. For his invaluable counsel, and for everything that I have learned from him, it is a pleasure to express to him my deepest gratitude.

C.G.
Rome, 1965

I THE NIGHT BATTLES

1

On 21 March 1575, in the monastery of San Francesco di Cividale in the Friuli, there appeared before the vicar general, Monsignor Jacopo Maracco, and Fra Giulio d'Assisi of the Order of the Minor Conventuals, inquisitor in the dioceses of Aquileia and Concordia, a witness, Don Bartolomeo Sgabarizza, who was a priest in the neighbouring village of Brazzano.[1] He reported a strange occurrence of the week before. He had heard from a miller of Brazzano, a certain Pietro Rotaro, whose son was dying from a mysterious ailment, that in an adjacent village, Iassico, there lived a man named Paolo Gasparutto who cured bewitched people and said that 'he roamed about at night with witches and goblins'.[2] His curiosity aroused, the priest, Sgabarizza, had summoned the fellow. Gasparutto admitted that he had told the father of the sick child that 'this little boy had been possessed by witches, but at the time of the witchery, the vagabonds were about and they snatched him from the witches' hands, and if they had not done so he would have died.' And afterwards he had given the parent a secret charm which could cure the boy. Pressed by Sgabarizza's questioning, Gasparutto said that 'on Thursdays during the Ember Days of the year they were forced to go with these witches to many places, such as Cormons, in front of the church at Iassico, and even into the countryside about Verona,' where 'they fought, played, leaped about, and rode various animals, and did different things among themselves; and . . . the women beat the men who were with them with sorghum stalks, while the men had only bunches of fennel.'[3]

Disconcerted by these strange tales, the good priest immediately went to Cividale to consult with the inquisitor and the patriarch's vicar; and chancing upon Gasparutto again, conducted him to the monastery of San Francesco. In the presence of the father inquisitor, Gasparutto readily confirmed his account and furnished new details about the mysterious nocturnal meetings: 'when the witches, warlocks, and vagabonds return from these games all hot and tired, as they pass in front of houses, when they find clear, clean water in pails they drink it, if not they also go into the cellars and overturn all the wine'; therefore, warned Gasparutto, addressing Sgabarizza, one must always have clean water on hand in the house. And since the priest did not believe him, Gasparutto offered to include him, along with the father inquisitor, in the mysterious gatherings: there were to be two before Easter, and 'having promised, one was then obliged to go.' And he declared that there were others who attended these reunions at Brazzano, Iassico, Cormons, Gorizia, and Cividale, but their names could not be revealed, because 'he had been badly beaten by the witches for having spoken about these things.' Trying confusedly to make some sense out of Gasparutto's tales, Sgabarizza concluded that there existed, or so it appeared, witches like Gasparutto himself, 'who are good, called vagabonds and in their own words benandanti . . . who prevent evil' while other witches 'commit it'.[4]

A few days went by. On 7 April, the priest of Brazzano reappeared before the Holy Office and reported that he had gone to Iassico to say Mass the Monday after Easter, and that he had run into Gasparutto there. After the Mass, as was customary, the priest had gone to a feast prepared in his honour. 'During the meal,' said Sgabarizza, 'I spoke about matters appropriate to the season, that is, guarding against sin and pursuing good and holy works.' But Gasparutto, who was present in his capacity as *commissario* (he must have been well-off: elsewhere there is a possible reference to his servants[5]), interrupted him to describe exploits of the usual company the night before: 'They crossed several great bodies of water in a boat, and . . . at the river Iudri[6] one of his companions became afraid because a fierce wind had come up, and the waters were rough, and he remained behind the others . . .; and . . . they were in the countryside not far away, and they jousted and busied themselves with their usual pastimes.' The priest, his curiosity greatly aroused, had not been able to contain himself: 'I brought him home with me, and treated him kindly so as to draw other details out of him, if I could.' But this was to no avail.[7]

The substance of Sgabarizza's depositions was confirmed by Pietro Rotaro, father of the child treated, though in vain, by Paolo Gasparutto. When Rotaro suspected that his son had been bewitched, he had appealed to Paolo, since the latter 'is known to go about with these witches and to be one of the benandanti'.[8] Also Gasparutto had talked at length with him about the nocturnal gatherings:[9]

> 'Sometimes they go out to one country region and sometimes to another, perhaps to Gradisca or even as far away as Verona, and they appear together jousting and playing games; and . . . the men and women who are the evil-doers carry and use the sorghum stalks which grow in the fields, and the men and women who are benandanti use fennel stalks; and they go now one day and now another, but always on Thursdays, and . . . when they make their great displays they go to the biggest farms, and they have days fixed for this; and when the warlocks and witches set out it is to do evil, and they must be pursued by the benandanti to thwart them, and also to stop them from entering the houses, because if they do not find clear water in the pails they go into the cellars and spoil the wine with certain things, throwing filth in the bungholes.'

At the judges' request, Rotaro added details about the way Gasparutto had said he went to these gatherings, namely, as we shall see later on, 'in spirit', and astride such animals as hares, cats, and so on. Rotaro also had heard it said that even at Cividale there was one of these 'witches', a public crier named Battista Moduco, who, talking to friends in the square, had declared that he was a benandante and that he went forth at night, 'especially Thursdays'. At his point Troiano de'Attimis, a noble of Cividale, was called to testify. He confirmed that he had learned from his brother-in-law, chatting in the piazza, that 'some of these witches were in Brazzano, and that there was one even in Cividale, not far from us.' Then Troiano had noticed Battista Moduco nearby and had asked him:[10]

> 'And you, are you one of those witches?' He told me that he is a benandante, and that at night, especially on Thursdays, he goes with the others, and they congregate in certain places to perform marriages, to dance and eat and drink; and on their way home the evil-doers go into the cellars to drink, and then urinate in the casks. If the benandanti did not go along the wine would be spilt. And he told other tall tales like these which I did not believe, and so I did not question him further.'

The vicar general, Maracco, and the inquisitor, Giulio d'Assisi, must have agreed with the scornful conclusion of the nobleman of Cividale; tall tales and nothing more. After this deposition, in fact, the interrogations set in motion by Gasparutto's revelations were halted. They were to begin again five years later, at the initiative, as we shall see, of another inquisitor.

Vague and indirect as this evidence may be, it does none the less allow us to state with assurance that there did in fact exist in the area around Cividale, in the second half of the sixteenth century, a complex of beliefs (not limited to an individual, private sphere), that were otherwise unrecorded, and were strangely blended with well-known traditions. The witches and warlocks who congregated on Thursday nights to give themselves over to 'dancing', 'games', 'marriages', and banquets, instantly evoke the image of the sabbat – the sabbat which demonologists had minutely described and codified, and that inquisitors had condemned at least from the mid-fifteenth century.[11] And yet there are obvious differences between the gatherings described by the benandanti and the traditional popular image of the diabolical sabbat. It appears that in the former, homage was not paid to the devil (in fact, there was no reference at all to his presence), there was no abjuration of the faith, trampling of crucifixes, or defilement of sacraments.[12] The essence of these gatherings was an obscure rite: witches and warlocks armed with sorghum stalks jousting and battling with benandanti armed with fennel stalks.

Who were these benandanti? On the one hand they declared that they were opposed to witches and warlocks, and their evil designs, and that they healed the victims of injurious deeds by witches; on the other, like their presumed adversaries, they attended mysterious nocturnal reunions (about which they could not utter a word under pain of being beaten) riding hares, cats, and other animals. This ambiguity was reflected even in the language. The notion of the profound difference, even real antagonism, between witches and warlocks (that is 'men and women who commit evil') and 'men and women benandanti', seems in fact to have been difficult to grasp even at the popular level. Thus, a country priest like Sgabarizza (who at first, significantly, used a rough translation for what he considered a strange word, 'vagabonds and in their language benandanti') and the miller Pietro Rotaro spoke of 'benandanti witches' – where the adjective gained meaning only when linked to a noun already firmly established. The benandanti were witches: but 'good' witches, Sgabarizza asserted, who tried to protect children or provisions in homes from the perfidy of the evil witches. Right from the start, therefore, the benandanti appear to us in the form of a contradiction which subsequently influences profoundly the course of their existence.

3

Five years later, on 27 June 1580, a new inquisitor, Fra Felice da Montefalco,[13] revived the case left unfinished by his predecessor and ordered one of the two benandanti, Paolo Gasparutto, to appear before him. Gasparutto declared that he did not know why he had been summoned. He had been going to confession and receiving communion from his parish priest annually; he had never heard it said that at Iassico 'there is anyone who is a Lutheran and leads an evil life.'[14] When Fra Felice asked if he knew anyone who was a witch or a benandante, Gasparutto replied in the negative. And then he suddenly exploded with laughter: 'Father, no, I really do not know . . . I am not a benandante, that is not my calling.' Then the inquisitor bombarded him with questions: had he ever tried to cure the son of Pietro Rotaro? Rotaro called me, Gasparutto replied, but I told him I knew nothing about such things and I could not help him. Had he ever spoken about benandanti with the previous inquisitor and with the priest of Iassico? At first Gasparutto denied this: later he admitted, with great mirth, that he had said he dreamed of fighting witches. But in the face of incessant questioning by the inquisitor, who reminded him of details from conversations held five years before, he repeated his denials, between peals of laughter. The friar finally asked: 'Why do you laugh so much?' Unexpectedly Gasparutto replied: 'Because these are not things to inquire about, because they are against the will of God.'[15] The inquisitor, more and more baffled, persisted: 'Why is it against God's will to ask about these things?' The benandante now realized that he had gone too far: 'Because you are asking about things that I know nothing about,' he replied, and resumed his denials. The questions continued: had he ever spoken of nocturnal battles with witches, had he ever invited Sgabarizza and the inquisitor to these gatherings? His eyes shut, Gasparutto obstinately insisted that he remembered none of this. After Fra Felice recalled for him his descriptions of witches and benandanti returning exhausted from their games, and how, when they did not find water in the houses, they went into cellars, 'urinating and spoiling the wine', Gasparutto exclaimed with mocking laughter, 'Oh, what a world.' But nothing could budge him from his silence and in vain did Fra Felice promise him pardon and mercy if he would only tell the truth. At this point the interrogation ceased and Gasparutto was imprisoned.

The same day the other benandante, the public crier Battista Moduco, nicknamed *Gamba Secura* was also interrogated. Born at Trivignano, he had lived in Cividale for the previous thirty years. He too declared that he had gone to confession and taken communion regularly, and that he did not know any heretics. But when he was asked about witches and benandanti, he quietly replied: 'Of witches I do not know if there are any; and of benandanti I do not know of any others besides myself.'[16] Fra Felice immediately inquired, 'what does this word "benandante" mean?' But Moduco seemed to have regretted his hasty reply and tried to turn the matter into a joke: 'Benandanti I call those who pay me well, I go willingly.' Nevertheless, he ended up admitting that he had told several people he was a benandante, and added: 'I cannot speak about the others because I do not want to go against divine will.' (We should note at this point that there is no evidence that Moduco and Gasparutto knew each other, or had even met.) Moduco did not hesitate to say of himself:

> 'I am a benandante because I go with the others to fight four times a year, that is during the Ember Days, at night; I go invisibly in spirit and the body remains behind; we go forth in the service of Christ, and the witches of the devil; we fight each other, we with bundles of fennel and they with sorghum stalks.'

It is not difficult to imagine the inquisitor's bewilderment over these benandanti who in so many ways themselves resembled the very witches against whom they acted as defenders of Christ's faith. But Moduco had not yet finished: 'And if we are the victors, that year there is abundance, but if we lose there is famine.' Later he clarified this:[17]

> 'In the fighting that we do, one time we fight over the wheat and all the other grains, another time over the livestock, and at other times over the vineyards. And so, on four occasions we fight over all the fruits of the earth and for those things won by the benandanti that year there is abundance.'

Thus, at the core of the nocturnal gatherings of the benandanti we see a fertility rite emerging that is precisely patterned on the principal events of the agricultural year.

Moduco added that he had not belonged to the company of the benandanti for more than eight years: 'One enters at the age of twenty, and is freed at forty, if he so wishes.' Members of this 'company' are all those who 'are born with the caul . . . and when they reach the age of twenty they are summoned by means of a drum the same as soldiers, and they are obliged to respond.' Fra Felice interrupted, trying to put difficulties in the way of the benandante: 'How can it be that we know so many gentlemen who are born with the caul, and nevertheless are not vagabonds?' (We can see that the friar, almost as if to keep his distance, was trying not to use the popular term which was foreign to him.) But Moduco stood his ground: 'I am saying everybody born with the caul must go.' All this seemed incredible to the inquisitor, who insisted on knowing the truth about entry into this 'profession'; and Moduco replied simply, 'nothing else happens, except that the spirit leaves the body and goes wandering.'

The benandante's replies must have aroused serious suspicions in the mind of Fra Felice, and he asked: 'Who is it that comes to summon you, God, an angel, a man, or a devil?' 'He is a man just like us,' Moduco informed him, 'who is placed above us all and beats a drum, and calls us.' And in response to another question, he added: 'We are a great multitude, and at times we are five-thousand and more . . . some who belong to the village know one another, and others do not.' The inquisitor would not give up: 'Who placed that being above you?' 'I do not know,' said Moduco, 'but we believe that he is sent by God, because we fight for the faith of Christ.' As for the captain, 'He is head of the company until he reaches the age of forty, or until he renounces it; . . . he's from Cologne . . ., a man of twenty-eight, very tall, red-bearded, pale complexioned, of noble birth, and he has a wife'; his insignia was white, 'the flag, that is the crosspiece that he carries above him, is black.' And he added: 'Our standard bearer carries a banner of white silk stuff, gilded, with a lion,' while 'the banner of the witches is of red silk with four black devils, gilded'; and their captain has 'a black beard; he is big and tall, of the German nation': they go to do battle in various places, in the region of Azzano, near Cuniano, and sometimes 'on German soil, in certain fields near Cirghinis'.

But the inquisitor demanded still more information, and above all, the names of the other benandanti. Moduco refused: 'I would be beaten by the entire company,' and he even declined to reveal the names of the witches.[18] 'If you say that you fight for God, I want you to tell me the names of these witches,' Fra Felice insisted. But Moduco was stubborn. He declared that he could not accuse anyone 'whether he be friend or foe . . . because we have a life-long edict not to reveal secrets about one side or the other. . . . This commandment was made by the captains of each side, whom we are obliged to obey.' Only after another of the friar's objections ('This is just an excuse; since you assert that you are no longer one of them, you cannot be obliged to obey them: so tell me who these witches are') did Moduco finally yield and furnish two names, one of which was that of a woman who had supposedly deprived livestock of their milk. Moduco's interrogation ended here; evidently his replies had not put him in such a bad light in the eyes of the Inquisition, since Fra Felice let him go.

5

On 28 June, Paolo Gasparutto was interrogated a second time. One day's imprisonment had convinced him of the futility of persisting in his denials. He admitted entering the company of the benandanti at the age of twenty-eight, summoned by the captain of the benandanti of Verona, of having remained in it for ten years, and of having abandoned it four years previously.[19] 'Why,' the inquisitor asked, 'did you not tell me this yesterday?' Gasparutto replied: 'Because I was afraid of the witches, who would have attacked me in bed and killed me.' But to the friar's next question, 'The first time that you went did you know that you were going with benandanti?' he responded at length: 'Yes, father, because I had been warned first by a benandante of Vicenza, Baptista Vicentino by name . . . thirty-five years of age, tall in stature, with a round black beard, well built, a peasant.' Battista had presented himself in 'the month of December, during the Ember season of Christmas, on Thursday about the fourth hour of the night, at first sleep.' And here the motif underlying the rites of the benandanti, which we saw in Moduco's interrogation, re-emerges especially clearly: 'He told me that the captain of the benandanti was summoning me to come out and fight for the crops. And I answered him: 'I do want to come, for the sake of the crops.'' '

Fra Felice interrupted: 'If you were asleep, how did you answer him and how did you hear his voice?' Gasparutto explained:

> 'My spirit replied to him,' and he added that it was his spirit that went forth, 'and if by chance while we are out someone should come with a light and look for a long time at the body, the spirit would never re-enter it until there was no one left around to see it that night; and if the body, seeming to be dead, should be buried, the spirit would have to wander around the world until the hour fixed for that body to die.'

The inquisitor then asked him if he had known Battista Vicentino prior to his appearance that night. 'No, father,' Gasparutto replied, unperturbed, 'but they know who is a benandante.' 'How do they know who is a benandante?' 'The captain of the benandanti knows it.'[20]

Here Gasparutto began to describe (with only a few slight differences from Moduco's account) the company of the benandanti to which he belonged: 'We are only six . . . we fight with viburnum branches, that is, with the staff which we carry behind the crosses in the processions of the Rogation days; and we have a banner of white silk, all gilded, and the witches have one that is yellow, with four devils on it.'[21] He added that they went to do battle in the country around Verona and Gradisca and, after an interruption by the inquisitor ('how do you know where you are supposed to go?'), he explained that 'during the Ember Days preceding, the benandanti and the witches challenge each other, and they name the place.' Then, to the friar, who had asked him if he had ever promised to take anyone to these 'games', he replied immediately, almost with annoyance: 'Yes, the last father inquisitor; and if he had come along, you would not be questioning me now.' Their captain was 'a person from Verona, I do not know his name, and I believe that he is a peasant of average height, a plump man with a red beard, about thirty years old'; Gasparutto did not know how he had become captain.

Gasparutto's story, like Moduco's, ended with the accusation of two witches – one from Gorizia, the other from the village of Chiana, near Capodistria. The inquisitor seemed satisfied and freed Gasparutto, ordering him to reappear within twenty days, this time not in Cividale but in Udine, at the monastery of San Francesco.

6

The proceedings described above took place on 28 June. On 24 September the inquisitor ordered that Gasparutto, who had not kept the appointment at Udine, (he later tried to excuse himself, claiming that he had been ill) be brought there, and had him incarcerated. Two days later the questioning of the benandante resumed.

Thus far Moduco's and Gasparutto's accounts match almost entirely. But now a difference appeared. Gasparutto modified his confession on one key point by introducing a new element: 'I have come to think that I should tell the truth,' he declared at the beginning of the interrogation. The inquisitor restated a question which was intended to undermine the most important theological point in his confession: 'Who led you to enter the company of these benandanti?' To this Gasparutto replied unexpectedly: 'The angel of God . . . at night, in my house, perhaps during the fourth hour of the night, at first sleep . . . an angel appeared before me, all made of gold, like those on altars, and he called me, and my spirit went out. . . . He called me by name, saying: "Paolo, I will send you forth as a benandante and you will have to fight for the crops." I answered him: "I will go, I am obedient." '[22]

How are we to explain this change? At first glance it would seem reasonable to suppose that, faced by the prolongation of the interrogations and the renewed imprisonment, Gasparutto might try to extricate himself from the clutches of the Inquisition by placing greater weight on the Christian motivation of his 'profession'. Perhaps he thought he could do this by introducing the theme of an angel, not realizing that he was thereby aggravating his own situation. But two points should be kept in mind: the detail of the angel who participated in the meetings of the benandanti (to whom Gasparutto referred) and who will reappear, if only briefly, in two later trials of 1618–19, and 1621;[23] and the fact that after he was led back to prison, Gasparutto mentioned the angel to Moduco. This undercuts the hypothesis that it was a spontaneous invention he concocted for his defence. All in all, it makes sense to suppose that in his first confession Gasparutto had kept silent about the appearance of the angel precisely because he discerned its intrinsic danger.

Gasparutto had barely finished speaking about the apparition of the angel 'all made of gold' when the inquisitor broke in with an abrupt insinuation: 'What did he promise you, women, food, dancing, and what else?' Gasparutto's allusion to the angel was all that was needed to convince Fra Felice of the basically diabolical character of the benandanti's 'games' and of their identity with the sabbat. Gasparutto vehemently denied this, and defended himself by shifting the accusation to the enemy, the witches: 'He did not promise me anything, but those others do dance and leap about, and I saw them because we fought them.' Now the inquisitor turned to another key point in Gasparutto's story: 'Where did your spirit go when the angel summoned you?' 'It came out because in the body it cannot speak,' Gasparutto replied. The exchanges now came in rapid succession: 'Who told you that your spirit had to come out if it was to speak with the angel?' 'The angel himself told me.' 'How many times did you see this angel?' 'Every time that I went, because he always came with me,' and a little later he added: 'He stays in person by our banner.'[24]

Thus far we have had what amounts to a monologue on Gasparutto's part, interrupted only by the inquisitor's requests for clarification. As long as the benandanti's tales of their nocturnal 'games' were merely startling facts, even though silently suspect, but at least not out of line with traditional demonological schemes, Fra Felice had maintained a passive attitude of mild astonishment and detached curiosity. But with the opening that Gasparutto had suddenly provided, the technique of the interrogation changed, becoming openly suggestive. The inquisitor now began in earnest to try and make the benandante's confessions conform to the existing model – the sabbat.

First of all he subtly endowed the figure of the angel with demonic attributes: 'When he appears before you or takes his leave, does this angel frighten you?' 'He never frightens us, but when the company breaks up, he gives a benediction,' Gasparutto stubbornly answered. 'Does not this angel ask to be adored?' 'Yes, we adore him just as we adore our Lord Jesus Christ in church.' At this point Fra Felice changed the subject: 'Does this angel conduct you where that other one is seated on that beautiful throne?' In Gasparutto's tale, needless to say, there had been no mention of devils or thrones. This time too the reply was prompt and tinged with exasperation: 'But he is not of our company, God forbid that we should get involved with that false enemy! . . . It is the witches that have the beautiful thrones.' The inquisitor persisted: 'Did you ever see witches by that beautiful throne?' And Gasparutto, gesturing with his arms, sensing that he had been caught in the inquisitor's trap: 'No sir, we did nothing but fight!' Fra Felice was implacable: 'Which is the more beautiful angel, yours or the one on the beautiful throne?' And Gasparutto, contradicting himself in his desperation: 'Didn't I tell you that I have not seen those thrones? . . . Our angel is beautiful and white; theirs is black and is the devil.'[25]

7

By now the trial was nearing its conclusion. On the whole, the inquisitor had managed to adapt Gasparutto's testimony to his own notions and theological preconceptions: the meetings of the benandanti and of the witches were nothing but the sabbat, and the 'company' of the benandanti which falsely proclaimed that it enjoyed divine protection and fought under the guidance and aegis of an angel was diabolical. Under the pressure of the inquisitor's questioning Gasparutto's self-assurance seemed to weaken, as if the reality of his beliefs had suddenly changed and was slipping out of his grasp. A day or two later, once more before Fra Felice, he declared: 'I believe that the apparition of that angel was really the devil tempting me, since you have told me that he can transform himself into an angel.' The same thing happened to Moduco in his interrogation of 2 October: 'Ever since I heard from that friend of mine who is in prison that an angel appeared to him, I have come to think that this is a diabolical thing, because our Lord God does not send angels to lead spirits out of bodies, but only to provide them with good inspiration.'[26] Were these retractions sincere? It is impossible to reply with certainty. What counts is that the events in this trial – the crisis of beliefs evidenced by the two benandanti, their incorporation, at the inquisitor's insistence, into the latter's mental and theological world – epitomised and anticipated the general evolution of the cult that was to define itself, little by little, over more than half a century.

But ancient beliefs are not so easily dispelled. Moduco had asserted that he was now convinced of the diabolical nature of his apparitions. But even though he may have been wary of expressing it, he could not help reaffirming what was for him an incontestable reality:[27]

> 'A certain invisible thing appeared to me in my sleep which had the form of a man, and I thought I was asleep but I was not, and it seemed to me that he was from Trivigniano, and because I had about my neck that caul with which I was born, I thought I heard him say "you must come with me because you have something of mine"; and so I told him that if I had to go, I would, but that I did not want to depart from God; and since he said this was God's work, I went at age twenty-two, or twenty-three.'

As for the 'caul' which he had already stated was a distinctive mark of the benandanti, Moduco asserted that he had always worn it about his neck; then, after losing it, he stopped going forth at night: since 'those who have the caul and do not wear it, do not go out.'

At this point, after a little more skirmishing, Fra Felice suddenly brought the indecisive course of the trial to a halt and took it firmly in hand: 'Did you see what the witches were doing out there?' This was a device, tried successfully with Gasparutto earlier, to compel Moduco to recognize the witches' sabbats in the meetings of the benandanti. And the fact that Moduco had already asserted that witches armed with sorghum stalks fought for the devil[28] made this misrepresentation easier. But Moduco avoided this trap: 'No sir, except on the Ember Days when we fought against them: but they go forth also on Thursdays . . . the witches always go out on Thursdays to hurt someone, and I do not know if anyone calls them out.' And he added: 'The witches do reverence and pray to their masters who go about with great solemnity in black dress and with chains around their necks, and who insist on being kneeled to.' The inquisitor's next question took a predictable turn: 'Do you benandanti kneel before your captain?' Moduco replied with martial pride: 'No, sir, we only pay our respects to him with our caps, like soldiers to their captain.' There was one more exchange: 'After they have knelt, do the witches play other games?' 'Sir, this I have not seen because they go hither and yon.' Then Fra Felice could no longer contain himself and exclaimed: 'How could you make yourself believe that these were God's works? Men do not have the power either to render themselves invisible or to lead the spirit away, nor are God's works carried out in secrecy.' It was an impetuous, frontal attack. And Moduco, rather than attempting a defence, offered excuses: 'That one begged me so much, saying, "dear Battista, get up," and it seemed as if I was both sleeping and not sleeping. Since he was older than me, I allowed myself to be persuaded, thinking it was proper.' But he admitted his error: 'Yes, sir, now I do believe that this was a diabolical work, after that other person told me of that angel of his.' However, he could not help insisting on the orthodox, even pious, character of the benandanti's gatherings:[29]

> 'The first time I was summoned . . . the captain took me by the hand and said "Will you be a good servant?" and I replied, "Yes". . . . He did not promise me anything, but did say that I was carrying out one of God's works, and that when I died I would go to paradise. There we did not mention Christ by name, nor the Madonna, nor any saint specifically, nor did I ever see anyone cross himself or make the sign of the cross: but in truth they did talk of God and the saints in general, saying: "May God and the saints be with us," but without naming anyone.'

Suddenly, provoked by yet another of the inquisitor's insinuations, he added: 'While waiting for the company we did not do anything, we neither ate nor drank; but on our way home, I wish I had a *scudo* for every time we drank in the wine cellars, entering through the cracks, and getting on the casks. We drank with a pipe, as did the witches; but after they had drunk, they pissed in the casks.' Irritated perhaps by such extravagant tales, the inquisitor cut the account short, and reproached the benandante for not having revealed these nocturnal diversions to his confessor. 'Dear sir,' Moduco replied with a mixture of astonishment and resentment, 'have I not told you that simply because I said a couple of things I was beaten terribly, so my sides were all black and blue and also my back and arms? And this is why I never told it to the confessor.'

8

The interrogations ended with the release of the two benandanti and an injunction to them to reappear whenever they might be summoned by the Holy Office. Because of a jurisdictional conflict between the patriarch's vicar and the commissioner of Cividale, pronouncement of sentence against them was delayed for over a year.[30] In fact, it was not until 26 November 1581 that the inquisitor conveyed to Moduco and Gasparutto the order to appear at the Church of San Francesco in Cividale *'ad audiendam sententiam'*.

In the sentences the heresies[31] contained in the confessions of the two men were listed in detail. Several points were singled out as being particularly worthy of censure: Moduco's statement that whoever was a benandante and fought for the faith against witches would be certain to go to paradise; the idolatry practised by Gasparutto in his adoration of the false angel; and finally, the sin of reticence of which the two became guilty by concealing their nocturnal activities from their confessors.[32] It is noteworthy, however, that in the sentence against Gasparutto, whose indictment was considered more serious because of his allusion to the presence of the ambiguous angel at the meetings of the benandanti, sharper language was used. Thus, it was not said, as in Moduco's case, 'You were with the benandanti,' but rather 'You were with witches whom you called benandanti'; moreover, 'diabolical arts' were explicitly mentioned. Further, a misconception was introduced into Moduco's sentence in another attempt to equate the diabolical sabbat with the meetings of the benandanti: 'You urged others to come with you . . . and to those who came you taught that they must not mention the holy name of God and of the saints, because they would then have had to remain.' According to Sgabarizza, Gasparutto instead had limited himself to saying: 'When we were there, even if we should see some wild dancing, we were to say nothing; otherwise we would have been forced to stay.'[33] Both were absolved from the more serious form of excommunication to which they were liable as heretics, and condemned to six months imprisonment. Moreover, prayers and penances were imposed which they were to fulfil during appointed days of the year, among which were the Ember Days, so as to obtain from God forgiveness for sins committed at these times. Soon after, the penalties were remitted, on condition that the two benandanti should remain within the city for a fortnight. That same day, after reading of the sentences, they solemnly abjured their errors 'in the presence of a great multitude'.[34]

As we will see, the picture that emerges from the recitals of the two benandanti would not be fundamentally modified for several decades. In a certain sense, in fact, this evidence is the richest source of information that has come down to us for this first phase of the beliefs being examined here. In this period the benandanti constituted, as we perceive from their confessions, a true and proper sect,[35] organized in military fashion about a leader and linked by a bond of secrecy – a relatively weak bond which the benandanti were continually breaking, either out of loquacity or naive boastfulness. The members of this sect (who were dispersed throughout the Friuli, and especially in the eastern sections) were principally united by a common element, that of having been born with the caul, in other words, wrapped in the amniotic membrane.

According to several bits of contemporary evidence, most of it emanating from the Friuli, various superstitions were attached to this object, the 'caul', or placenta: it was supposed to protect soldiers from blows, cause the enemy to withdraw, and even help lawyers to win their cases.[36] Certainly, it was an object endowed with magical powers. To increase these powers Masses were even celebrated over it, as we know from a superstitious practice already in vogue in the time of San Bernardino, who condemned it in one of his sermons.[37] Battista Moduco asserted that he had been given the caul with which he was born by his own mother, together with the warning that it should always be worn. Once, when he was in Rome, Moduco had a monk celebrate more than thirty Masses over this caul which had been baptized with him. In his turn Gasparutto confessed: 'About a year before the angel appeared to me, my mother gave me the caul in which I had been born, saying that she had it baptized with me, and had nine Masses said over it, and had it blessed with certain prayers and scriptural readings; and she told me that I was born a benandante, and that when I grew up I would go forth at night, and that I must wear it on my person, and that I would go with the benandanti to fight the witches.' Thus, a specific power was added to the general properties of the caul; that of predestining the individual born wrapped within it to the 'profession' of the benandanti; moreover, Moduco affirmed 'those who have the caul and do not wear it, do not go out.' There was a strong tradition in the folklore of many parts of Italy, including the Friuli and Istria (where it was an echo of the very belief we are examining here), that children born with the caul were condemned to become witches.[38] But this similarity does not tell us how the connection between being 'born with the caul' and becoming benandanti could have evolved. We will attempt to clear up this point with the help of additional evidence.

The initiation of the benandanti took place at a specific age, corresponding approximately to the reaching of maturity (Moduco entered the 'company' at age twenty, Gasparutto at twenty-eight); as in an army, after a time, say ten or twenty years, one became freed from the obligation of marching forth at night to fight. In any case, the moment of initiation did not come without warning; in fact, it was expected, as we saw from the admonishments of Gasparutto's mother to her son. As Moduco said, when those born with the caul 'reach the age of twenty they are summoned by means of a drum the same as soldiers.' Regardless of whether this was done by an angel or a benandante, they already knew that 'they had to go.'

10

We have been talking of the benandanti as a sect: a very special sect, whose ceremonies, in the words of the benandanti themselves, had an almost dream-like character. But actually, the benandanti were saying something different; they never doubted the *reality* of those gatherings which they attended 'in spirit'. An identical attitude is discernible in witch trials in other parts of Italy, and elsewhere as well. We can use as an example the case of Domenica Barbarelli, a witch of Novi, prosecuted by the Modenese Inquisition in 1532. She had testified that 'she wanted to go to the games of Diana at all costs and because others knew this, she was watched so that she could not get away. She lay as if dead for about two hours, but finally, after frequent shaking by the bystanders, seemed to awake and spoke these words: "I did indeed go there in spite of you": and she reported many evil deeds which she said she had done in the games.'[38] Here too, the going in a dream, 'in spirit', was perceived as something real. For this reason the witch taunted the bystanders: she believed that she herself, or her spirit, had truly gone to the 'games'.

Later we will investigate the significance of this going 'in spirit' on the part of witches and benandanti. Meanwhile we should note first of all that both groups claimed that, before setting out for their meetings, they fell into states of profound prostration, or catalepsy, the causes of which have been widely discussed. Doubtless, this is a marginal problem in the interpretation of witchcraft. Even if we could (and we cannot) determine with certainty the nature of these cataleptic states, we would still need to explain the really important element: *the meaning* of the visions claimed by both witches and benandanti. There is no doubt that the question should at least be asked.

The explanations that have been suggested are basically of two types: either it has been supposed that witches and warlocks were individuals afflicted by epilepsy, hysteria, or other mental diseases not well defined; or else the loss of consciousness accompanied by hallucinations, described by them, have been attributed to the effect of ointments containing sleep-inducing or narcotic substances. Let's begin by discussing the second of these possibilities.

It is well known that witches anointed themselves before going to the sabbat. Already in the mid-fifteenth century the Spanish theologian, Alfonso Tostado, in his commentary on *Genesis*, noted in passing that Spanish witches, after uttering certain set words, smeared themselves with ointments and then fell into a deep sleep which made them insensible even to fire and to injuries. But upon waking they declared that they had been to this or that, perhaps very distant, place, to meet their companions, feasting and philandering.[39] A half century later Giovanni Battista Della Porta obtained a similar result when he had an old woman reputed to be a witch anointed, recording in minute detail the ingredients of the unguent used. The experiment was repeated with conflicting results by two scholars in modern times.[40] It seems reasonable to suppose, nevertheless, that if not all, at least some of the confessed witches, used unguents capable of inducing states of hallucination and delirium.

It is not so easy, however, to extend this hypothesis to the benandanti. Neither Gasparutto nor Moduco ever mentioned ointments. They spoke only of deep sleeps and of lethargic states which rendered them insensible, thereby allowing the spirit to leave the body. Even in later benandanti trials we find only two references to ointments. A cowherd of Latisana, Menichino, admitted being a benandante and asserted that he went out at night in the form of smoke to fight the witches. During his trial by the Venetian Holy Office in 1591 the inquisitor asked him, in the usual insinuating manner, if 'when he went forth as smoke, as he says, did he anoint himself with any unguent or oil, or . . . did he utter any words?' At first the defendant reacted violently to this suggestion: 'No, by the saints, God, and the Gospels I did not oil myself or say any words.' But later when the interrogations were being read back to him he did admit that the benandante who had persuaded him the first time to go out at night had told him to grease himself 'with lamp oil the evening before he was to go forth'.[41] This was a cautious and perhaps incomplete admission and it does not find much more solid corroboration in the testimony of a carpenter from Palmanova who denounced as a benandante a well-known prostitute named Menica of Cremons to the inquisitor of Aquileia: 'She herself admits that when she goes out she greases herself with oils and creams, and the body remains while the spirit departs.'[42] As we will see, this is second-hand and also very late evidence (the trial took place in 1626), and should probably be taken as an early sign of that association of benandanti with witches which was beginning to be made in this very period.[43] All in all, the evidence for the use of unguents by benandanti is really too sparse, in relation to the number of surviving trials, to allow us to use it as an explanation for their behaviour.

Let's pass now to the first-mentioned hypothesis. It is an established fact that many witches were epileptics, and that many demoniacs suffered from hysteria. Still, there seems little doubt that we are confronted with many manifestations which can not be explained on pathological grounds. First, this is so in terms of statistics, since in the face of such large numbers of 'sick' people, even the boundaries between a healthy and diseased state become vague; secondly, the so-called hallucinations, instead of being confined to an individual, private sphere, have a precise cultural basis. For example, their recurrence in a circumscribed period of the year – the Ember Days – immediately comes to mind. They are of a type befitting a specific popular religiosity or a particular aberrant mysticism. The same reasoning applies to the benandanti. It would seem obvious to ascribe the catalepsy and the lethargy by which they claimed to be afflicted to epileptic fits. The fact is, however, that only one benandante – a woman named Maria Panzona, tried by the Holy Office first at Latisana and later in Venice in 1618–19 – appeared to have suffered from the 'ugly ailment' (*'bruto male'*), epilepsy.[44] To be sure, in her case, the attacks which beset her continually, even during questioning, must have seemed at certain times – during the Ember Days – much like the benandanti's ritual lethargies. The documents available to us, however, do not give sufficient information, and the nature of the benandanti's catalepsy remains a mystery. In any case, whether it was induced through ointments containing drugs, epileptic fits, or specific ecstatic techniques, the puzzle of the benandanti and their beliefs must be resolved on the basis of the history of popular religiosity not on that of pharmacology or psychiatry.[45]

The loss of the senses, a condition common to both witches and benandanti, was understood as a separation of the spirit from the body. Margherita of San Rocco, condemned to the stake in 1571 by the mayor and elders of Lucca, declared that 'the visits to the games which I have made did not take place in person, but *in spirit, leaving the body at home*.'[46] And one of her companions, Polissena of San Macario (who met the same fate) testified: 'I allowed myself to be persuaded by an aunt of mine, Lena of Pescaglia, to enter into witchcraft; after her death I did nothing for about a year, and then I began to go out in this way, that is, she called me and said "let us go", and only I could hear her voice, and then I greased myself with the ointment I had brought with me . . . and was transformed into a cat, *left the body at home*, descended the stair, and went out by the door.'[47] These were words uttered during torture, or at least in the course of a trial heavily influenced by it.[48] But what counts here is not their sincerity but rather the evidence they furnish for the widespread existence of certain beliefs which, as we will see, were not shared by the judges.

This departure of the spirit from the body, which was left lifeless, was understood as an actual separation, an event fraught with perils, almost like death. To the mayor and elders of Lucca, Margherita of San Rocco declared (and this particular recurs in the confessions of her companion Polissena) that when they went to the sabbat 'if perchance we were turned over face down we would lose the spirit and the body would die';[49] moreover, if the spirit 'did not return before dawn at cock's crow, we would not change back into human form, and the body would stay dead and the spirit remain a cat.'[50] For his part, the benandante Gasparutto told Rotaro that 'when he [Gasparutto] went to these games his body stayed in bed and the spirit went forth, and that while he was out if someone approached the bed where the body lay and called to it, it would not answer, nor could he get it to move even if he should try for a hundred years; and . . . they wait twenty-four hours before returning, and if one should say or do something, the spirit would remain separated from the body, and after it was buried, the spirit would wander forever'.[51] The soul which left the body to go to the witches' conventicles or to the jousts of the benandanti was considered in both cases as something very real and tangible, usually an animal. In another Lucchese trial (this one dating from 1589) an old woman accused of witchcraft, Crezia of Pieve San Paolo, declared: 'Forty years or more ago, I knew a witch called Gianna, and once when she fell asleep I saw a mouse come out of her mouth; it was her spirit and I do not know where it was going.'[52] When Gasparutto's wife was interrogated by Fra Felice da Montefalco on 1 October 1580, she claimed not to know whether her husband was a benandante; however, she did remember that one winter night she had woken in a fright and called to Paolo for comfort: 'And even though I called him ten times and shook him, I could not manage to wake him, and he lay face up'; a little later she had found him mumbling to himself: 'These benandanti say that when their spirit leaves the body it has the appearance of a mouse, and also when it returns, and that if the body should be rolled over while it is without its spirit, it would remain dead, and its spirit could never return to it.'[53] Later corroboration of this belief that the soul was a 'mouse' (which was not limited to the Friuli[54]) was provided in a 1648 trial against a child who claimed to be a benandante: at the sabbat which he had attended (by that time the identification of benandanti with witches had been pretty well accomplished) some of those present were 'in spirit and in body, in male and female forms', while others instead were 'in the shape of mice', that is, only 'in spirit'.[55] The concept of the soul as something material had such deep roots among the benandanti that Menica of Cremons, denounced in 1626, declared that she went to the conventicles leaving her body behind so that she might assume another one like it.[56] Moreover, this belief was known even beyond the circles of witches and benandanti. In Verona, for example, early in the sixteenth century Bishop Gian Matteo Giberti had to suppress the popular custom of removing the roofs of houses of the recently deceased so that their souls might be freed and ascend to heaven.[57]

12

Not all witches asserted that they went to the sabbat 'in spirit'. A woman of Gaiato, Orsolina, nicknamed 'la Rossa', tried by the Modenese Inquisition in 1539, was asked by the judge whether she always made her way to the sabbat 'physically or in sleep'. She replied that 'there are many who go in spirit only, but some also in their bodies'; as for herself, 'she always went there physically'.[58] From the very first persecutions, controversy had raged, among those who debated the true nature of witchcraft, over the two alternatives – whether witches betook themselves to the sabbat 'in dreams' or 'physically'.

Obviously, this is not the place to retrace the long history of this controversy.[59] It will suffice to sum up the arguments of the respective positions. The advocates of the reality of the 'games' (by far the majority until the second half of the seventeenth century) found justification by evoking venerable authorities for their position, in addition to the *consensus gentium*. The utterances of witches were too alike despite differences in the physical constitution, social condition, and place of origin of the accused to be attributed to dreams or fantasies.[60] In other words, everything was real: the magical properties of the diabolical ointments, the transformation of the witches into animals, their nocturnal flights to perhaps very distant places, the devil's presence at the conventicles, and so forth. On the other side were those who argued that the sabbat was unreal; they judged it to be the fruit of the delirious fantasies of 'base-born old folk or ignorant and simple people, vulgar rustics', or of women, as Andrea Alciato jeered, who deserved hellebore more than the stake. They confronted their opponents with the celebrated *Canon Episcopi* (derived from a German penitential work, probably of late ninth-century origin) and maintained the impossibility of the witches' nocturnal flights on both natural and supernatural grounds.[61] This thesis, supported by the physician Johann Weyer whose arguments were already partially rationalistic, began gradually to predominate in the course of the seventeenth century, until little by little it prevailed uncontested, during that very period which saw the persecutions of witches come to a peak almost everywhere in Europe.

These alternatives formulated by inquisitors, jurists and theologians naturally were also those faced by the judges of the two benandanti. Should the nocturnal gatherings and the battles which they described be understood as dreams and fantasies, or as real events? There were no doubts on this score, as we have seen, among the benandanti themselves: conventicles and battles were very real, even if only their spirits participated. But the judges refused to go along with this division: in the sentences concluding the trial, Gasparutto and Moduco were condemned for having 'gone' with the benandanti, and for having dared 'to believe and affirm' that the spirit could, on these occasions, abandon the body and re-enter it at will. Similar distortions turn up, and not by chance, in many other witchcraft trials. As they sought to control, by articulating it, the painful sense of profound disorientation experienced during their lethargies, witches and benandanti alike spoke of the spirit leaving the body in the guise of a cat, a mouse, or some other animal (these were the metamorphoses discussed at such length by theologians and inquisitors). But this experience could not be successfully conveyed, and the statements about the departure of the soul from the body were condemned. The confessions of the witches and benandanti were wilfully incorporated into the inquisitorial *schema* with its contrary concepts of a real tangible sabbat and one of fantasy and imagination.

13

What we have noted thus far helps to explain the reason for the queries attempted by Fra Felice da Montefalco during the interrogation. It is not surprising either, that in the final session the notary observed that Gasparutto's wife cried without shedding tears, a fact considered obvious evidence of witchcraft and of ties to the devil;[62] and that Gasparutto's and Moduco's trial was routinely filed under the rubric *'Processus haeresis contra quosdam strigones'* ('heresy trial against certain witches').

When we turn, however, to the rites which, according to the benandanti, were practised at their nocturnal gatherings, it is clear that they bore no resemblance to the sabbat. They were rites that hardly need to be explained, so explicit and transparent is their significance: we are not dealing with hardened superstitions mechanically repeated, but with ceremonies that were intensely and emotionally experienced.[63] The benandanti, armed with bundles of fennel who fought witches and warlocks armed with stalks of sorghum, did so with the consciousness that they were locked in a struggle 'out of love for the crops', to assure their community abundant harvests, a plenitude of food, of small grains, and of the vineyards, in fact, 'all the fruits of the earth'. It was an agricultural rite which survived with extraordinary vitality almost to the end of the sixteenth century in the marginal area of the Friuli, left relatively untouched by the main routes of communication.[64] It is hard to say when it originated, but even today, it is possible to discern the complexity of the cult which expressed itself through this rite.

The benandanti went forth on Thursday nights in the Ember seasons: festivities which had survived from an ancient agricultural cycle and which were eventually incorporated in the Christian calendar,[65] that symbolized the changes of the seasons, the perilous passage from the old to the new time of year, with its promise of planting, harvest, reaping and autumn vintage.[66] It was during these occasions, on which the prosperity of the community depended, that the benandanti went forth to protect the produce of the earth from witches and warlocks, and from those forces that they thought secretly threatened the fertility of the fields: 'And if we are the victors, that year there is abundance, but if we lose there is famine.'

To be sure, the benandanti were not alone in fulfilling this propitiatory function. The church itself laboured to protect the harvests and ward off those all too frequent and ruinous famines by means of Rogations, processions around the fields, usually during the three days preceding the Ascension: and for a long time the tradition was preserved of forecasting harvests from each of these days – the first for vegetables and grapes, the second for wheat, and the third for hay.[67] And, in this period, the disasters caused by foul weather were frequently attributed, especially in the Friuli, to punishment inflicted by God for past sins: on 9 April 1596 Clement VIII absolved the district of Polcenico from an excommunication which it feared it had incurred as evidenced by the barrenness of the crops; he did the same on 26 March 1598 with the district of San Daniele, whose harvests had been repeatedly struck by hail.[68] But if the processions of the Rogation Days and papal absolutions were not considered sufficient, here, in tacit competition, emerged the rites of appeasement of the benandanti. It certainly was not accidental that the benandanti's weapon in their battles to protect the fertility of the fields was, as Gasparutto described it, the wayfaring tree or viburnum, 'that rod which we carry behind the crosses in the Rogation processions.' This mixture of the sacred and the diabolical led the inquisitor to forbid Gasparutto (and the prohibition was intended to include his domestics) from bearing these rods in the Rogation processions, and in fact to order them kept at home.[69]

Obviously, we are not suggesting by this that Friulian peasants at the end of the sixteenth century attempted to safeguard their crops and their harvests exclusively by means of religious processions or superstitious practices, but the careful performance of work in the fields could and in fact did easily co-exist with faith in the benefits of ecclesiastical rituals or even in nocturnal battles fought victoriously by the benandanti. In these very years and among these same peasants there is evidence of attitudes that were deeply and fiercely naturalistic; such as a magnificent statement by Niccolò Pellizzaro, a peasant of Villa in Carnia, whom the Inquisition condemned in 1595 for having maintained 'that the benedictions which priests pronounce over fields, and the holy water which they sprinkle over them the day of Epiphany, in no way help the vines and trees to bear fruit; only dung and the industry of man do that.'[70] But even more than a 'humanistic' exaltation of man's power over nature, we may see here the echo of a religious polemic; Pellizzaro, in fact, was suspected of Lutheranism, and by his statement he may have been conveying his scorn for priests and Catholic ceremonies.

So the benandanti with fennel stalks battled witches armed with stalks of sorghum. It is not clear why sorghum was the weapon of the witches – unless it could be identified with the broom, their traditional symbol (the so-called 'broom sorghum', one of the most common varieties of sorghum, is a type of millet). It is a compelling theory, especially in light of what we will say about the nocturnal gatherings of the witches and benandanti as the antecedents of the diabolical sabbat – but obviously this is a theory which should be advanced with caution. In any case, for the benandanti the sorghum seemed to symbolize the evil power of the witches. The parish priest of Brazzano, Bartolomeo Sgabarizza, reported having had this conversation with Gasparutto: 'He begged me not to sow sorghum in my field, and whenever he finds any growing he pulls it up, and he curses whoever plants it; and when I said that I wanted to sow it, he began to swear.'[71] To fennel, instead, whose healing qualities were recognized in popular medicine, was attributed the power of keeping witches away: Moduco affirmed that the benandanti ate garlic and fennel 'because they are a defence against witches'.[72]

It may be supposed that this combat re-enacted, and to a certain extent rationalized, an older fertility rite in which two groups of youths,[73] respectively impersonating demons favourable to fertility and the maleficent ones of destruction, symbolically flayed their loins with stalks of fennel and sorghum to stimulate their own reproductive capacity, and by analogy, the fertility of the fields of the community.[74] Gradually the rite may have come to be represented as an actual combat, and from the uncertain outcome of the struggle between the two opposed bands would magically depend the fertility of the land and the fate of the harvests.[75] At a later stage these rites would cease to be practised openly and would exist precariously, between the dream-like and the hallucinatory, in any case on a purely internal emotional plane – and yet without quite sliding into mere individual fantasizing.

But these are pure conjectures that can be confirmed only on the basis of solid evidence, unavailable at present, about preceding phases of the cult. There is absolutely nothing in the statements of the benandanti that can be interpreted as a relic of this hypothetical original rite. More plausible perhaps is the analogy between the battles of benandanti against witches and ritual contests between

Winter and Summer (or Winter and Spring) which used to be acted out, and still are today, in some areas of north-central Europe.[76] Consider, for example, the plant parts with which both contestants are draped: Winter with pine branches or other plants of the season, Summer with ears of grain, flowers, and so forth. Is there something analogous, even though the two plants flourish in the same season, in the sorghum and the fennel of which the benandanti spoke? It should be noted, in particular, that the contest between Winter and Summer is linked, in some areas, to a presumably older rite, that of the expulsion of Death, or of the Witch.[77] In this ceremony, undoubtedly intended to procure abundant harvests, an effigy of Death, or of the Witch, is beaten with a stick, stoned, and finally solemnly driven from the village. Is there an analogy between this symbolical removal of the wintry season, and the blows inflicted on the witches by the benandanti? Possibly; but along with these similarities there are also notable differences. First of all, the ritual struggle between Winter and Summer was celebrated everywhere once a year, whereas the benandanti claimed that they fought the witches on four occasions each year (the Ember seasons); secondly, and this is even more important, the content of the two rites appears to be totally dissimilar. In the contests between Winter and Summer a peaceful alternation of the seasons is symbolized, and the victory of Summer is inevitable;[78] on the contrary, the battles between benandanti and witches were a clash, with an uncertain outcome, between abundance and famine, a real battle conducted according to a precise ritual. Here the contrast between old and new seasons was experienced dramatically, virtually a contest to decide the actual physical survival of the community.[79]

14

In the confessions of these benandanti, religious elements of very different origin were superimposed on this agrarian rite, seemingly self-sufficient in its internal motivations. Moduco and Gasparutto both asserted that they could not discuss the nocturnal conventicles in which they participated because by doing so they would be flouting the will of God; and Moduco clarified this point: 'We go forth in the service of Christ and the witches in the service of the devil.' The company of the benandanti was a divine entity, virtually a peasant army of the faith established by God ('we believe that it is given by God, because we fight for the faith of Christ'): at its head, according to Gasparutto, was an angel of God; within the group, Moduco related, God and the saints were piously invoked, and its members were certain to go to paradise after death.

The contrast between fighting 'for love of the crops' and fighting 'for the faith of Christ' is indeed glaring. To be sure, in this popular religiosity, so composite, interlaced with the most varied elements, such syncretism is not surprising. But we should ask ourselves the reason for this Christianization of agrarian rites performed by the benandanti – which undoubtedly was 'spontaneous' in this period and widespread throughout the Friuli. Perhaps it was a method adopted in a distant past to shield from the eyes of the church a rite that was not quite orthodox (just as the groups of young people celebrating ancient fertility rites placed themselves under the protection of a patron saint);[80] or it may be that the ancient agrarian rite gradually received a Christian motif from those who ingenuously joined the good cause of the fertility of the fields with the holy cause of the faith of Christ. Finally, we may even suppose that, in the face of the progressive assimilation (to be discussed below) of diabolical elements on the part of their enemies, the witches, the benandanti instinctively and correspondingly identified their cause with that of the faith.

There may be some truth in each of these assumptions. At any rate, it is clear that this attempt at Christianization did not (and could not) succeed, and indeed was not favourably received by the Inquisition. It faded away within a few decades. Two primary elements coexisted within the medley of beliefs of which the benandanti were the bearers: an agrarian cult (probably the more ancient of the two) and a Christian cult, and in addition a number of other elements capable of being assimilated by witchcraft. When inquisitors failed to understand the first and decisively rejected the second, this composite of myths and beliefs, for lack of other outlets, inevitably had to debouch in the last direction.

15

Thus far we have spoken principally of the benandanti. The time has come to talk about their adversaries: the witches and warlocks. They appear from the confessions of Gasparutto and Moduco first of all by

way of contrast – a contrast that here too is physical and tangible – with the benandanti: 'Our captain was somewhat pale of face, and the other one swarthy,' 'our standard bearer carries a banner of white silk, gilded, with a lion . . . the banner of the witches is of red silk with four black devils, gilded.'[81] But what did witches and warlocks do in their conventicles? Besides fighting with the benandanti, 'they dance and leap about,' Gasparutto stated. There is no trace, as we have already noted, of the elements that would later impress a diabolical stigma on the traditional sabbat: presence of the devil, profanation of the sacraments and apostasy from the faith. To be sure, certain details were there pointing to a tendency in this direction – the devils depicted on the banner of the witches and Moduco's statement: 'We go forth in the service of Christ and the witches in the service of the devil.' But these are isolated matters, and may have been appropriated at a later date. These witches were characterized not in terms of crimes theologically defined, but rather in terms of the destruction they brought to the harvests and famine, and the sorcery they worked on children. But even in this second instance they had to overcome the strenuous opposition of the benandanti. The son of the miller Pietro Rotaro 'had been possessed by witches, but . . . at the time of the witchery the vagabonds were about and they snatched him from the witches' hands.' In fact, the benandanti could recognize immediately the victim of an act of witchcraft: 'It can be ascertained,' said Gasparutto, 'because they do not leave any flesh on the body, . . . and they remain dried up and withered, nothing but skin and bones.' If the benandanti arrived in time they could attempt to save the bewitched child: it sufficed to weigh him three successive Thursdays, and 'while the child is weighed on the scale, the captain of the benandanti uses the scale to torment the witch that has caused the injury, even to the point of killing him; . . . when the child gains in weight . . . the witch withers and dies, and if the child withers, it is the witch that lives.'[82]

The fact that this trial is the first Friulian evidence of witches' conventicles might be considered pure chance. But this coincidence becomes remarkable and probably no longer casual when we notice that it is not until 1634 (and after more than 850 trials and denunciations to the Holy Office of Aquileia and Concordia) before we encounter a full description of the traditional diabolical sabbat. There are many accounts before this time of nocturnal conventicles of witches and warlocks, but benandanti were always present in them, and the rites were always somewhat unusual, much like those described by Gasparutto and Moduco. It is a relationship that recurs too often and over too long a period to be attributed to chance.

Something must have taken place in the Friuli akin to what has been documented for another part of the peninsula, the area around Modena:[83] the gradual but continuous transformation of ancient popular beliefs, which, under the unconscious pressure from inquisitors, finally crystallized in the pre-existing mould of the diabolical sabbat. In Modena, the earliest references to nocturnal meetings of witches in fact do not concern the adoration of the devil, but the cult, still innocuously magical, of a mysterious female divinity, Diana, about which we have knowledge in northern Italy at least from the end of the fourteenth century.[84] When it was said of a witch (who was mentioned in a trial in 1498, although she herself was not tried) that she used to go *'in striacium'*, that is to say, to the sabbat, what is described is merely a peaceful nocturnal gathering of individuals assembled together until dawn to eat 'the turnips of a field or garden'.[85] It is not until 1532 that one encounters descriptions of the desecration of the cross and of the host, intercourse with devils, and so forth. And it should be noted that in this later context the person of Diana, although transformed, was still present.[86]

We see that the acceptance of the diabolical sabbat in the Modenese area long preceded – by a century in fact – a similar development in the Friuli. This too reflects what we have called 'the marginal quality' of the Friuli, as well as, perhaps, the greater complexity and vitality of the benandanti's beliefs compared to the cult of Diana (a cult from which these beliefs were an offshoot). In both cases, however, it seems fair to assert that the belief in the diabolical sabbat is something that was initially foreign to the popular mind. Indeed, even if this observation could be applied to many other localities, the problem of the origins of the diabolical sabbat would still persist.[87]

16

The trial of Gasparutto and Moduco was the first in a long series involving the benandanti (both men and women) who declared that they fought at night with witches and warlocks to secure the fertility of the fields and the abundance of the harvests. This belief (we have hinted at its presumbly ritual origins) does not appear to the best of our knowledge, in any of the countless trials for witchcraft or superstitious practices held outside the Friuli. The sole and extraordinary exception is furnished by the trial of a Livonian werewolf which took place at Jürgensburg in 1692 – more than a century after the trial of Gasparutto and Moduco, and at the other extremity of Europe.[88]

The accused, a certain Thiess, an old man in his eighties, freely confessed to his judges that he was a werewolf (*wahrwolff*). But his account seriously differs from the concept of lycanthropy which was widespread in northern Germany and the Baltic countries. Thiess related that he once had his nose broken by a peasant of Lemburg named Skeistan, who at that time was already dead. Skeistan was a witch, and with his companions had carried seed grain into hell to keep the crops from growing. With other werewolves Thiess had also gone down into hell and had fought with Skeistan. The latter, armed with a broom handle (again, the traditional symbol of witches) wrapped in the tail of a horse had struck the old man on the nose. This was not a casual encounter. Three times each year on the nights of St Lucia before Christmas, of Pentecost, and of St John, the werewolves proceeded on foot, in the form of wolves, to a place located 'beyond the sea': hell. There they battled the devil and witches, striking them with long iron rods, and pursuing them like dogs. Werewolves, Thiess exclaimed, 'cannot tolerate the devil'. The judges, undoubtedly astonished, asked for elucidation. If werewolves could not abide the devil, why did they change themselves into wolves and go down into hell? Because, old Thiess explained, by doing so they could bring back up to earth what had been stolen by the witches – livestock, grains, and the other fruits of the earth. If they failed to do so, precisely what had occurred the previous year would be repeated: the werewolves had delayed their descent into hell, found the gates barred and thus failed to bring back the grains and buds carried off by the witches. For this reason last year's harvest had been very bad. But this year, instead, things had been different, and, thanks to the werewolves, the harvest of barley and rye, as well as a rich catch of fish, were assured.

At this point the judges asked where the werewolves went after death. Thiess replied that they were buried like other people, but that their souls went to heaven; as for the souls of witches, the devil claimed them for himself. The judges were visibly shaken. How was it possible, they asked, for the souls of werewolves to ascend to God if it was not God they served but the devil? The old man emphatically rejected this notion: the werewolves were anything but servants of the devil. The devil was their enemy to the point that they, just like dogs – because werewolves were indeed the hounds of God – pursued him, tracked him down, and scourged him with whips of iron. They did all this for the sake of mankind: without their good work the devil would carry off the fruits of the earth and everyone would be deprived as a consequence. The Livonian werewolves were not alone in their fight with the devil over the harvests: German werewolves did so as well, although they did not belong to the Livonian company and they journeyed to their own particular hell; and the same also was true of Russian werewolves who that year and the one before had won prosperous and abundant harvests for their land. As soon as the werewolves managed to snatch away from the devil the seed grain he had stolen, they cast it up into the air so that it might fall back down to earth and be spread over the fields of rich and poor alike.

At this juncture, as might have been foreseen, the judges tried to get Thiess to confess that he had entered into a compact with the devil. The old man reiterated, in vain, with monotonous obstinacy that he and his companions were 'the hounds of God' and the enemies of the devil, that they protected men from dangers and guaranteed the prosperity of harvests. Then the parish priest was summoned, who scolded him and called on him to abandon the errors and diabolical lies with which he had tried to cover up his sins. But this too was useless. In a burst of anger Thiess shouted at the priest that he was tired of hearing all this talk about his evil doings: his actions were better than the priest's, and moreover he, Thiess, would neither be the first nor the last to commit them. The old man remained steadfast in his convictions and refused to repent; on 10 October 1692 he was condemned to ten lashes for his superstitious beliefs and acts of idolatry.

This was not a case, clearly, of more or less ill-defined similarities, or of the repetition of metahistorical religious archetypes.[89] The beliefs of the old werewolf Thiess substantially resemble those which emerged at the trial of the two Friulian benandanti: battles waged by means of sticks and blows, enacted on certain nights to secure the fertility of fields, minutely and concretely described. Even details such as the broom handles with which the Livonian witches were armed recalls the stalks of sorghum or millet used by the witches of the Friuli. In the Friuli the struggle was primarily over the vineyards, in Livonia over barley and rye, but the struggle for fertility was understood as a work that was not merely tolerated but was even protected by God, who actually guaranteed entrance into paradise for the souls of the participants. There is not much doubt about any of this. Obviously, what we have here is a single agrarian cult, which, to judge from these remnants surviving in places as distant from one another as were Livonia and the Friuli, must have been diffused in an earlier period over a much vaster area, perhaps the whole of central Europe. On the other hand, these survivals may be explained either by the peripheral positions of the Friuli and Livonia with respect to the centre of diffusion of these beliefs, or by the influence, in both cases, of Slavic myths and traditions. The fact that in Germanic areas, as we shall see, there were faint traces of the myth of nocturnal combats waged over fertility, might lead us to lean towards the second possibility. Only intensive research may be able to resolve this problem.

But it is not just the beliefs of old Thiess that remind us of the Friulian benandanti. The reaction of the Jürgensburg judges resembles, even in particulars, that of the Udine inquisitors: both rejected, with mingled shock and indignation, the paradoxical boasts of the benandanti to be the champions of 'Christ's faith', and of the werewolves to be 'the hounds of God'. In both cases the judges tried to identify the benandanti and the werewolves with the witches who were followers and worshippers of the devil. There is a difference to be noted, however. Gasparutto and Moduco, to the best of our knowledge, were the first benandanti tried by the Holy Office; the very name 'benandanti' was unknown to the inquisitors. Only gradually would the benandanti assume the traits of diabolical witches. In that late seventeenth-century Livonian trial we are witnessing the opposite phenomenon. The figure and negative attributes of werewolves, the ferocious scourge of flocks and herds, were well known to the judges of Jürgensburg. But a totally different picture was painted by old Thiess: werewolves were defenders of the harvest and of livestock against the constant threat from the enemies of the prosperity of mankind and of the fertility of the land – the devil and the witches. This revival of presumably ancient beliefs can probably be explained by the fact that at the end of the seventeenth century Livonian judges had ceased to use judicial torture or even rely on leading questions in the interrogation of defendants.[90] That the favourable image of werewolves was much older than the end of the seventeenth century is shown first of all by Thiess's venerable age: presumably he must have acquired these beliefs in his distant youth, which brings us to the early years of the century. But there is an even more compelling bit of evidence. In mid-sixteenth century Caspar Peucer, during a digression on werewolves and their extraordinary exploits, inserted into his *Commentarius de praecipuis generibus divinationum* an anecdote about a young man of Riga who had suddenly fallen prostrate to the ground during a banquet. One of the onlookers had immediately recognized him as a werewolf. The next day the youth related that he had fought a witch who had been flying about in the guise of a red-hot butterfly. Werewolves, in fact, Peucer commented, boasted that they kept witches away.[91] This *was* an ancient belief, then. But, just as with the benandanti in the Friuli, under pressure from the judges, the original

positive qualities of the werewolves began gradually to fade away and become corrupted into the execrable image of the man-wolf, ravager of livestock.

In any case, on the basis of this surprising Livonian counterpart, it seems appropriate to suggest that there is a real, not an analogical, connection between benandanti and shamans. Such phenomena as trances, journeys into the beyond astride animals or in the form of animals (wolves or, as in the Friuli, butterflies and mice) to recover seed grain or to assure the fertility of the land, and as we will note shortly, participation in processions for the dead (which procured prophetic and visionary powers for the benandanti) form a coherent pattern which immediately evokes the rites of the shamans. But to trace the threads which tied these beliefs to the Baltic or Slavic world obviously falls outside the scope of this particular investigation. So let us return to the Friuli.

II THE PROCESSIONS OF THE DEAD

1

Towards the end of the year 1581 the inquisitor general of Aquileia and Concordia, Fra Felice da Montefalco, received a denunciation against a woman of Udine, the widow of Domenico Artichi, called Anna la Rossa, who claimed that she could see the dead and converse with them. The accusation was wholly confirmed during the interrogation of the witnesses. It seems that Anna had gone to visit a woman of Gemona, Lucia Peltrara, who was confined in a hospital, and told her that at the sanctuary of Santa Maria della Bella she had 'seen' a deceased daughter of Lucia's wrapped in a sheet and 'in a dishevelled state'. The dead girl had beseeched her to convey her last wishes to her mother: namely, that she should give a shirt to a certain Paola, and go on pilgrimages to some nearby sanctuaries. At first Lucia hesitated 'between yes and no'; later, torn by remorse, spurred on by the exhortations of her friends ('at least give it [the shirt] to her, which will be for the love of God') and at Anna's urging, she obeyed the wishes of her departed daughter, and thus finally put her own mind at rest.[1] Another witness, Aurelia of Gemona, confirmed Anna's extraordinary powers. The latter, for example, had been able to describe, without actually having been present, the details of a squabble occurring the night before between two brothers. Anna said that she had her information from the deceased mother of the two rivals who had been at the altercation and had tried, though invisible, to restore peace. Generally, it was common knowledge that Anna la Rossa could see the dead, and she herself made no secret of it.[2]

On 1 January 1582, it was Anna's turn to be interrogated by the Holy Office. At first she evaded the inquisitor's questions; eventually she admitted that 'many people' asked her whether she had seen their departed loved ones, but she drove them away angrily. It was a weak sort of defence: put on the spot 'she did not know what to say.' She was sent home, and the interrogation resumed the following day. Her skirmishing was of short duration. She quickly confessed that she had told Lucia Peltrara about the apparition of her daughter for a reward of five *soldi*: 'To support my husband and my children,' she gave as her excuse. For a similar reason, to obtain 'a few mouthfuls of bread', she had come up with the story of the fight between the two brothers.

The inquisitor was not satisfied, however, and wanted to get to the bottom of the matter: 'Have you been able to speak about what happens at night in the houses of others? How did you come to know all this? What sort of an art is it?' Anna 'did not know what to say.' This silence, Fra Felice warned her, made her gravely suspect of witchcraft. Anna burst into tears and 'cried exceedingly': 'No one will ever be able to say that I make medicines and that I am a witch.' And yet, the inquisitor reminded her, she had told someone 'that his mother was of good cheer, visited Santa Maria della Bella and had been holding Terentia by the hand'; and to another she had said that 'Master Battista goes around with his head down, worried-looking, saying nothing.' How had she come by these ideas and where had she seen these dead people? 'They just came into my head,' Anna replied. And, seeing that she was not going to confess, she was allowed to go, on condition that she remain at the disposal of the Holy Office.[3]

Fra Felice continued to investigate the case. On 7 March he summoned Lucia Peltrara to testify again. She supplied new particulars about Anna's powers, adding that 'she . . . goes about saying that the rest of us cannot see the dead, but she can, because she was born under that sign; and she also says that, if anyone wants to see their deceased father or mother, she can arrange it, but she worries that this might provoke some evil.'[4]

The facts that have emerged thus far are sufficiently clear. Anna la Rossa was trying, it would appear, to alleviate her own and her family's poverty by exploiting an extremely common but also insatiable desire, the longing to know something about the fate of a departed loved one (and linked with the hope of life beyond the tomb), mingled inextricably with the instinctive inability to think of a dead human being without restoring to it the life it no longer possessed. But this desire is tinged with remorse: remorse for not having lived up to what those beings had expected from us in life, here both alleviated and accentuated by the thought that there might be a way to do something for them, to directly better their otherworldly lot. This was undoubtedly the reason why Lucia Peltrara acceded to the last requests communicated to her by Anna: perhaps the shirt given in charity and the pilgrimages to the sanctuaries would shorten her daughter's suffering. The man who had come to Anna to hear about his dead mother must have rejoiced to learn that she 'was cheerful'; on the other hand, the parents of Master Battista who went about in the other world 'with his head down, worried-looking, saying nothing' must have been saddened. From this game of contrasting emotions Anna la Rossa squeezed out sometimes five *soldi*, sometimes a mouthful of bread. This was a seemingly direct, uncomplicated sort of behaviour. And yet it becomes charged with unforeseen implications in light of some later evidence.

Aurelia of Gemona, who was interrogated again on 7 March, declared that Anna 'said she knew many things which the dead themselves had told her, but that if she should tell some of these things, they would beat her fiercely with those stalks of sorghum which commonly grow in the fields.' And Anna herself added that 'on Fridays and Saturdays beds had to be made early, because on those days the dead would come in exhausted and throw themselves on the beds in their own houses.'[5] There is more: the denunciation which had provoked the investigation of Anna concluded with the statement that:[6]

> this woman used to be called by her husband many times at night while he was alive, and even though he elbowed her vigorously, it was as if she was dead, because she would say that the spirit had set out on its journey and thus the body remained as if dead; and when the spirit returned, she told her husband that when he found her in that state he should not become so infuriated, because she was in great pain and torment. And so her husband desisted and left her in peace.

A connection with the accounts of the benandanti appears from these facts, which must remain unexplained for the time being. It was not stated that Anna la Rossa was a benandante,[7] in fact the word was not even mentioned. But the lethargies into which she periodically fell, accompanied by the withdrawal of the spirit from the body which remained as if dead, recalls the tales of the benandanti (remember the testimony given by Gasparutto's wife) as well as those of the witches. Just like Anna, Polissena of San Macario, the Lucchese witch who was a victim of sudden deep fainting spells, said to her mother-in-law who had tried to revive her: 'When I am in the condition I was in last night, do not bother me, because you do me more harm than good.'[8] Moreover, Anna, going with her spirit to visit the dead, claimed to learn from them things she dared not repeat lest she be beaten with the stalks of sorghum which grew in the fields – the same weapons used by witches to punish benandanti who had not kept silent about the nocturnal gatherings. Finally, just like the witches described by the benandanti, the dead entered houses on given days to be restored. These are scattered elements which still do not constitute a coherent pattern: nevertheless, that some connection existed between the two seems unquestionable.

Could a presentiment of this connection also have struck the inquisitor entrusted with bringing the case of Anna la Rossa to a conclusion – the same Fra Felice da Montefalco who not long before had condemned the two benandanti to six months in prison? We cannot be certain. After hearing the new evidence he ordered, threatening excommunication *latae sententiae* in case of disobedience, that Anna should present herself within three days before the tribunal of the Holy Office. She was to testify about facts which, if verified, would render her suspect in matters of the faith. But when the time came, Anna could not be found: it seems that she had gone to Spilimbergo. Her husband and daughter came forward to ask that the date set for her appearance be postponed since Anna was far away and could not be reached on such short notice. The request was granted and the date moved back a month. On 30 March 1582 Anna voluntarily placed herself at the inquisitor's disposal. The latter discharged her, enjoining her to reappear at the end of Easter week.[9] But there is no trace that she did so. The trial was left unfinished and the new inquisitor, Fra Evangelista Sforza, discerned this deficiency in the course of sorting the papers inherited from his predecessor. A note inserted in the trial records by an unknown hand briefly summed up the results of the interrogations and concluded: 'Perhaps it would be better to pursue the trial, at least for the sake of her reputation.'[10] Was this veiled criticism of the way in which Anna's inquest had been conducted? It does indeed seem to suggest the intention of continuing the case and bringing it to a conclusion. But evidently it was not of such great concern even to the new inquisitor. On 1 February 1585 (three years later), Paolo Bisanzio, vicar general of the patriarch of Aquileia, Fra Evangelista Sforza, inquisitor general of Aquileia and Concordia, Pietro Gritti, provincial governor for the *Patria* of the Friuli, and other officials of lesser account met at Udine in the Church of San Giovanni a Platea. On this occasion the tribunal of the Holy Office, 'since it finally intended to come to a resolution . . . of the present trial,' and because the trial itself was 'of little . . . moment', ordered the inquisitor to wind it up personally, as soon as he had a chance to go to Gemona on other business.[11] In any case this conclusion never took place.

The connection between the benandanti and those who, like Anna la Rossa, claimed to see the dead emerges even more clearly in a trial begun in 1582 of the wife of a tailor, Aquilina, residing at Udine *in vico Grazzani*.[12] In the city as well as in all the neighbouring villages it was said about her that 'she makes a profession of seeing,' and cured diseases of every kind with spells and superstitious remedies. A 'great multitude of people' came to her, and there were rumours that she earned (since 'she wants to be paid and well paid at that . . . and can tell at a glance those who are able or unable to pay') perhaps a hundred, perhaps even more than two hundred ducats a year. There were those who claimed she was a witch, but 'if they call her witch she chases them away and becomes very angry because she wants them to call her Donna Aquilina.'[13] The depositions were numerous and in agreement: but it turned out to be impossible to question Aquilina. As soon as she learned of the suspicions piling up against her she fled, and found refuge, it seems, at Latisana. This inquest too broke off. Only after a year did the Holy Office decide to resume it. At that time it became known that among the sick who had come to Aquilina there had been a woman of Pasiano 'who used to say that she could see the dead.' When confronted, Aquilina replied that 'she must have been born with the caul.' This is a new link in the chain to add to those mentioned earlier.

On 26 August, 1583, Fra Felice da Montefalco went to the home of Aquilina, who claimed to be ill, with the intention of interrogating her. But the woman 'because of the great fear and fright given her by so many horsemen,' that is, by the emissaries of the Holy Office, slipped away and hid in the house of a neighbour. The inquisitor came upon her there, still in a state of terror. When he asked her why she had fled and thereby disobeyed the orders of the Holy Office, she replied: 'Because I am afraid.' 'Afraid of what?' 'Afraid,' she replied. On 27 October, after a series of delays sought and obtained by her husband, the moment of the interrogation finally came. Aquilina had recovered her composure, and responded in a defiant manner to the inquisitor's threat of excommunication: 'Even the excommunicated eat,' she said, 'there will be a pardon, and I will have myself absolved so that I won't die excommunicated.'[14] She declared that she was not able to recognize children who had been bewitched, and added impetuously: 'Nor do I know what is meant by witches . . . I have even been asked where I store the ointment which I use to grease my feet when I run up the chimney; but what do I know about running up chimneys?' Similarly, she denied being acquainted with any of the benandanti: she knew only that persons born with the caul were benandanti. And, in reply to a question from Fra Felice, she related that one day a woman of Pasiano had come to her in tears and told her 'that she could see the dead but she did not want to see them.' Aquilina said to her 'that it would satisfy her curiosity if she could see a daughter of her own who was dead, and who was dressed in such and such a way.' But then she stated that she no longer believed that the dead went wandering about, 'because,' she said ingenuously, 'I had a husband and a daughter who loved me very much, and if they could go about, they surely would have come to visit me.'[15]

The aftermath of Aquilina's trial – the prohibition against using cures based on spells and superstitions, the denunciations which followed without interruption until 1591 despite penances which had been imposed two years earlier by a new inquisitor – does not concern us here except as further confirmation of the relative lack of interest (evidenced by the slackness in the judicial process, the interruptions, the postponements) on the part of inquisitors in these widespread superstitions and beliefs, considered harmless in comparison with contemporary heretical infiltrations throughout the Friuli.

3

In that same year, 1582, Fra Felice da Montefalco investigated a woman of Cividale, the widow of a certain Andrea of Orsaria, named Caterina la Guercia, accused of practising 'various maleficent arts'.[16] When she was interrogated on 14 September, she declared that her occupation was 'to sew and to weave'; but she knew how to cure children's sicknesses by uttering certain words, which she did not consider superstitious. This prompted Fra Felice to ask her, abruptly, whether she was a benandante. Caterina denied it: 'No sir, not I, I am not one of the benandanti, but my deceased husband was; he used to go in procession with the dead.'

Here then was explicit confirmation of a link which had been suggested hypothetically: whoever could see the dead, went with them that is, was a benandante. Caterina la Guercia's husband even used to fall into a sort of swoon: 'I would remove his shoes, and he lay on the bed . . . still, and he was not to be touched until he returned from the procession, because his spirit solemnly went out, and even though I might call him, he would not respond.' And she added: 'There were many people who wanted him to show them their dead, but he never would, saying that later the dead would have beaten him, and I knew that there were some among them who even wanted to give him bushels of grain.' But she was not able to say who accompanied her husband on these processions, and she herself did not go: 'Because I did not possess that grace; God did not give it to me as it was given to him.'[17]

In the case of Anna la Rossa, one could suppose, at least initially, that the alleged ability to see the dead was no more than a device to earn a little money. Gradually, instead, this 'power' took the form of a widespread belief (and not just of an individual stratagem), and for those who claimed to possess it, namely the benandanti, it became a destiny. It was a thing that weighed heavily on life, marking it indelibly – sometimes accepted as a grace from God, sometimes as a 'fate' from which they longed to flee, but could not, as with the unknown woman of Pasiano. At times, even witches asserted that they proceeded to the sabbat impelled by an irresistible interior force. The Lucchese witch, Margherita of San Rocco, replied to a judge who had asked her 'what reward they received, or hoped to receive from such servitude': 'I did not expect to get anything, and since I was born with that disgrace I used to go [to the sabbat] and experience certain pleasures.'[18] But it was principally 'the going out' to fight the witches that became the inevitable necessity for Gasparutto and Moduco. When they reached the predetermined age they were called 'by means of a drum in the same way that soldiers are called, and . . . they are obliged to respond.' And for them too the fact of being summoned was a sign from God: 'I cannot teach this art to anyone,' declared Gasparutto, 'when our Lord God has chosen not to teach it Himself.'[19] This was an additional link between the benandanti who went out at night 'in spirit' to observe the dead, and the benandanti who went out 'in spirit' to contend with the witches over the harvests. We are faced here with two branches – presumably not independent of one another, as the points of contact between them suggest – of a single belief with roots stretching far back into time.

In his instructions to bishops, Regino of Prüm (d. 915) along with various other superstitions, condemned the belief of women who, deceived by the devil, claimed that they rode on certain nights with Diana, the pagan goddess, and her entourage of women, travelling to remote places.[20] This passage, taken up time after time by various authors, and finally introduced by Gratian into his great collection of canon law, provoked an interminable round of debate in the demonological literature: the same passage, in fact, described nocturnal cavalcades and conventicles (more or less resembling the sabbat of the witches) as phenomena that were not rooted in reality and were produced by diabolical illusion. According to some authorities, consequently, the celebrated *Canon Episcopi* constituted an argument against the persecution of witches, poor women who were the victims of the deceptions and seductions of the devil.

The long discussion which ensued on this subject does not concern us here. It is important, instead, to note that this belief in nocturnal cavalcades had a wide diffusion, as witnessed by the ancient German penitential works. In these writings, however, the name of Diana was occasionally replaced by such popular Germanic divinities as Holda, endowed with attributes which, in a contradiction frequently encountered, were related to both life and death. Holda, in fact, like her sister deity in southern Germany, Perchta, was at the same time goddess of vegetation, and thus of fertility, and the leader of the 'Furious Horde' or 'Wild Hunt' (*Wütischend Heer, Wilde Jagd, Mesnie Sauvage*) – namely of the ranks of those who had died prematurely and passed through village streets at night, unrelenting and terrible, while the inhabitants barricaded their doors for protection.[21] There is no doubt that the nocturnal cavalcades of Diana's female followers are a version of the 'Wild Hunt'. And this explains the astonishing presence of Diana 'the pagan goddess' in these popular myths – an identification, helped by certain superficial similarities, made on an educated level by inquisitors, theologians and preachers. Even Diana-Hecate, in fact, was followed in her nocturnal wanderings by a band of the dead for whom there was no peace: people taken by death before their time, children snatched away at an early age, victims of a violent end.[22]

There is a reference to these nocturnal hordes guided by a female figure in a work by William of Auvergne (d. 1249). According to the common people, a mysterious divinity (but in reality a devil, William explained) called Abundia or Satia, wandered at night through houses and cellars, accompanied by her followers, eating and drinking whatever they could find: if she came upon food and bread left as offerings, she bestowed prosperity on the house and its inhabitants; otherwise she withdrew and refused her protection.[23] There also is an allusion to *dame Abonde* and to her followers in the *Roman de la Rose*, written towards the end of the thirteenth century. It relates that there were those who believed (although the poet himself thought all this was *'folie orrible'*) that the thirdborn were obliged to go thrice weekly to the homes of neighbours in the company of *dame Abonde*. Nothing could stop them, neither walls nor barred doors, since only their souls travelled while their bodies remained behind, immobile: if the body should be turned over, however, the soul would never return to it.[24]

In many respects these narratives resemble the accounts of the benandanti. Regarding the propitiatory offerings, we remember that Gasparutto had urged the priest of Brazzano to always keep some 'clean water' handy, since when witches, warlocks, and benandanti 'return from these games all hot and tired, as they pass in front of houses, when they find clear, clean water in pails they drink it, if not, they also go into the cellars and overturn all the wine.' This piece of evidence is actually somewhat imprecise: even in the present circumstance, as Moduco explained, we have a distinct contrast between the behaviour of the 'evildoers' (*malandanti*), the witches, and that of the benandanti: 'Getting astride the casks,' he said, 'we drank with a pipe, as did the witches; but after they had drunk, they pissed in the casks.'[25] On the other hand, the same element recurred, but with a different meaning, in the stories told to her neighbours by Anna la Rossa – one of the benandanti who claimed she could see the dead: 'On Fridays and Saturdays,' she said, 'beds had to be made early, because on those days the dead would return exhausted and throw themselves on the beds in their own houses.'[26] Even food was prepared, in this variant of the myth, not to propitiate, but to assist the dead, who on certain days were seized by longing for their former homes and, fatigued from their wanderings, asked to be received, to rest and be fed. The belief has been preserved, in this very form, in Italian popular traditions (and not in Italy alone) from Piedmont to the Abruzzi and Sardinia. In these places, on 2 November, All Souls' Day, the deceased pass through the town in long processions, carrying candles, and re-enter their former homes where the charity of the living has placed food, drink and clean beds at their disposal.[27]

Another similarity between the followers of *dame Abonde* and the 'agrarian' benandanti is, of course, the journey accomplished by the soul alone, with the inanimate body remaining behind. Even the fact that if a body was turned over, the soul would never be able to re-enter its natural home can be found in the accounts of the benandanti ('if the body should be rolled over while it is without its spirit, it would remain dead, and its spirit could never return to it'). On the other hand, this detail is encountered also in the confessions of witches, as emerges from a Lucchese trial cited above ('if perchance we were turned over face down we would lose the spirit and the body would die')[28] – one thread of evidence among many (if we look beneath later incrustations built up around the devil) connecting these ancient beliefs to actual witchcraft. We should note especially that, just like the benandanti born with a caul, the thirdborn followers of *dame Abonde* had the duty, imposed on them by destiny, to secure prosperity and abundance.

But, as we have said, Abonde is only one of the many names assumed by this popular deity. A woman tried by the Milanese Inquisition in 1390 for having asserted that she belonged to the 'society' of Diana, declared that the goddess accompanied by her followers wandered at night among the houses, chiefly those of the well-to-do, eating and drinking: and when the company came to dwellings that were well swept and orderly, Diana bestowed her blessing.[29] Two centuries later, instead, in Bavaria, we again find the name of Abonde, employed, significantly, as synonymous with Perchta. The *Thesaurus pauperum*, written in 1468, actually condemned the idolatrous superstition of those who left food and drink at night in open view for Abundia and Satia, or, as the people said, Fraw Percht and her retinue, hoping thereby to gain abundance and riches. The same superstitious practice of offering salt, food and drink to Perchta, *'alias domine Habundie'*, on specific days had been noted and condemned a few decades previously, in 1439, by Thomas Ebendorfer von Haselbach in his treatise *De decem praeceptis*.[30]

5

Evidence such as this indicates that there was a connection, still of a rather general nature, between the popular divinity of the many names – Abundia-Satia-Diana-Perchta[31] – and the complex of beliefs which revolved about the benandanti. We can be even more precise regarding this convergence.

The Dominican J. Nider (1380–1438), in his *Praeceptorium divinae legis* recorded the names of those who had contravened the first commandment by superstitious acts and beliefs. Among them were those individuals who thought they could be transported to the conventicles of Herodias, and, immediately following, women who 'during the Ember Days, out of their senses, boasted of having seen the souls in purgatory and of many other fantasies'. After these women recovered from their swoons, they related extraordinary things about souls in purgatory or in hell, about stolen or lost objects, and so forth. According to Nider these poor wretches had been deceived by the devil, and it was not surprising, if during their obscure trances, they did not even feel the burn from the flame of a candle: the devil possessed them to such a point that they were aware of nothing, just like the victims of epilepsy.[32]

This passage in Nider (who referred continually in his works to superstitions encountered in the Germanic world) reminds us closely of the benandanti's own accounts – in particular, of the female benandanti who claimed that they could see the dead during the Ember Days. But, significantly, Nider, while stressing the diabolical character of these hallucinations, compared them not so much to witchcraft as to the visions of those who claimed they participated in the gatherings of Diana, of Herodias, or of Venus, synonymous with the female divinity who was believed to wander about at night followed by her retinue of women.

The distinction between these pre-witchcraft beliefs and witchcraft proper shows up, with striking clarity, in a passage of the chronicle (which should be dated several decades after Nider's death) of Matthias von Kemnat, a chaplain at the court of the Upper Palatinate. After describing the characteristics of the evil 'sect *Gazariorum*', namely diabolical witchcraft, which included the sabbat, pacts with the devil, crimes and such things, Kemnat mentioned another, less infamous sect which had been persecuted at Heidelberg *c.* 1475, and about which he was not able to say very much: it concerned women who 'travelled' during the Ember Days, provoking storms and casting non-fatal spells on men.[33] Here too, however, the mysterious wanderings of these women during the Ember Days was linked to a cluster of beliefs with which we are already familiar. Kemnat cited in this context an episode from the life of San Germano in the *Legenda Aurea* of Jacopo da Voragine. The reference was to propitiatory offerings destined for 'the good women who go forth at night' and to strange nocturnal journeys.[34] It seems plausible to suppose that this 'less infamous' sect, whose traces were beginning to disappear, was nothing other than a residue of popular beliefs to which true witchcraft was being grafted towards the end of the fifteenth century (Kemnat was writing before the publication of the *Malleus maleficarum*). It probably was not accidental that in the first witchcraft trials held in the canton of Lucerne and in the Tyrol, the defendants stated that they went to the sabbat on Thursdays in the Ember Days, while later in these same regions they spoke only of Thursdays without other particulars.[35]

6

Thus, the mysterious journeys by wómen during the nights of the Ember seasons was an ancient motif and not limited to the Friuli. Moreover, it always seemed to be closely connected to the myth of the nocturnal travels of the band of women led by Abundia-Satia-Diana-Perchta, and thus also to that of the 'Wild Hunt' or 'Furious Horde'. An identical connection recurs, at the beginning of the sixteenth century, in the Strasbourg sermons of Geiler von Kaisersberg, collected under the title *Die Emeis*. Here, Geiler, discussing witches and others who stated that they went at night to see 'Fraw Fenus' (Venus), mentioned women who, during the Ember Days, fell into swoons which rendered them insensible to pricks or scaldings. When they revived, they related what they had seen, declaring that they had been in heaven, and spoke of stolen or hidden objects.[36] These were diabolical visions, Geiler commented, virtually repeating the words of Nider cited above: and yet the popular, immediate tenor of his sermons, which developed in the form of answers to questions and doubts advanced by the faithful, makes rather improbable the theory that the passage is simply a literary allusion, unrelated to the actual popular beliefs of the time. The fact that Geiler returned to the theme of the superstitions associated with the Ember seasons also favours this interpretation: in these periods, and especially during the Ember Days of Christmas, the holiest of all according to popular belief, the 'Furious Horde' appeared, composed of people who had died before their time, as for example, soldiers who had perished in battle and were compelled to wander until their allotted time on earth had elasped.[37] But even this fact takes us back to the benandanti and their tales. We recall how Gasparutto had stated,[38]

> 'and if by chance while we are out someone should come with a light and look for a long time at the body, the spirit would never re-enter it until there was no one left around to see it that night; and if the body, seeming to be dead, should be buried, the spirit would have to wander around the world until the hour fixed for the body to die.'

Plate 1 Geiler von Kaisersberg, *Die Emeis*, Strasbourg 1516, f. xxxvii r (by permission of the British Library)

What really characterized this kernel of traditions and myths is the fact that it had absolutely no connection with the educated world, if we except the attempt to portray such popular deities as Perchta or Holda in the guise of Diana or Venus, who were better known as such to the authors of the writings that we have discussed above. The volume of Geiler's Strasbourg sermons is a striking example of this disassociation. We know only two editions of the work. In the first, the sermon dealing with the 'Furious Horde' ('Am dürnstag nach Reminiscere von dem wütischen heer') is accompanied by an engraving which, at first glance, may seem a surprising choice: in a charming wood the carriage of Bacchus approaches, preceded by a satyr playing on a bagpipe and by an inebriated Silenus, with his head thrown back and wreathed with bunches of grapes, riding an ass (see Plate 1). It is difficult to see how this scene from classical mythology could have been expected to suggest to readers the shadowy myth of the 'Furious Horde', so well known to them. The artist had taken the

Plate 2 *Publii Virgilii Maronis Opera* . . , Argentorati 1502, f. lxi r (by permission of the Bodleian Library, shelfmark: DOUCE V SUBT 21)

illustration from an edition of Virgils's works published by Sebastian Brant in 1502, confining himself to removing the figure of the poet seated at his desk, on the left of the picture (see Plate 2). In itself there was nothing exceptional about this. But in the present case the gulf between the text being commented on and the figure was so great, that the illustrator of the *Emeis* did not even bother, as he had done elsewhere, to delete the labels with the names 'Bachus', 'Silenus', 'Satirus'.[39] For the 'Furious Horde', to be sure, there was no iconographic tradition to fall back on, but Bacchus's peaceful cavalcade could not have satisfied Geiler's readers, just as it does not satisfy us today. In 1517, a year after the first edition, the *Emeis* was republished, again in Strasbourg, with some changes in the illustrations, including a substitution for the engraving accompanying the sermon on the 'Furious Horde'. Bacchus's cavalcade was replaced, not with an original engraving, but with an image based on an illustration in Brant's *Stultifera navis* (Basel, 1 August 1497), modified here and there (for example, the horoscope upper left is lacking; see Plates 3 and 4).[40] Obviously, Brant's wagon-load of fools seemed more suitable than a group of Bacchus's followers to express the aura of mystery and terror surrounding the myth of the 'Furious Horde'. But the substitution also

Plate 3 Geiler von Kaisersberg, *Die Emeis*, Strasbourg 1517, f. xxxvii r (by permission of the National Library of Paris)

tells us something about the difficulty of attempting to translate into visual imagery a popular belief which, in contrast to doctrines concerned with witchcraft, lacked points of reference in the world of the educated classes.[41]

7

So then, the nights of the Ember Days in which the journeying of the women condemned by Nider and Geiler took place (as well as those of the female Friulian benandanti) were also, according to a tradition widespread in central Europe, the nights in which the 'Furious Horde' appeared.[42] Needless to say, this morbid vision differs greatly from the processions of the dead we have encountered in the trials of the female benandanti. The tradition of the 'Wild Hunt' or of the 'Furious Horde' which expressed an ancient, pre-Christian fear of the dead seen as mere objects of terror, as unrelenting maleficent entities

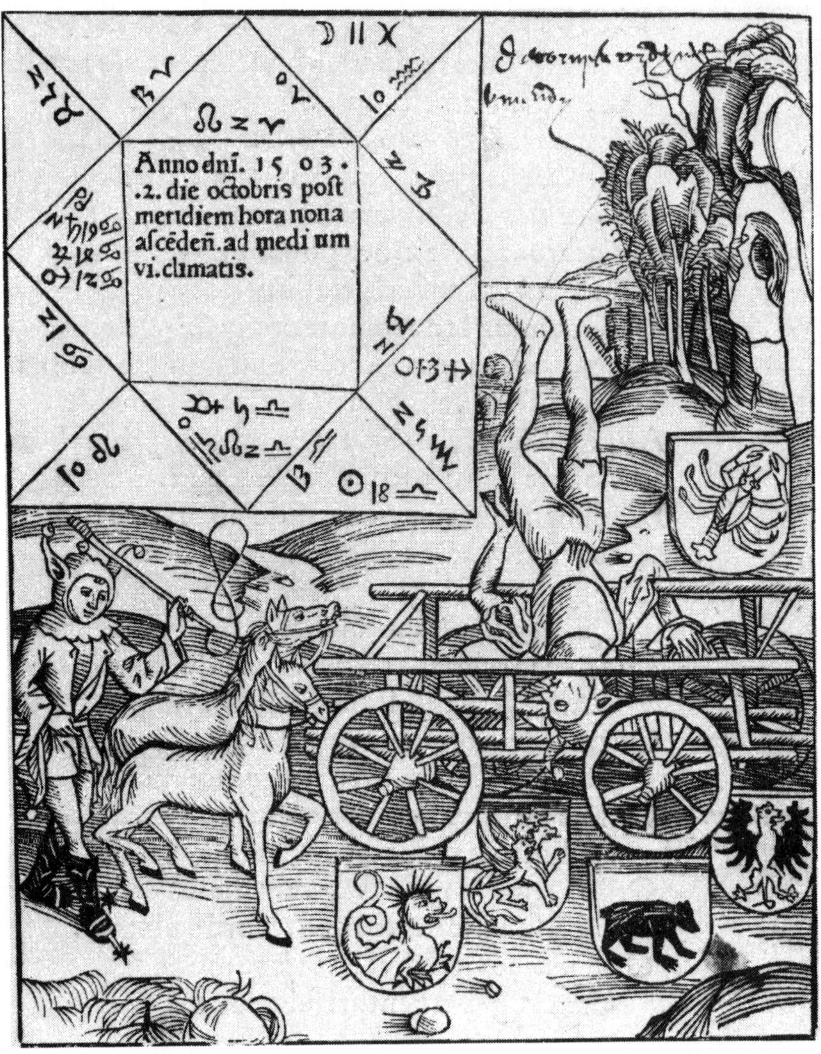

Plate 4 S. Brant, *Stultifera navis*, Basel 1497, f. cxlv r
(by permission of the British Library)

without the possibility for any sort of expiation, began to experience attempts at Christianization very early. The first evidence of this is a passage in the *Ecclesiastical History* of Orderic Vitalis. Under the year 1091 he inserted an account of an extraordinary event occurring in 'a village called Bonneval', the present-day Saint-Aubin de Bonneval. One night, a priest strolling along a path suddenly heard a clamour resembling an army on the march. Immediately an enormous being armed with a club stood before him, followed by a great multitude of men and women, some on foot, others on horseback, all cruelly tormented by demons. Among them the priest recognized many individuals who had died only a short time before and he heard their pitiful cries. He saw assassins, lewd women, clerics and monks (and even many commonly believed to be among the saved): and then it dawned on him that he was face to face with the *'familia Herlechini'*, whose existence he had always doubted, even when confronted by the most tangible kind of evidence. The dead spoke to him, describing their suffering, and gave him messages for their loved ones on earth.[43] Here, clearly, the dead were no longer a dark and terrible presence passing like a whirlwind through village streets: they had been introduced into the framework of the Christian afterlife and had assumed the traditional function of instructing and admonishing the living.[44] Obvious traces of the ancient beliefs lingered in this initial, tentative attempt at Christianization: thus, the company of the dead was led by the legendary Wild Man, here possessing some of the characteristics of the devil Herlechinus (gradually, he will exchange the club, symbol of the savage, for a bat, assuming the well-known traits of Harlequin's disguise)[45] who elsewhere appears as the head of the 'Wild Hunt'. But this first timid attempt to give a new and pious content to the ancient myths, was significantly transformed in the popular traditions of the region around Saint-Aubin de Bonneval: in these accounts it was a horde of men dressed in red whom the priest encountered. They led him to a field and there asked him to forsake God and the faith.[46]

These two elements – the deity at the head of the 'Wild Hunt' and the procession of the dead – are both still present but in a modified form in a trial held at Mantua in 1489. The principle defendant, Giuliano Verdena, was a weaver, as were also the witnesses summoned to testify – the master and two of Giuliano's companions in the trade. It came out in their depositions that Giuliano was accustomed to tell fortunes by filling a vase with water (sometimes holy water), setting it beside a lamp and then getting a boy or girl to gaze into it and murmur a well-known magical formula ('White angel, holy angel, etc.'). The proceedings were the customary ones, but the purpose of the spell was unusual, inasmuch as Giuliano only rarely permitted himself to make the reflections of perpetrators of petty thefts appear on the water of the vase.[47] Usually, he read from a book, while he urged the children to pay close attention to what they would see form on the surface of the water: and the children might say that they saw 'many, many who seemed to be Muslims,'[48] or 'a great multitude of people some of whom were on foot, others mounted, a few without hands,' and sometimes 'a large man seated with a servant on either side.'[49]

Giuliano explained to the children that the 'Muslims' were spirits, and the mysterious personage was Lucifer, *'magister artis'*. The latter clutched a closed book in his hand, in which many hidden treasures were recorded: and Giuliano stated that he wanted to copy that book at all costs,' for the sake of Christianity, in order to proceed against the Turk and destroy him.'[50] At other times the children discerned in the water of the vase a figure which Giuliano recognized as the 'mistress of the game', (a designation used alternately for Diana and Herodias) who 'clothed in black, with a chin to her stomach', appeared before Giuliano himself, saying she was ready to reveal to him 'the properties of herbs and the nature of animals'.[51] But in these figures which Giuliano saw as a multitude of spirits we perceive a remnant of the tradition of the procession of the dead, some on foot, others on horseback, described by Orderic Vitalis. Sometimes Giuliano might ask the girl to look in that same vase of water to learn 'whether he would go to hell, or not'; and the girl beholding him 'in a cauldron, Lucifer above him, holding him down with a sort of mattock', would keep silent, 'lest Giuliano beat her.' In turn, Giuliano showed her her dead father, and the girl, declaring that she had seen him 'in purgatory and ascending to heaven', burst into tears. And another time Giuliano 'out of his own imagination' caused a cleric who was helping him with the incantations to see an unidentified 'illustrious Lord Robert . . . damned in hell, in a fiery cauldron, above whom was Lucifer, Barbariza . . . Zanetin and other spirits.'[52] All this testifies to the fact that the ancient motif of the wandering dead assumed a new emotional content with the passing of time. It ceased to instruct the living by portraying for their benefit the punishments attending them in the afterlife. Through divinatory magic it became an outlet for an acute and painful anxiety about both the problem of individual salvation as well as regret and longing for dead relatives.

8

With the trial of Giuliano Verdena we seem to have lost sight of the benandanti: the only point of contact between them seems to be the mention of the procession of souls and their fate beyond the tomb. Actually, here too, even if only marginally, we are dealing with a similar set of beliefs. This becomes clear if we compare Verdena's revelations to those of a woman of Burseberg in the Tyrol, Wyprat

Musin, tried for her superstitions on 27 December 1525. Two years earlier, during a night in one of the Ember seasons, she testified, a great multitude appeared before her led by a woman who said she was called Fraw Selga and was the sister of Fraw Venus.[53] Fraw Selga ordered the terrorized Musin to follow her, or face death, in the processions that took place in various parts of the parish on Thursday and Saturday nights. Musin had to join in, whether she wanted to or not, Fraw Selga affirmed, since she had been predestined to them from birth. The processions were composed of souls in purgatory, as well as of the damned who were suffering various punishments; and these souls reassured Musin by telling her that those who participated in these processions had to keep themselves virtuous, not committing sins, and giving alms. During their conventicles, which took place in the Ember Days, they gazed into a sort of basin, which was also a fire (Musin was not able to explain herself better: what she meant, as it became clearer from some related evidence, was a basin in which the fires of hell appeared)[54] in which the likenesses of the members of the parish who were destined to die within the year could be seen. In addition, Fraw Selga told Musin that she knew places where there was much buried treasure intended for those who served and prayed to God.

There are obvious similarities between this tale and Verdena's: the feminine divinity (in one case described simply as Fraw Selga, in the other as 'the mistress of the game'), the buried treasures, the band of souls, the theme of otherworldly fate, and even the detail of the basin filled with water which reflected the images of those who were soon to die. But in this second case, the woman, compelled by an inescapable destiny to take part in the processions of souls, went forth at night during the Ember seasons – and, we can be sure that if she had lived on the other side of the Alps, in the Friuli, she would have called herself a benandante. In any case, her confessions confirm the deep ties existing between these benandanti, whom we could dub 'funereal', and the beliefs attached to the 'Furious Horde'.

9

We do not know if Wyprat Musin was accused of being a witch: in any case, elements that were explicitly diabolical or related to witchcraft were missing from her account. In other places, people who asserted that they had seen the souls of the dead in nocturnal processions were condemned straight away as witches. Consider the case of a woman of Küssnacht whom we know only by her very revealing name of *Seelenmutter*, mother of souls. She was denounced in 1573 at the council of Schwyz because of her 'unchristian fantasies' and burned as a witch a few years later.[55] Just like the female benandanti of the Friuli she put her vaunted powers to practical use and, in return for a little money, provided information about the otherworldly destiny of men and women who had died or disappeared long before. Occasionally her revelations were exposed sensationally. Once, after her announcement that a shoemaker had died among the Lutherans and, thus, alms had to be given and prayers offered for his soul in the church of Our Lady at Einsiedeln, he reappeared six months later, alive and flourishing.[56] There is no evidence that the *Seelenmutter* claimed to see hordes of the dead on the nights of the Ember seasons. We do know, however, that in Lucerne, in the canton of Schwyz and to some extent in Switzerland as a whole, the belief in nocturnal processions of the prematurely dead was extremely widespread. In this version, even living beings could participate through their souls, leaving their bodies behind in bed, and as a result be deemed particularly fortunate and pious.[57] Moreover, the *Seelenmutter* herself had told a necromancer, whom she had instructed in the art of evoking spirits, that if he was born during the Ember Days, of spirits he would be certain to see many.[58] Thus, here too, there are features that we have already encountered in the tales told by the female Friulian benandanti, but in a state of confusion due either to the sketchy nature of the evidence, or because we are on the boundaries of the area of diffusion of these beliefs.

Perhaps the second is the true explanation. Indeed the evidence which bears the closest resemblance to the Friulian is Bavarian. It concerns a trial held at Oberstdorf in 1586 (even the dates correspond), of a shepherd named Chonradt Stöcklin, thirty-seven years of age. He told the Oberstdorf judges that eight years before on his way to the forest to cut down fir trees, the drover Jakob Walch, a townsman of his who had died eight days before, suddenly appeared before him. Walch confided that he was being compelled to wander for three years before experiencing the pains of hell, and exhorted him to live honestly and piously, and always to keep God before his eyes. These apparitions were repeated; after a year the dead cowherd appeared before him again, dressed all in white, with a red cross on his chest, and invited him to follow. Suddenly, Stöcklin experienced a loss of consciousness, and found himself in a place where he saw suffering and joy – hell and heaven he thought – inhabited by people he did not know. There he was urged to pray often (thirty thousand Ave Marias during the Ember Days), take his wife and children to Mass, abstain from sinning and venerate the sacraments. On still another occasion the dead cowherd Walch told him, in reply to a question, that the almighty God had turned him into an angel and that there was not anything sinful in his wandering about. In fact, Stöcklin explained at the trial, there were three ways in which one might wander: the first, was by being one of the 'nocturnal band', to which he himself belonged; the second, as one of the deceased, waiting for their destined hour; the third, by joining witches going to the sabbat, but about this last he did not know anything, because he had never participated. The journeying of the 'nocturnal band' took place during the Ember Days, on Fridays and Saturdays, almost always at night. Prior to setting out one fell into a swoon and remained in an inert state: it was the soul (at least so he supposed) which departed, leaving the body behind immobile and lifeless for an hour or a little more. Woe, however, if the body, meanwhile, be turned over, because that would make the re-entry of the soul painful and difficult. To one of the judges' questions Stöcklin replied that he knew only one member of the 'nocturnal band', but not his name. However, he was able to furnish the names of many witches of Oberstdorf and their misdeeds, which he had learned about during his mysterious nocturnal journeys; he asserted that he could cure men and beasts stricken by witches, and that he had done so many times through the grace of God, by imposing prayers and fasts.

The judges challenged Stöcklin's startling statements down to the smallest detail, but without success; in no way could they extort an admission from him that he was a witch, that he had participated in a sabbat or that he had bound himself to the devil. Obstinately, he repeated that he had nothing to do with the devil and with witchcraft. But when Stöcklin was interrogated anew on 23 December 1586, he began to vacillate: first of all, he admitted that at age sixteen he had received an ointment from his mother which he used to bewitch both men and animals; then, pressed hard by the judges, he confessed that he had gone to the sabbat many times, and that he had abjured God and the saints before the great devil. Not yet fully satisfied, the judges had him tortured, and obtained a fuller confession and a long list of accomplices. In the end, Stöcklin was condemned to the stake together with the various women whom he had accused.[59]

A nucleus of fairly consistent and compact beliefs stand out from these dispersed and fragmentary pieces of evidence – beliefs which, in the course of a century, from 1475 to 1585, could be found in a clearly defined area which included Alsace, Württemberg (Heidelberg), Bavaria, the Tyrol; and, on the fringes, Switzerland (the canton of Schwyz). Intensive research of a kind which has not been attempted yet (and these brief remarks are not intended to be a substitute for it) may be able to furnish a fuller and more detailed picture of this diffusion. Even so, it seems possible to establish the existence of a thread linking the various pieces of evidence that have been examined thus far: the presence of groups of individuals – generally women – who during the Ember Days fell into swoons and remained unconscious for brief periods of time during which, they affirmed, their souls left their bodies to join the processions of the dead (which were almost always nocturnal) presided over at least in one case by a female divinity (Fraw Selga). We have also seen that these processions were linked to an older and even more widely diffused myth, that of the 'Wild Hunt'. It was precisely these elements that reappeared, as we shall see more clearly, in the confessions of the female Friulian benandanti. Their accounts even occasionally included the mention of a multiformed feminine divinity. A benandante of Latisana, Maria Panzona, who was tried in 1619, claimed that she entered the valley of Josaphat many times in spirit, astride an animal, and that with the other benandanti paid homage 'bowing her head to a certain woman called the abbess, seated in majesty on the edge of a well.'[60]

But what was the connection between the female benandanti who could see the dead and the 'agrarian' benandanti, such as Moduco and Gasparutto, who said they went out at night during the Ember seasons to fight for rich harvests against witches and warlocks? The name they shared, first of all, and the swoons into which they fell on the nights of the Ember Days, conceived as the journey of the disembodied soul, immediately suggest that theirs were two offshoots of a single belief. Moreover, other elements crop up in the confessions of the Bavarian shepherd, Chonradt Stöcklin, which also help to connect the two currents – the faculty to recognize witches and their crimes, and the power to cure the victims of spells. Furthermore, evidence collected earlier has demonstrated the association between the deity and her retinue of the dead (Abundia-Satia-Diana-Perchta), and wealth and abundance. But there was no mention of the Ember Days: and even abundance was understood in general terms, without specific allusions to the fertility of the fields. This last piece of the mosaic is provided by another group of beliefs in which the feminine divinity who presided over the ranks of the dead reappears under another name: Holda (Frau Holle) or Venus.[61]

11

For the year 1544, Martin Crusius, in his *Annales Svevici*, cites a curious tale, borrowed from an older chronicle.[62] Wandering about the Swabian countryside at that time were certain *clerici vagantes* who wore yellow nets draped about their shoulders in the place of capes. They had approached a group of peasants and told them they had been on the Venusberg and had seen extraordinary things there. They claimed knowledge of the past and could foretell the future; they had the power to discover lost objects and possessed charms which protected both men and animals from witches and their crimes; they could even keep hail away. With such boasts, intermingled with fearsome words mumbled ominously through clenched teeth, they stunned both men and women, especially the latter, and extorted money from them. As though this was not enough, they also declared that they could call up the 'Furious Horde', made up of children who had died before they were baptized, of men slain in battle and of all 'ecstatics' – in other words of those whose souls had had to abandon their bodies, never to return.[63] These souls, they said, were accustomed to gather in deserted places on the Saturday nights of the Ember seasons and on Thursdays of Advent, wandering about, sorrowing, until the appointed time of their deaths, when they could be received among the blessed. These *clerici vagantes* claimed that they had two lengths of rope, one for grain, the other for wine: if one of them was buried, the price of grain or wine would increase that year.

Once again, if this evidence had come from the Friuli instead of Swabia, we can be certain that these *clerici vagantes* would have added being benandanti to their boasting. Here too there are obvious similarities: the journey to the mysterious kingdom of Venus (where, in the popular mind, there was believed to be a real afterlife as we shall see later) gave them the power to cure spells, and, during the Ember Days, to summon the ranks of those who had died prematurely, to which 'ecstatics' like themselves belonged, whose souls had not been able to return to their bodies; it also gave them the ability to obtain wealth for farmers by working their magic, not on the fertility of fields, as did their Friulian counterparts, but curiously enough, on the prices of agricultural products. This was the year 1544, forty years before the trial of Gasparutto and Moduco: but it would be hasty to conclude that these beliefs arrived in the Friuli from Germany, merely because there are no Friulian trials recorded prior to the first half of the sixteenth century. At any rate, groups of *clerici vagantes* who claimed to have been on the Venusberg appeared at Lucerne in 1576 (significantly they were compared to the *Seelenmutter* of Küssnacht discussed earlier) and again in 1599 and 1600.[64] A similar group, belonging to an association called *Johannesbrüderschaft*, was tried at L'vov in 1694: like their Swabian fellows of a century and a half before, these *clerici vagantes* searched for treasures, claimed to have seen the souls of the dead on the Venusberg and tried to call them forth.[65]

12

The connection between the world of the dead ('Furious Horde', Venusberg) and the fertility of the fields, mentioned by Crusius, stands out even more sharply in a trial of a sorcerer, Diel Breull, held at Hesse in 1630.[66] He had been tried the year before for casting spells while gazing into a crystal ball and was condemned to be banished. In the course of the second trial, Breull related that eight years back, during a period of profound depression (he had lost his wife and children), he happened once to fall asleep and, upon waking, found himself on the Venusberg. The deity of the place, 'Fraw Holt' – the Germanic Holle, considered synonymous with Venus – showed him the strangest things reflected in a basin of water: magnificent horses, men feasting or seated in the middle of a fire, and, among them, people he knew who had died long before. They were there, Fraw Holt explained, because of their misdeeds. Diel Breull then realized that he was a member of the nocturnal band, a *'nachtfahr'*, the same expression used by the Bavarian herdsman Chonradt Stöcklin almost fifty years before. Subsequently, he returned to the Venusberg four times in the course of the year during the Ember Days. That year the harvests were abundant. Here too, then, whoever had the power, after waking from a mysterious lethargy, to travel during the Ember seasons to the world populated by the dead over which Holle-Venus presided, became a guarantor of fertility – the last in the series of episodes confirming the extremely close links between the two faces of this cult, the 'agrarian' and the 'funereal'. But even Diel Breull's account was forced into the mould of the diabolical sabbat: he was made to confess under torture that he had abjured Christ and surrendered himself to the devil. As a consequence, he was executed in 1632. The association of these beliefs with witchcraft was inevitable. So it is not surprising that the inquisitor, Ignazio Lupo, asserted in a treatise which had appeared a few decades before, that the witches of the area surrounding Bergamo congregated on Thursdays of the Ember Days on the mountain of Venus, the Tonale, to adore the devil and indulge in orgies.[67]

13

The myth of the benandanti is connected by innumerable threads to a much larger complex of traditions which was widely scattered for almost three centuries in an area stretching from Alsace to the eastern Alps. But we still are not able to assert with certainty that the Friulian version was of Germanic origin. With the exception of the trial of the Livonian werewolf, there has been no mention in the evidence that has come down to us of anything resembling the battles described by the 'agrarian' benandanti – battles between the witches armed with stalks of sorghum and benandanti armed with bundles of fennel. At best, we might recall that Burchard of Worms threatened to impose penances on women who believed they flew up into the clouds in the dead of night to engage in mysterious battles – an allusion which only faintly recalls the battles of the benandanti and which should more likely be seen, (indeed, it has) as an echo of the traditions of the 'Wild Hunt'.[68] It is possible, though, to find a deviant form of the benandanti's nocturnal rites in the folklore of the Tyrol, specifically in the so-called *Perchtenlaufen*. These are ceremonies in which, on set occasions, two groups of peasants square off against one another, the first masked as 'beautiful' and the other as 'ugly' Perchte, brandishing wooden canes and sticks – undoubtedly a remnant of the ancient ritual battles. Even the distinctive purpose of this rite, that of achieving fertile harvests, recalls the battles between benandanti and witches.[69] This carries us back to an area bordering the Friuli, and to Perchta, the polymorphous popular divinity who was supposed to lead the 'Furious Horde': nothing new here, apparently. But traces of this ritual skirmishing between the two troops of Perchte, the 'beautiful' and the 'ugly', have been identified in the Balkan peninsula. According to a daring and controversial theory, these traditions arose in the Middle East and then spread into central Europe, precisely through the Balkans, in the first centuries of the Christian era.[70] Is it reasonable to conclude from this that belief in the benandanti – particularly the motif of battles for the sake of prosperous harvests, so clearly recognizable in Livonia – was of Slavic, or even Middle-Eastern origin? Granted, traces of popular beliefs resembling those of the benandanti have been identified, as we shall see, even in Dalmatia. But due to a lack of systematic, in-depth research of areas outside the Friuli, we are not entirely sure if they spread from Germany into the Friuli, and from there to Dalmatia, or vice versa. The dates of the available sources seem to tip the scale in favour of the first alternative: Nider's allusion to women who fell into trances during the Ember Days dates from the mid-fifteenth century; the trial of the Bavarian herdsman as well as the earliest proceedings against the Friulian benandanti took place about 1580; while the evidence for similar beliefs in Dalmatia dates from 1685–90, in other words, more than a century later. It is impossible to say if such a clearly drawn line of diffusion is due merely to the scantiness and, thus, to the accidental nature of the evidence collected, or not.

In conclusion, the Germanic origins of the myth of the processions of the dead is practically certain; but the question remains unresolved as far as the battles over fertility are concerned. To be sure, the presence of this second myth in Livonia and among the Slovenes seems to suggest a tie to the Slavic world. In the Friuli, where Germanic and Slavic currents flowed, the two myths might even have converged and formed the more comprehensive one of the benandanti.

14

But if the question of origins appears necessarily unsolvable and, furthermore, abstract, there is no doubt, instead, about the significance of these beliefs, particularly the profound bond which joined the two currents, the 'agrarian' and 'funereal' benandanti. It is not simply a matter of the identity of names, or of the trances which were common to both during the Ember Days. There is more: both the conventicles of witches and the processions of the dead could be reached by the benandanti only 'in spirit' with the body left behind, sunk in a deep lethargy as if dead. In both cases, this going forth 'in spirit' was, and we have emphasized this repeatedly, a kind of death: a fictitious death, but one which the benandanti saw, just the same, as a dangerous event, one which could indeed lead to real death, if the spirit failed to return from its nocturnal rendezvous in time to reclaim possession of the abandoned corpse. And that state of lethargy – provoked by the use of sleep-inducing ointments or by a catalepsis of an unknown nature – was sought after as the ideal way to reach the mysterious and otherwise unobtainable world of the dead, of those spirits that wandered over the face of the earth without hope of peace. In the 'agrarian' version of the cult these spirits retained the fearful traits of the ancient 'Wild Hunt', whereas in the 'funereal' form they assumed an aspect which was more orderly and conformed more closely to the Christian tradition of that procession which was first described by Orderic Vitalis. Thus we discern the fundamental similarity between the wandering dead and the witches against whom the benandanti fought at night. The *clerici vagantes* described by Crusius in his chronicle stated that the souls of 'ecstatics' which had not returned to their proper bodies also belonged to the 'Furious Horde' of the unrelenting dead. Similarly, according to Gasparutto, the spirits of benandanti which 'wait twenty-four hours to return' from the nocturnal conventicles or which commit some crime or other, remained 'separated from the body, and . . . later when the body is buried, the spirit goes wandering and is called a *malandante*,' that is an evildoer, or a witch, compelled to wander without respite 'until the time appointed for that body to die, like an evil, hostile presence.' 'These *malandanti* devour little children.'[71] So, the dead punished the benandanti who penetrated the secret of their nocturnal processions, beating them with stalks of sorghum which grew in the fields – just as did the witches against whom Moduco and Gasparutto claimed they fought.[72] Envy of the living and their works, a sentiment also popularly attributed to beings torn prematurely from life, is what characterized these witches, portrayed at this point only for the spells they cast on children and as destroyers of the harvests, not yet as followers of the devil or enemies of the faith. At Lucca and Bergamo during the sixteenth century healers cured not only the victims of sorcery, by the use of spells and charms, but also others who had been 'afflicted by the dead' or by 'shadows'.[73] Fear of the wandering bands of the prematurely deceased was a widespread phenomenon. A woman named Grana of Villa Marzana, a spinner by trade, was tried by the Modenese Inquisition in 1601. She was accused of having cast spells *'ad amorem'* and of being 'reputedly a witch'. She stated that as a girl she had learned from her nurse that the victims of witchcraft would be attacked by 'shadows' if they were not protected with appropriate defences. These 'shadows' were 'the souls of the lost and the dead, which go about doing evil, and if any one runs up against them and his feet are touched by them, they enter inside him and cause him grief'. A little later she added, forcefully: 'Also I do believe and consider true that when someone dies before his appointed time on earth, he is compelled to wander, inclined to do evil and remains lost until he reaches the appointed day.' She had heard this notion (which she herself believed because of an actual experience) upheld even by a priest, whose name she had forgotten. Then when she was severely admonished by the judge and exhorted to retract her error ('if the Church tells you that it is false to assert that the souls of the dead wander about lost and doing evil, will you hold with the Church or follow popular opinion?'), Grana submitted: 'I would sooner believe the Church because it stands higher in such matters.'[74] The dread of witches also arose out of this substratum of fantasies and fear, even though an actual demoniacal dimension was missing from it.

Obviously, this identity between witches and wandering dead was an identity *sui generis*: probably one should not make a series of rational, hard and fast relationships out of these kinds of popular beliefs, so fluid, contradictory and yet stratified. It is easy to note that witches and warlocks, according to the accounts of the benandanti, besides taking part in the nocturnal conventicles 'in spirit', also had ordinary lives to live – they were, in fact, men and women of flesh and blood, not disembodied wandering souls. But such an unresolved duplication of levels is characteristic of this popular mythology.[75] It would really be more precise, then, to speak of a common participation in a mythological sphere which originally had been undifferentiated, rather than of a distinct identity. In succeeding stages it became particularized and assumed different aspects; it took on the traits of the witches in the 'dreams' of Gasparutto and Moduco, and was made concrete by the image of deceased relatives in those of Anna la Rossa.

But who inherited this destiny, be it power or curse, to 'go forth at night' and 'see the dead', as did Anna la Rossa, or to fight against witches and warlocks as did Moduco and Gasparutto? Here, presumably, the significance of the tangible factor which bound all the benandanti – having been born with the caul – becomes clear. The caul was considered to be the seat of the 'outer soul' in several European and even non-European popular traditions. It crops up as a link to the world of wandering souls, of the prematurely deceased, a bridge, a point of passage between their world and that of the living. This explains why in certain countries – Denmark, for example – the ability to see ghosts was attributed to being born with the caul.[76] In the eyes of the benandanti the caul became the necessary precondition for 'going forth'. And so, the benandante who appeared before Moduco the first time said: 'You have to come with me because you have something of mine.' This 'thing' which Moduco had was the amniotic membrane in which he was born: 'I always wore that caul of mine around my neck, but I lost it, and after that I was never again [at the nocturnal gatherings].'[77]

The sixteenth-century Friulian peasant born with the caul thus learned very early – from his relatives, from his friends, from the entire community – that he was born under a special 'sign'. The caul about his neck, which might have been blessed by a priest in some cases, bound him to a destiny from which there was no escape. When he reached adulthood, on a Thursday of the Ember Days, the benandante would embark on his 'profession' by falling into a mysterious lethargy, inhabited by figures and events, a state destined to repeat itself, with scant variations, for years to come. It provided an outlet for collective aspirations and fears – the terror of famine, hopes for a good harvest, thoughts about the afterlife, forlorn longing for the dead, anxiety over their otherworldly fate. Actually, it is difficult for us to conceive in the first place, of this tradition taking the form of a rigid, irresistible, internal impulse; in the second, of its long existence without loss or impoverishment, even though within the narrow confines of a purely interior, reflective life; and in the third place of the richness and above all the subjective consistency of these 'dreams', of these 'fantasizings'. Where we might have expected to encounter the individual in his (presumed) non-historic immediacy, we find instead the force of the community's traditions, the hopes and needs tied to the life of society.

15

The emotional implications of the myth of the processions of the dead emerge very clearly in a trial which took place in 1599. The proceedings got underway on the heels of a precise and carefully detailed accusation lodged by a priest of Udine, Sebastiano Bortolotto, pastor in the parish of San Cristoforo. He began by stating that he was trying to live up to his proper churchly duties, as well as to a recent Inquisitorial edict: 'I feared the piercing sword of excommunication which threatened me, if I did not come forward to make a denunciation within fifteen days of learning about things which pertained to the Holy Office.' So he was there to state that donna Florida, wife of the notary Alessandro Basili (who had himself cured the sick through prayers) 'goes about sowing all sorts of discord', telling her neighbours that every Thursday night she had to join the processions of the dead, and that among them she had spotted 'the former messer Bartholomio del Ferro, with run-down stockings, a rosary in his hand, who stays there very unwillingly, and . . . the former messer Valentin Zanutti, who died about six days ago, hatless, and with riding boots, because of which he is unable to walk, and also many others.' Florida used to conclude her accounts by saying 'that she cannot help herself because she is a benandante, and if she reveals more, the dead would beat her severely.'[78]

The denunciation of the priest was dated 2 September; four days later women who had heard and believed Florida's tales and had been enjoined by their repective confessors to denounce her to the Holy Office, appeared before the inquisitor Gerolamo Asteo. Specifically, it seems that Florida had claimed to be a benandante, able to recognize in the processions in which she participated 'those who are in purgatory and in hell,' and to point out 'those who are in paradise.' (From another piece of evidence we learn that the souls of the blessed did not participate in the benandanti's processions, just as they did not in the processions described by Orderic Vitalis). Moreover, Florida explained 'that she fights witches, and that she has been beaten twice for revealing certain details, and for having taken payment.' Florida had told a youth who did not want to believe such 'visions' to go 'to the canton of Povaro on Thursday, where he would be shown these processions of the dead.' Here too, as we see, the two branches of the myth intertwine and overlap. Florida insisted that she could behold the dead and join in their processions, and at the same time that she fought witches.

On the same day, 6 September, Florida herself appeared voluntarily before the tribunal of the Holy Office. She stated that she had told her neighbours about seeing their dead relatives only 'in jest' (although later she would admit that she had begun to divulge her alleged visions in the hope of earning a ducat). She had added certain details simply to make her stories seem more plausible. She said she had seen a dead woman nicknamed la Mozza 'in hell, with a hand over her eyes', because 'of a great sin which I heard this Mozza had committed, and so it is likely that she is in hell.' Of another departed one she had said that 'he has gone to paradise, basing myself on the good reports that his confessor has given about him.' News of these tales spread and other women had come to Florida importuning her. She persevered in her inventions, partly so that she could butt into other peoples' business, partly with the intention of doing some good:

> 'Hearing that . . . the widow Francesca was thinking of going to live with her mother, I said to Francesca that . . . the deceased Valentin told me that she [Francesca] should not remain alone, but go and live with her mother. Similarly, I pretended that this Valentin informed me that his people should restore what he had taken in excess from those he had served as steward; in the same way I made believe that Valentin had told me that his wife must not quarrel with a baker of Aquileia, with whom Valentin had accounts to settle.'

It reached the point that four or five people came every day to ask Florida 'various things about the dead': among them was 'Betta, who is pregnant now thanks to the cook of monsignor the most illustrious patriarch, and she came to me to learn if her husband, who had left Udine, was dead or alive, since she would like to marry this cook of monsignor the patriarch.' Florida intervened in this case too and tried to set things to rights: 'As was my habit, I pretended to know that he wasn't dead, so that she would not seem a sinner.' Thus, in this setting of neighbourhood intrigue and gossip the myth of the nocturnal processions of the dead retained its original admonitory function, with a particular emphasis on its moralistic side.

As for such details as going forth Thursday nights, being a benandante, and so on, Florida declared that these too were complete fabrications, modelled on the tales of a woman, now deceased, whom she had known eleven years earlier at Preclus, who used to say that she was a benandante and could see the dead. And Florida added:

> 'I said I was a benandante, but it was madness of me . . . to win that person's trust I pretended that I did not want to receive anything, saying . . . I would not accept even a hair, because I know that those who did were beaten, and so, my father, you can see my madness, because I did these things without reward . . .'

For the same reason, she said, 'I pretended that I had been born with the caul, that I am compelled to go out every Thursday night, and that we fight the witches on St Christopher's square, and that wherever the banner dips, there someone dies.' Florida concluded her account by asking to be forgiven for her frivolity, and was let go.

But the accusations against her continued. Florida had told all her neighbours that she was a benandante and that she was compelled, since she had been born 'under that sign', to go out on Thursday nights 'to see the dead in body and soul, and that it was wrong to say that one went only in spirit.' And, chatting with a neighbour, after her appearance before the Holy Office, she had exclaimed: 'I have been before the father inquisitor, and what did these people here think he could do to me? If it wasn't for us benandanti, witches would devour children even in their cradles': and everybody heard her say this 'since there were many people in the street and leaning out of windows.' What comes through so clearly, once again, is the prideful certainty of the benandanti in their role as defenders of the community against the evil forces that threatened it: they were not witches, and it was not even conceivable that their good works would be persecuted by the inquisitors. Thus emboldened, Florida Basili cried out her innocence and her powers as a benandante to her neighbours. But precisely in the light of this subsequent evidence, Florida's alleged confession appears incomplete, if not downright untruthful. To another friend Florida had said, significantly: 'I have been to the father inquisitor and he said nothing to me, and so I am not afraid of anyone, except my husband; but I was born this way, and I am forced to be a benandante, and I cannot do otherwise.'

This new evidence did not stir the inquisitor to revive his investigation of Florida Basili. A decision to summon her was finally taken on 11 May 1601 by a congregation of the Holy Office composed of the patriarch, Francesco Barbaro, and the commissioner of the Inquisition, Fra Francesco Cummo of Vicenza, among others. After two fruitless interrogations, held on 16 and 28 May, the woman was incarcerated. At last, on 6 July, she resolved to acknowledge, in a general way, everything of which she had been accused in the trial. The next day two witnesses came forward as her bondsmen and Florida was released. But after a few months, in November, a new denunciation against her reached the Inquisition. This time it was not a case of seeing the dead, nor of benandanti: Florida was accused of having treated by supernatural means (an egg tied by a thread, bones from a corpse) a certain Maddalena, a whore, who feared that she had been 'doctored' by her lover. She died after a few days 'with a great effusion of blood'. On this occasion the Holy Office did not bestir itself at all, and we know nothing more about Florida Basili.

By her stories, Florida Basili unconsciously served to gratify the fantasies, the anxieties, the fears and the longings which surrounded the world beyond the grave in the minds of the people; and at the same time, ingenuously, she provided momentary glimpses of the lives of the deceased, describing their bewilderment, their gloom, and their reactions to the afterlife and its laws. She told a woman neighbour 'that she had not seen her [the woman's] former son-in-law in purgatory, but that she had indeed seen her deceased husband, who was amazed that his son-in-law had only spent three months in purgatory'; to another she said 'that a little dead child of hers doesn't have a dress and can't go among the roses like the others, and therefore is sad.' It was to learn these 'various things about the dead' that her neighbours thronged to Florida Basili's door.

Florida's ability to approach the dead and to communicate with them was obviously widely recognized – even though one of her neighbours did say to the inquisitor who was interrogating her (how sincerely it's hard to tell) 'some of us think she is crazy.' We might have expected Florida's power to shield children from the attacks of witches, which she flaunted publicly, conscious of her worth to the community, would have been equally recognized. But it was not like that at all. A servant who lived in the neighbourhood asserted that it was being whispered about the *contrada* that Florida 'has the evil eye'. 'What does it mean, to have the evil eye?' asked the inquisitor. The girl explained what she meant: 'We say that those women have the evil eye who dry up the milk in nursing women; they are witches who eat little children.' This was a startling about-face – Florida herself was being accused of harming infants, she, a benandante, who claimed to defend them in the cradle against witches' attacks: she of all people to be accused of witchcraft! We might suppose that her husband, notorious for his ability to heal illness of all sorts by supernatural means, had ended by casting a shadow even over powers possessed by Florida. And yet, we have seen that the woman tried to take the place of her husband, and even attempted to cure a sick person by the same means. This was an isolated, still embryonic contradiction, but one, as we'll see, destined to develop in unforeseen directions.

16

In the same year as the last of the denunciations against Florida Basili, a Dominican monk, Fra Giorgio de' Longhi, presented himself of his own accord before the commissioner of the Inquisition, Fra Francesco Cummo of Vicenza. The deposition (dated 5 April 1601)[79] was directed against a female benandante who fits squarely into the current that we have been examining. The case concerned a blind woman named Gasperina who lived in Grazzano, near the house which had once belonged to the 'great Aquilina'. The Dominican was undoubtedly alluding to a famous healer, herself an inhabitant of Grazzano, who had been prosecuted a few years earlier by the Holy Office. Gasperina had been accustomed to visit in the home of the monk's mother, and it was the latter who had extolled Gasperina's virtues to her son, asserting that 'she was a saintly woman, and . . . discussed many things concerned with God, our Lord, and also that she beheld and spoke with the Lord, and she [Gasperina] had told her that our Lord God had let her know that if she wanted to regain her sight he would restore it to her, but she had not wanted it.' Moreover, Gasperina used to say that 'she had a caul, which she wore, that had been blessed by the pope' and 'on the eves of St John the Baptist and Epiphany, and Thursdays in the evening' she went 'in procession with a multitude of people dressed in red, and when she went along, she could see.' For Gasperina, as for Moduco and Gasparutto, being a benandante was a divine gift, and she attributed even this fleeting and miraculous disappearance of her blindness to God.

Fra Giorgio had listened to his mother's stories with suspicion – a suspicion perhaps nurtured in part by the allusion to the eve of St John, which as everybody knew was a day given over to all sorts of popular superstitions. He warned her 'since she was a simple and ignorant person that this Gasperina was doing things which were not right, that in fact were contrary to our faith.' And meanwhile he had tried to talk to that woman 'with the firm intention of issuing a sound warning to see if he could extricate her from her errors.' At first Gasperina simply ignored the Dominican's pressing invitations to appear at his monastery but finally she cried that 'she did not want to go and talk to monks.' (It should be noted that Florida Basili also had warned her neighbours not to confide what she told them to their confessors, but rather to make a full confession 'before an image; this was the way our Lord God granted pardons.') The Dominican's suspicions were confirmed when he learned that Gasperina (who frequented the homes of the great ladies of the city) could not help joining in the processions to which she was called, and that if she revealed the names 'of those in her company who took part in the aforesaid processions, she would be beaten.' 'So, because I had read certain books, I was even more firmly convinced,' the Dominican added, addressing himself to the commissioner of the Inquisition, 'that this Gasperina was a benandante.' This is a very interesting statement: what sort of books would have provided Fra Giorgio the kind of information permitting him to recognize the blind Gasperina as a benandante? Could they have been Nider's *Praeceptorium* or Geiler von Kaisersberg's sermons? In any case, this mention testifies to growing interest, even among the clergy, in the beliefs of the benandanti. Less than twenty-five years before, the inquisitor Fra Felice da Montefalco did not even know the name 'benandanti'. But even if they were now better informed, inquisitors still did not seem to want to change their ways: the denunciation against Gasperina was dropped without further investigation.

17

The basically uniform character of this complex of beliefs reappears particularly clearly in the confessions of a benandante of Latisana, Maria Panzona, already mentioned, who was tried in 1619. She gave a vivid description of a journey she had taken into the beyond, 'in body and spirit', in the company of her godfather, the first to show her the 'sign' under which she was born:

> 'Before setting out he told me that I must never speak, and he led me to heaven, to the meadow of the Madonna, and to hell; and in heaven I saw God and the Madonna with many small angels, and everything was filled with roses; and in hell I saw devils and smaller devils being boiled and I also saw one of my godmothers.'

This had occurred at the time of her initiation: on later occasions instead, Maria Panzona had participated in the benandanti's battles against the witches in 'Josaphat's field', 'in defence of the faith', and also to ensure abundant harvests.[80]

Another vestige of the processions of the dead turns up in a denunciation to the Holy Office of Aquileia in 1621 against a shepherd named Giovanni, reputed to be a benandante.[81] We will take up his case, as well as Maria Panzona's later; for the moment it must suffice to note simply one passage in the shepherd's recital. He related how at those nocturnal conventicles, 'both men and women cavorted, and sometimes ate, and . . . they also were accustomed to go with lighted candles to the small church [of San Canziano] inside and out.' Among the witches, 'there was an old man who had knowledge of the dead, that is, he saw them in the sufferings they were enduring; he saw those who had stolen boundary markers from the fields of others, and were carrying them on their shoulders . . .'[82] Here we have another echo of that ancient procession of the dead described by Orderic Vitalis, and of its original purpose: the depiction of the punishments of sinners for moral and religious edification. But it is only an echo: before long the myth became emptied of its content and almost all that remained was the symbolic element, nocturnal processions of the dead with candles in hand. This development was not yet evident in the denunciation registered by the canon Francesco Baldassarri with the Holy Office of Cividale (on 23 February 1622) against a peasant woman of Iplis, Minena Lambaia.[83] The testimony was based on third-hand information and contained a jumble of familiar facts:

> 'Thursdays of the Ember Days she goes out in procession, candle in hand . . . and . . . they go up into the mountains, and there is food there, and they walk around her house, moaning, so that she must go out to them, and because she revealed this and other things, an aunt of hers beat her, and she had shown him her back all black and blue, and although she knows many things, she will not talk about them any more.'

But in later trials this current clearly appears to have spent itself. A denunciation made on 15 January 1626 to the inquisitor Fra Domenico d'Auxerre against a prostitute who claimed to be a benandante,[84] referred in general terms to 'crowds of young people in procession'. As for a certain Morosa, a benandante of Prutars, who was denounced to the Holy Office in 1645, it was said more specifically that 'on the night of San Giusto she saw processions that began near her home and went as far as Anconeta, and all the marchers were clutching candles in their hands, and on one occasion she had even seen her father and mother in a procession, and they begged for alms, but she replied that she would give them nothing.'[85] All that remained now was a myth drained of its meaning and reduced to pure externals. And in a clumsy parody of romantic drama, written by Pietro Zorutti, the most renowned Friulian poet of the nineteenth century, and first performed at Udine with great success on 2 February 1848,[86] the 'lighted taper' in the hands of a *'Bellandante'* had long before lost its significance and become nothing more than a case of formalism, pure and simple.

On the whole, in the Friuli the myth of the processions of the dead occupied a relatively marginal place, as far as its diffusion and persistence is concerned, in that complex of beliefs that we associate with the benandanti. On the other hand, a much more involved history and richer future awaited the other myth, the agrarian myth of combats fought against witches and warlocks over the harvests.

III THE BENANDANTI BETWEEN INQUISITORS AND WITCHES

1

Between 1575–80 and 1620, roughly, the myth of the 'agrarian' benandanti was recorded, with the basic characteristics that we have noted, throughout the Friuli. Only superficially was it a static phase in the events that we are describing, actually paving the way for a subsequent period of swift, almost violent change.

In the early months of 1583 the Holy Office at Udine received a denunciation against Toffolo di Buri, a 'herdsman' of Pieris, a village near Monfalcone – across the Isonzo river and thus outside the natural borders of the Friuli, although still under the spiritual jurisdiction of the diocese of Aquileia. This Toffolo 'asserts that he is a benandante, and that for a period of about twenty-eight years he has been compelled to go on the Ember Days in the company of other benandanti to fight witches and warlocks in spirit (leaving his body behind in bed) but dressed in the same clothing he is accustomed to wear during the day.' So Toffolo went to the conventicles 'in spirit', and for him too the act of 'going forth' was like dying: 'When he has to go out to fight he falls into a very deep sleep, and lying there on his back when the spirit leaves him three groans are heard, as people who are dying sometimes make.' The spirit went forth at midnight, and 'stays out of the body for three hours between going, fighting and returning home'; and if he did not set out punctually Toffolo was severely beaten. 'These benandanti, witches and warlocks who number about three thousand and even more, come from Capo d'Istria, Muggia, Trieste and the territory about Monfalcone, and other places of the Carso.' The benandanti ('some on foot and others on horseback') were armed with 'stalks of fennel',[1] while the warlocks 'use as weapons the slabs of wood for scouring the ovens before bread is baked; as for the witches, they use slimy canes, and some of them ride cocks, others cats, or dogs and billy-goats,' and 'when they fight they administer great blows to the benandanti with these canes.' Here too the benandanti were drawn up in military formation: 'It is like seeing an army, because there is a drummer-boy, a bugler, and captains.' The bugler was from Trieste, the drummer from Capodistria: as for the captain, Toffolo, (who was the standard-bearer for the benandanti) 'he does not want to say what place he is from, because he is afraid he would be beaten if he did.' Once again, the battles were over the fertility of the fields: 'The benandanti had been victorious three Ember seasons, and . . . if they should prevail also during the Ember Days of Lent, witches and warlocks would have to tip their caps to them,' since, 'when the benandanti are victorious, that year there is abundance, and when their enemies win, storms prevail, and so there is a famine that year.'[2] Moreover, benandanti fought witches 'who with the devil's own cunning eat the flesh of little children,' making them die slowly, 'leaving them only skin and bone'. So once, when Toffolo spotted a woman 'who had lit a fire to burn a little creature born only a short time before,' he had yelled: ' "Oh, what are you doing?" and then she let the creature go, transformed herself into a cat and ran off.'[3]

Thus far there is absolute agreement with the facts obtained from the confessions of the Cividale benandanti. But a popular myth that was not tied to a particular cultural tradition and therefore was uninfluenced by factors tending towards unification and homogeneity (a role which sermons, printed books, and theatrical representations sometimes played in this period) inevitably ended up attracting to itself individual and local accretions of every sort, eloquent testimony of its currency and vitality. There is a variant of this in the denunciation against Toffolo. He had asserted that 'even Turks, Jews and Heretics in infinite numbers have military exercises and fight as armies do, but separated from the sects named above,' by which he meant benandanti, witches and warlocks. This is indeed an extraordinary notion which may have existed elsewhere in the territory of Monfalcone, but this is the only trace of it that has come to our attention. In any case, it demonstrates that the benandanti too suspected their gatherings of being heterodox if they compared them to the jousts of Turks, Jews and heretics. And this awareness could cause them anguish of the kind to which Toffolo admitted (and which reminds us of the desperation of the unknown woman of Pasiano who had tearfully begged Aquilina, the sorceress of Udine, to free her from the necessity 'of seeing the dead'): 'He desires greatly to rid himself of his duty as standard bearer . . . and he says that he would consider himself happy if he could be so freed.' Why did Toffolo want this? He realized that his activities as a benandante were contrary to the teachings of the Church, and this troubled him: 'He goes to confession and takes communion, and he believes what the Holy Roman Church believes, but he cannot help going out as was mentioned before; and it seems to me,' continued the anonymous author of the denunciation, 'that he said something about a caul in which some people are born.'[4]

On 18 March the members of the Holy Office of Udine met to decide about Toffolo. The same day they wrote to Antonio Zorzi, mayor of Monfalcone, requesting him to arrest the benandante and have him brought to Udine, 'so that we may have his testimony and thereby judge what should be done in this case.'[5] The arrest took place (as the mayor of Monfalcone communicated by letter on 20 March) but as for sending the prisoner to Udine, that was not so simple: he did not have men to escort him there. But in Udine no one stirred. And after waiting in vain for either the Holy Office or the patriarch to send the necessary guards to Monfalcone, the mayor let the prisoner go.[6] Toffolo's case was forgotten. Three years later (November 1586) the old denunciation surfaced in the archives of the Holy Office, prompting the inquisitor of Aquileia to visit Monfalcone and look into the matter. But Toffolo did not respond to the summons enjoining him to present himself to answer charges which rendered him 'suspect . . . in the faith'. A notary of the Inquisition was sent to Pieris where he learned that the benandante had left the village more than a year before, and no one knew his whereabouts.[7]

Once again the basic indifference of the inquisitors is obvious from the way these investigations were lazily protracted over the years. And it is symptomatic that in the span of almost a half-century (1575–1619), no trial against a benandante was brought to a conclusion, with the exception of the first one known to us, the trial in which Gasparutto and Moduco were condemned. In other cases which were obviously deemed more urgent – the repression of Lutheranism, for example – the activity of the Holy Office of Aquileia was extremely effective.

Then too, the traditional vigilance which Venice exercised over the Holy Office must have been applied with special care in matters as controversial as superstitious practices. The Venetian attitude is summed up in a message sent in 1609 by magistrates of the Republic to their officials in Udine, exhorting them to oppose the pretensions of inquisitors 'who are always attempting . . . to stretch the just limits of things and extend their jurisdiction.'[8] In fact, lamented Paolo Bisanzio, the patriarch's vicar, in a letter to his superior dated December 1582, inquisitors were always seeking to enlarge their field of competence even to the point of prosecuting 'certain poor women who, under the pretext of healing and being paid a little money for it, were using some superstitious practices that had nothing to do with heresy.' He asked for instructions on how to proceed since for his part he firmly believed that 'the inquisitor should not meddle with superstitions which have nothing to do with manifest heresy.'[9] In point of fact, these power struggles must have helped to shield the benandanti from persecution by the Holy Office, among other reasons because inquisitors felt constrained to discover heretical propositions in the confessions of the benandanti (as we have seen from the sentences against Gasparutto and Moduco), not an easy matter, despite the pressure and twisting of meaning in the interrogations.

The insistence and cajoling on the part of inquisitors during the trials, which we have emphasized on several occasions, do not conflict with their basic lack of commitment in prosecuting and condemning benandanti. Once they gave up the attempt to force the confessions of the benandanti into the schemes and categories of the demonology treatises, the judges adopted an attitude of indifference. This is confirmed by the fact that when, towards the second decade of the seventeenth century, the benandanti began to assume the known, codified characteristics of sabbat-attending witches, the mood of the judges also changed, becoming harsher (if only relatively) and several trials actually concluded with mild condemnations.[10]

This judicial indifference seems to filter through in letters from the vicar Paolo Bisanzio to the patriarch, residing in Venice, bringing him up to date on the situation in the Friuli. On 4 July 1580 – the interrogations of Gasparutto and Moduco had occurred only recently – he wrote that four individuals had been discovered (only two, really) who made 'professions of being benandanti'. He gave assurance that 'they would be prosecuted to the full extent of the law so as to give a permanent lesson to the many others who exist and lie hidden in this land.' This show of diligence was negated a couple of months later by Bisanzio's own off-hand reference to 'two minor trials against benandanti and witches', as well as by the gentle punishment, which was anything but exemplary and immediately commuted, that was imposed on the two benandanti of Cividale.[11] A year or two later, on 12 February 1582, Bisanzio wrote to the patriarch in the same tone: 'A few days ago when I went to Gemona . . . a woman who speaks to the dead and is held in very low repute was denounced to me and we shall not fail to bring her to trial,' speaking of the benandante Anna la Rossa. 'We shall see,' he continued with good-natured sarcasm, 'whether she is a new Pythoness who can summon Samuel to the presence of Saul

. . .'[12] It does not surprise us that the questioning of the 'new Pythoness', after delays, postponements and solemn but ineffectual threats of excommunication, should have terminated with the recognition of the scant importance of the case, which was left to the inquisitor to conclude at some appropriate moment, in other words, never. What was lacking, after all, between benandanti and inquisitors was some mutual meeting ground, even if based only on hostility and repression. The benandanti were ignored as long as possible. Their 'fantasies' remained enclosed within a world of material and emotional needs which inquisitors neither understood, nor even tried to understand.

2

A few years after the accusations against Toffolo di Buri a new piece of information about the benandanti reaches us, this too from Monfalcone. On 1 October 1587 Don Vincenzo Amorosi of Cesena, a priest in the town, denounced Caterina Domenatta, 'midwife', to Fra Giambattista da Perugia, the inquisitor of Aquileia and Concordia.[13] 'When a certain woman gave birth to an infant who came into the world feet first, this guilty sorceress,' ran the accusation, 'persuaded the mother that if she did not want her child to become a benandante or a witch, she should place him on a spit and turn him over the fire, I do not know how many times.' The priest urged that Caterina be jailed, because she was 'a woman of low life, full of incantations and sorceries,' before she could get beyond the reach of the Holy Office. In this particular case the new inquisitor showed himself to be more energetic than his predecessors, and on 22 January 1588 he went to Monfalcone to collect depositions concerning Caterina. The witnesses confirmed the accusations of the priest, and even the midwife freely admitted that she had committed the superstitious act of which she was accused. She added, however, that she had been authorized to do so by the parents of the child: 'Old midwives always have been accustomed to place infants born feet first on a spit and turn them three times over the fire, so that they will not fall into witchcraft; thus with the permission of the father and mother I turned him over the fire with my hands.'[14] As a consequence of all this she was condemned to make public penance[15] and an abjuration ('she told the populace in a loud voice why this penance had been imposed on her . . .').

What makes this trial interesting is not only the evidence of a belief comparable to that of being born with a caul, which predestined the child to going out at night with the benandanti, but that here too, it is a destiny enveloped in a frightening aura. One of the witnesses, Pasqua, the wife of Battista Furlano, mother of the 'enspitted' child, declared that she did not know whether 'there was anyone who was a benandante or practised witchcraft' in Monfalcone. But her father had been a benandante 'because he was born with the caul and kept it.' Caterina's husband, now dead, also had been a benandante, 'because,' she said, 'he was born with the caul, and he told me many things about going out, and since I did not believe him he told me that if I wanted to go too I would see.' But to the inquisitor's questions ('do you believe these benandanti go forth in spirit only? Do you believe that the works of the benandante are God's good works or evil?') Caterina Domenatta replied evasively, perhaps holding something back: 'I really do not know, he told me that he went out . . . I do not know.'

3

The motif of benandanti acting as defenders of the faith against witches and warlocks is absent in these trials from the area of Monfalcone. It does reappear, however, in the deposition of a cowherd of Latisana, Menichino della Nota, made in October 1591 before the commissioner general of the Venetian Inquisition, Fra Vincenzo Arrigoni da Brescia, who happened to be in Latisana adjudicating the cases of some women accused of sorcery and maleficence.[16] Menichino had been denounced as a benandante by the curate of the Church of San Giovanni Battista in Latisana and the substance of the accusation was confirmed by Menichino's own master, messer Machor Maroschino. The latter stated that the youth used to tell him, and anyone else who cared to listen, 'that he goes to the sabbat, in other words that he loses himself in a dream, and he imagines finding himself in a field of flowers, where flowers and roses bloom even in winter, and he asserts that when he is there he fights for the faith against witches who oppose the Christian faith; and he also says "sometimes we are the victors." He adds too that he cannot help going forth.' At first Menichino tried to dodge the inquisitor's inquiries when he was himself called to testify: 'I have many dreams but I cannot tell you about any one of them in particular. And to the peremptory demand to know 'whether he is a wanderer, that is does he go to the sabbat,' a question suggesting an identification which ended by visibly enlivening the entire interrogation, Menichino replied: 'One of my uncles, Olivo della Notta, who is dead now, told me that I was born with the caul, but even though I never had one I went out as in a dream into the woods, over meadows and fields to pasture animals, and into briar patches.' The inquisitor interrupted him brusquely: 'Stick to the subject and force yourself to tell the truth.' Menichino replied obediently: 'Sir, I will tell the truth. Three different seasons, that is three times a year, I have been to a field . . . which I had heard about from companions of mine whom I do not know (no one knows anyone else, because it is the spirit that goes, and the body remains behind in bed) and it is called the field of Josaphat, according to what my abovementioned companions told me.'[17] He had visited this field at night 'at the time of the feasts of St John, of Corpus Christi and of St Matthias.[18] And, urged on by specific questions from the inquisitor, he continued:

> 'I went on those three days because others told me to . . . the first one to tell me to go was Giambattista Tamburlino . . . he informed me that he and I were benandanti, and that I had to go with him. And when I replied that I would not go, he said, "When you have to come, you will come." And to this I declared, "You will not be able to make me," and he, in turn, insisted "You will have to come anyway, one goes as though in a smoky haze, we do not go physically," and said that we had to go and fight for the faith, even though I kept saying that I did not want to go. And a year after these conversations I dreamed that I was in Josaphat's field, and the first time was the eve of St Matthias, during the Ember days; and I was afraid, and it felt as if I was in a field, wide, large and beautiful: and it had a scent, that is it emitted a good odour, and there appeared to be flowers and roses in abundance.'

And he added:

> 'I did not see the roses, because there was a sort of cloud and mist, I could only smell these flowers . . . I had the impression there were many of us together as though in a haze but we did not know one another, and it felt as if we moved through the air like smoke and that we crossed over water like smoke;[19] and the entrance to the field seemed to be open, and I did not know anyone within, because there no one knows anyone else.'

In that place, Menichino continued, 'we fought, we pulled each other's hair, we punched each other, we threw each other to the ground and fought with fennel stalks.' 'Why did you fight?' the inquisitor asked. 'To preserve the faith, but we did not say which faith,' the benandante replied. Fra Vincenzo's questions grew more subtle: 'Were other things going on in that field?' 'No sir,' Menichino replied, 'they only said that they fought against witches for the faith.' And the inquisitor, with growing insistence: 'Was there dancing, music, singing or eating in that field, were there beds, trees or other things?'

If benandanti were prisoners of a myth in which they were constrained to go out in a dream-like state to contend with witches during the Ember Days, inquisitors too, in a different way, were locked into a reflexive response where the benandanti were concerned – in Udine as in Latisana, for Fra Felice da Montefalco as well as Fra Vincenzo da Brescia – which virtually predetermined their course of action. They all took for granted the image of the diabolical sabbat proposed by Fra Vincenzo, an orgy of banquets and dances under the legendary walnut tree. But Menichino vehemently rejected the inquisitor's insinuation:

> 'We did not do anything else, we benandanti, except that when the combat was finished, which lasted about an hour, we all had to return and be at home by cock's crow, or else we would die, as the aforesaid Giovambattista Tamburlino told me, and everyone returned home as smoke . . . and Tamburlino also said that if our bodies should be turned over while we were away, we would die.'

These souls, separated from their lifeless bodies 'like smoke' (Menichino's wife had once believed that her husband 'had died in bed, because he did not move at all') pursued their combat with the witch-dead, according to the benandanti, in the great field where all the dead, at the end of time, would come together – the valley of Josaphat.

The inquisitor asked another provocative question, 'whether when he went forth in the form of smoke, as he had said, did he first anoint himself with any sort of unguent or oil, or did he pronounce any words?' After his initial indignant denial,[20] Menichino acknowledged that he had greased himself 'with lamp oil' at Tamburlino's suggestion. But after admitting this, he denied that he had made Tamburlino 'any sort of promise or oath' as the inquisitor suggested that he might have done. No, the benandante declared: 'I told him that if it was under my sign I would go, and if not I would not go.' This had occurred fifteen or sixteen years before, one night while Menichino and Tamburlino were walking alone 'proceeding in single file on the way to Tisanotta where we were going to have some fun, and it was winter, on the road at night after supper.' No one else had ever invited him to go forth at night. But he knew that Menico Rodaro was a benandante, and spoke about it with him: 'One night, walking single file I asked him if he was a *buonoandante* because Tamburlino had told me he was, and Menico replied, "Yes, I am a benandante" '; and he too acknowledged that he went forth to fight for the faith. Of the other benandanti, he only knew their names. Menichino had talked about these things with many people, 'discussing them like that at night, walking single file, as was customary'. Finally, replying to another of the inquisitor's questions, he concluded: 'I told my master that when the benandanti won it was the sign of a good harvest, and I also said that this year there would be a good harvest, without storms, because we had won.'

The inquisitor had not succeeded in shaking Menichino's self-confidence. His last attack lacked conviction ('during this time that you were a benandante were you forbidden to go to confession, take communion or go to Mass?') and Menichino energetically rejected it, even perhaps, with a trace of astonishment: 'Nor sir! I was never forbidden either to confess myself, take communion, or go to Mass; in fact, Tamburlino used to tell me that one should stay on good terms with God.' The benandante was then set free, after his master, messer Machor Maroschino, agreed to stand surety for him with the sum of a hundred ducats.

Two days later (18 November 1591) one of the persons whom Menichino had called a benandante was questioned, a certain Domenico Rodaro. Virtually nothing can be gleaned from his deposition. He limited himself to saying: 'I only know that I was born with the caul, and I have heard that anyone so born is a benandante, and I know that I was born with the caul because my mother told me so.' In vain did the inquisitor attempt to break his silence by asking him, who had told him that 'those born with the caul are benandanti, and what does he really mean by the term benandante.' 'I do not know who told me,' Domenico Rodaro replied, 'because I heard it said everywhere by so many people that those who are born with the caul are benandanti. And I believe that benandanti are Christians like others.'

Aside from this disarming reply, the inquisitor obtained nothing. Rodaro also was set free. It had not been possible to probe more deeply into a key element which had emerged from Menichino's testimony, the act of initiation performed not by an angel (as Gasparutto had affirmed) nor by a benandante appearing 'in spirit' (as Moduco had declared), but rather by a man of flesh and blood like Tamburlino and on the most banal of occasions – while walking on a winter's night in search of a bit of merrymaking in a nearby village. Was this initiation imaginary or real? And, more generally speaking, to what extent were these rites confined to individuals; or were there instead, confidences exchanged, meetings, real encounters of a sectarian type among the various benandanti? This question must remain unanswered since, up to now, except for the present case, we have only come across accounts of benandanti unconnected to one another.

4

A few of the benandanti encountered thus far – Gasparutto, Florida Basili, Toffolo di Buri – claimed that their struggles with witches and warlocks were meant to preserve children from harm. This ability to dispel malicious forces and to heal bewitched children was explained simply in the light of the benandanti's extraordinary powers, and principally attributed to their 'going forth' at night to fight witches and warlocks. In fact, combat with witches as a propitiatory fertility rite never succeeded in gaining a foothold outside the narrow circle of the benandanti, although it seems to be the very essence of their beliefs and is the most interesting element for us. Instead, it remained in the background, merely an esoteric detail. By the early years of the seventeenth century two characteristics distinguished the benandanti in the eyes of the peasants and artisans who believed in them: the ability to heal the victims of sorcery and to recognize witches. Actually, the first was not a particularly distinguishing trait. In this period rural areas in Italy and throughout Europe were overrun by healers, sorcerers, and witches who cured every sort of malady through the use of ointments and poultices seasoned with magic and superstitious prayers; and undoubtedly benandanti were confused with this heterogeneous and motley crowd. But this sort of association was dangerous, for it exposed them to the risk of prosecution by the Holy Office. The ability to heal bewitched individuals, in particular, was considered a probable indication of witchcraft. 'Who knows how to heal knows how to destroy,' categorically affirmed a woman who was called to testify in a trial held before the Modenese Inquisition in 1499.[21] As confirmation of this axiom the majority of confessed witches asserted that they worked their spells on children whom they then proceeded to cure, in exchange for small sums or other compensation.[22] Thus, there was a strong inclination to view the benandanti-healers as 'good' witches, but witches none the less – as the priest of Brazzano defined them, if we recall his discussions with Paolo Gasparutto. (Even at that point, the myth was marked by an intrinsic weakness.) On the contrary, the second element – the ability to recognize witches – obviously worked in a sense opposed to the assimilation mentioned above, especially because it provoked sensational and *real* hostility (resembling the hostility of which the benandanti dreamed) between individual benandanti and individual witches, or presumed witches. But we should not get ahead of ourselves: it suffices to note that these two contradictory tendencies, together with the one mentioned before exercised by inquisitors as they began to identify benandanti with witches, determined in these decades the course of the beliefs we are studying here.

5

An early appearance of the 'healing of the bewitched' as a characteristic of the benandanti, bringing with it the danger of prosecution by the Holy Office, occurs in two depositions made in 1600 by the *'magnifica domina'* Maddalena Busetto of Valvasone to Fra Francesco Cummo of Vicenza, the commissioner of the Inquisition in the dioceses of Aquileia and Concordia.[23] The lady testified ('to unburden her conscience') that when she was visiting the village of Moruzzo her curiosity led her to try to discover the perpetrator of an injury to the child of a friend. To this end she struck up a conversation with a person who was presumed to be the guilty party, an old woman with the name of Pascutta Agrigolante, who confided to her that she was a benandante and knew witches. 'And I,' Maddalena related, 'not understanding what benandante meant,' (the cultural and social chasm to which we have already alluded was especially marked, significantly enough, on a linguistic plane) 'tried to find out; and she [Pascutta] told me that women born with the caul were benandanti, but they were not witches, and they went forth only when the witches committed some evil; and that a few days before, these benandanti had fought with witches and had won and as a result there would be an abundance of sorghum' (on this point the account is obviously confused). Pascutta named various other benandanti, including the priest of Moruzzo and a certain Narda Peresut. Then Maddalena, filled with curiosity by now, went looking for this Narda who did indeed admit that she was a benandante and also volunteered: 'The daughter, who has been bewitched . . . will have a terrible sickness the Ember Days of the most Holy Trinity, and if you want me to heal her, I will do so, but you must promise not to tell anyone about it, especially near Udine or Pordenone where you go, not even your confessor, because you know how they bothered that woman called Cappona de Cervignan in Udine.'[24] Narda Peresut must have feared being prosecuted by the Holy Office for her activities as a healer, so 'she practised her art of benandante at Grao,[25] and not in these parts, because she knew that there she would not be punished in any way, but here she would.' Finally she had told Maddalena Busetto that the female benandanti

'went out invisibly in spirit, and that the body remained behind as if dead, and if perchance it was turned face down it died, and as for herself, being an invalid, she was assigned a rendezvous that was closer by.' She went to these gatherings riding a hare: 'When she had to go out to perform her functions as benandante . . . this creature came to her door and created a great clatter with its paws until she opened it, and went where she had to go.' But, exclaimed Maddalena, at the conclusion of the first of her depositions, 'as for me I do not believe any of this.' In reality, considerable behind-the-scenes activity lay behind these proceedings, as we discover from a letter written by Maddalena's husband, Antonio Busetto, which is attached to the dossier of the inquest. Busetto's letter, dated 17 January 1600, was addressed to his brother-in-law: 'When my wife was in Morucis in April, thinking she would get some fun out of it, she mixed in with a crowd of gossiping women to see if she could discover who among them might be a witch or a benandante, for no other reason, as she states, except as a joke.' (Obviously, Busetto was trying to downplay his wife's mistake, but his disdain for the 'gossiping women' and their foolish beliefs was genuine). His wife's confessor had not wanted to absolve her without the concurrence of the father inquisitor. Consequently, Busetto was now asking his brother-in-law to interest the inquisitor in the case so as to spare his wife a trip to Udine. And, in fact, a week later Fra Francesco Cummo visited the Busetto home, a short way from Valvasone, to gather the testimony we have just reviewed.

In light of the accusations which had been made against the two benandanti, Pascutta Agrigolante and Narda Peresut, Fra Francesco Cummo resolved to continue the investigation (the decision was taken at the congregation of 19 April 1600). However, there is no further mention of the two women. Once again the inquisitor's good intentions remained confined to paper.

6

Maddalena Busetto's depositions can be compared to a group of denunciations lodged against Bastian Petricci of Percoto in 1600.[26] In a group of people who had been discussing witches and warlocks, he had been overheard saying: 'I too am a benandante,' but the witness who reported this fact also commented, 'I did not believe him, because I am not convinced that these benandanti exist; although,' he prudently added, 'I defer to the Holy Church.' Bastian had also told a woman of Percoto that her child was ill because three witches were sucking away its blood, and he had asked for a reward in return for revealing their names. A few years later in 1609, Bernardo, a peasant of Santa Maria la Longa, was denounced to the Holy Office.[27] He asserted that he was a benandante, 'forced to go forth thrice weekly to the sabbat', that he could recognize warlocks and witches, especially those who 'eat children' and that he possessed the power 'to keep them all away'. But a few years later the identification of benandanti with witches began to take shape on a linguistic plane. In 1614, a certain Franceschina 'from the village of Frattuzze' presented herself at the monastery of San Francesco in Portogruaro to denounce a woman called Marietta Trevisana who, in her own words, had 'wasted and bewitched her'.[28] Franceschina declared that she had visited someone known as Lucia, 'the witch of Ghiai', in order to be cured. The judges reproved her: why had she gone to Lucia of Ghiai, 'knowing that it was forbidden and a sin to go to such people?' The woman's reply is revealing: 'I believe she is not a witch, but she punishes witches; and then too, I went because many people go to her to have signs made over them, and they even come from beyond the mountains.' ('Not a witch, but she punishes witches.') If the 'witch of Ghiai' had been interrogated in person she probably would have defended herself by saying that she was not a witch but a benandante. But the fact that to her clientele, to women like Franceschina who came to her to be treated, she was 'the witch of Ghiai', is eloquent testimony of the homogenizing process to which we have alluded. Could it be that in their more or less conscious attempt to avoid this ever incumbent association with witches the benandanti accentuated the Christian motifs of their profession? In any case, even the witch of Ghiai tried to give an orthodox colouring to her practices. First, she told Franceschina, 'I cannot say [who bewitched you] because the bishop has given me licence to make signs over rich and poor without revealing their names, but even though I cannot reveal the names I will give you a clue: you have quarrelled with a woman, and she has cast a spell over you.' And then Lucia made signs over her 'with two rosaries and two crucifixes which she keeps in a small box, and also with a coral that had been sent to her by the Pope.'

Donato della Mora of Sant' Avvocato near Pordenone, accused a few years later in 1630,[29] was considered by everyone to be 'a sorcerer who can identify the victims of spells,' and he disclosed the names of witches in exchange for some small compensation. Not only did he claim that he owned 'a book from which he had learned all this,' but he also boasted that he was not afraid 'since he had received full authority from monsignor the vicar of Porto Gruaro.' This Donato also seemed to possess the characteristics of the benandante, just as did one Piero 'the sorcerer', named by a peasant woman accused of witchcraft by the Holy Office in 1616:[30] 'It is true that I went,' she said, 'to seek out this Piero . . . because people said he could recognize witches, and since I had been accused of witchcraft I went to him so that he could tell me if I was a witch; and he said that it was not true I was a witch and when he asked to be paid I gave him a linen cloth half an arm's length.' So strong was the conviction that benandanti could identify witches, that a negative judgment from Piero 'the sorcerer' carried enough weight in the eyes of the community to ward off suspicions, curses, or accusations.

7

The element 'identifying of witches' clearly was still only of secondary importance in a somewhat earlier trial held at Palmanova in 1606.[31] The central themes of this complex of beliefs reappeared, relived with great immediacy.

An artisan of Palmanova, Giambattista Valento, went to Andrea Garzoni, superintendent general of the *patria* of the Friuli, and informed him that his wife Marta 'has for a long time been afflicted with unusual ailments, and there is the suspicion that she has been bewitched by means that are diabolical and prohibited by Holy Mother Church.' The denunciation did not fall on deaf ears. Garzoni ordered that the patriarch of Aquileia be immediately informed in the event that the alleged crime fell under the jurisdiction of the Holy Office, and the same day (17 March) the inquisitor general, Fra Gerolamo Asteo,[32] went to Palmanova to investigate the matter. Obviously, the suspicion of witchcraft preoccupied the civil and ecclesiastical authorities of the Friuli more profoundly than the rites practised by benandanti in their dream-states. Actually, there was a benandante implicated even in this case, Gasparo, an eighteen-year-old shop-boy who had been going about saying that 'if he could be sure he would not be killed by the witches . . . he would reveal many of these witches' names.' At Palmanova everybody was convinced that Valento's wife had been the victim of witchcraft – and Valento's wife herself believed this as much as anyone. At the suggestion of a friend she searched her own bed looking for possible concealed charms, and found 'such strange things as nails, needles with threads of damask and sendal, finger nails, bones, long strands of hair curiously wound together.' It was whispered about that the sorceress, the 'charmer,' was Agnabella of San Lorenzo, a woman who had stood as godmother with Marta Valento.

But the evidence against her was so inconsistent that the inquisitor did not even trouble to question her. His attention was soon drawn to the benandanti: Gasparo and Tin, the son of Gasparo's master, a child of eight, who had been born with the caul (the women of the house had preserved it scrupulously), who asserted that 'he had not yet begun to go out like the benandanti'; 'but perhaps,' a witness commented, 'it is only because he is still a boy that he has not yet gone out.' When the child was called to testify he related that one day Gasparo told him ('I do not really know if he was making fun or was speaking seriously, because he is a joker'): 'Tin, I have been calling you, and you have not come; and if you do not come this first time, you never will be able to again.' Then the inquisitor fixed his gaze on the boy and commenced to instruct him on the true Catholic doctrine: 'These are mere fables and lies that men are compelled to go out at night to fight or for other such activities, which is what is said about benandanti and witches, because the devil cannot compel any man.' Then he ordered Gasparo to appear before him and began the interrogation with the customary question: did he know or at least guess the reason for his summons? 'I will be brief about it,' Gasparo began. 'My lord, I will tell you, everybody says that I am a benandante, but I know neither witches nor about going out.' But had he or hadn't he said that he was a benandante? Gasparo denied it. 'What does benandante mean?' the inquisitor pressed him. Visibly flustered, the young man replied: 'They say that I go out.' The monk urged him to speak the truth freely, and Gasparo, thus reassured, began his tale:

'I have told various people at various times that I am a benandante, but really I am not; I have heard it said that benandanti go forth at night to certain country areas, some to one place, some to another, that they go to fight for God's faith, that is, the witches fight with sticks or staves like those used for scouring ovens, but we benandanti,' – and while saying this he placed a hand on his chest, the notary recorded, (the initial ingenuous fiction had been quickly cast aside in the ardour of telling the story) – 'carry stalks of fennel, and it is said that the witches beat us; actually it is true that it also seems to me that I go out as a benandante in a dream, but we do not know where we go, and we have the feeling that we are going about the countryside with those fennel stalks.' The inquisitor was incredulous and asked obtusely, 'whether he in fact held these stalks of fennel.' Gasparo denied it, and provided other details about his dreams: 'We believe that we go out to fight on Wednesday nights before Thursday dawns, but never other nights. . . . No one knows anyone else.' Right here, predictably, the inquisitor laid his trap: did Gasparo 'imagine that he was going out with women or looking for women in that company, or to feast and drink?' 'No sir,' Gasparo replied calmly, 'we do not go out to do anything except fight.' As if he could not believe what he had heard, Fra Gerolamo repeated the question: 'You really thought you were fighting?' 'We really did think we were fighting,' Gasparo replied unperturbed. And then he added: 'We go out all together to fight against the witches, and we have our captains, and when we perform our duty well, the witches try to give us a good thrashing'; but all this without experiencing pain ('we do not feel anything, nothing hurts afterwards'). As for the leader of the benandanti, Gasparo said, 'I do not know him, but when we are all together, we hear people say, "this is the captain," and almost in a dream we see a man larger than the others.' As his insignia this captain carried, 'a thick bundle of fennel, and in place of a flag, branches of fennel; and we all always have our cauls, and we never see the witches, but they can easily see us.' There are, as we can see, endless variations on the theme of the struggle between benandanti and witches. It is worth repeating that we are not dealing here with a fossilized superstition, a dead and incomprehensible remnant from a too distant past, but with an actual living cult.

This vitality expressed itself not only in the proliferation of colourful details, the lion for example (an echo of the lion of St Mark?) which was inscribed, according to Moduco, on the gilded flag of the benandanti, but is replaced here by fennel, a symbol more ancient and closer to the remote origins of this fertility cult. Even the mood in which the cult was experienced varied from individual to individual. Paolo Gasparutto went to the nocturnal reunions 'for the sake of the crops'; Menichino of Latisana, instead, was impelled by a dark fatalism ('if it was my sign I would go, and if it was not I did not go'). What was Gasparo's own attitude? To the inquisitor who asked him 'did they fight out of hate to kill the witches, or what,' he had answered impetuously, almost scornfully: 'Oh no sir, I wish they would kill each other!' And when his interrogator continued to insist on learning 'what motivates their going out,' he replied: 'It is said that when we assemble we benandanti must fight for the faith of God, and the witches fight for the devil's.' But, 'for the faith of what God do they fight?' the inquisitor wanted to know, with a mixture of wheedling and suspicion. And the benandante replied solemnly: 'For the God who sustains life, who is the true God whom all we Christians know: Father, Son and Holy Ghost.'

The inquisitor still was not satisfied and continued to ask, despite what the benandante had said, whether the battles and conventicles he had described were really only dreams. Obstinately he inquired 'if it comes to them in a dream every Wednesday, at night, as Thursday dawns, and if they always see the same thing.' 'No,' Gasparo explained, 'it does not seem to me that every Wednesday night we go and see the things I have related; it only happens to us benandanti once every five years, as far as I can tell.' He thought he had only gone twice, 'and the last time was this year on the Wednesday of the Ember season of Christmas last, and also five years before on the same Wednesday night I think I went.' And he added:

> 'When the harvest is good, that is, when the crops are plentiful and beautiful, that is a year when the benandanti have won; but when the witches win, the harvest is bad. But our captain does not tell us how the harvests were until twenty years later, and he still has not told me anything during the two times I have gone.'

The central motif of the battle over fertility recurs here, but with a difference: the benandanti no longer went out four times a year but only once (still, however, on one of the Ember Days) every five years: for this reason, perhaps, they had to wait twenty years, in other words the span of four battles, to learn about the outcome of their efforts.

As the interrogation drew to a close, the inquisitor asked: 'Did you know that particular Wednesday of the Ember Days, which you mentioned, was the one when you would have to go out, and were you expecting it to be that night?' Gasparo replied in the affirmative: 'They all said that they had to go out that night.' 'Who are these "all" who said this?' The young man explained that they were two inhabitants of San Lorenzo: 'They too are benandanti, even though they do not want to admit it, because they say they have the caul . . . and it was they who asserted that benandanti would be going out that night.' But he did not want to reveal the names of any of the witches because he was afraid: 'It is said that they give sound beatings.' The inquisitor reassured him: he need not fear a thing since individuals interrogated by the Holy Office could not be harmed 'either by witches or by benandanti'. Thus reassured, Gasparo named the various witches of the neighbourhood, among whom was Agnabella, although he did not know anything precise about her. But evidently Fra Gerolamo did not place great weight on Gasparo's accusations; in fact, the examination ended there.

In Gasparo's case as well, we have observed the inquisitor twist the interrogation in an attempt to make the young man's account fit into the traditional patterns of witchcraft. This sort of suggestive questioning, though it took a very different form, resembled the attitude which was beginning to develop spontaneously, especially among country folk, in those circles which were in the most direct contact with the benandanti. As a result, the latter were practically caught in a crossfire.

But pressure from the dominant class was not restricted to the inquisitorial sphere. This is very clear from a kind of memorandum compiled and submitted to the Holy Office in 1621 by a citizen of Udine, Alessandro Marchetto, evidently a person of means.[33] The document began by accusing a fourteen year old boy, a servant with a family in Udine, of being a benandante. But this denunciation was inserted into a description of a long series of strange happenings – bewitchings, spells, transformations of women into cats, extraordinary 'feats' of benandanti – described in an emotional tone: 'The entire city is full of witches and evil people performing a thousand evils and a thousand injuries against their neighbours, and there is an abundance of such misbegotten people; there are many who speak of this boy's deeds and of many other similar things.'

This boy, who was thought to be a benandante, had once successfully healed the child of one of Marchetto's companions, Giovan Francesco Girardi. The youth had miraculously broken the spell by recommending that 'garlic and fennel' be placed under the victim's pillow or bedside (another instance of fennel serving as a weapon against witches) 'so that at night witches would not molest the creature.' After several days the child had passed a restful night. The next day Girardi struck up a conversation with the benandante and asked him about his wonderful powers, about witches, and so forth. Suddenly, 'he saw the boy lower his head and blood flow out of his mouth.' Where did this blood come from? The youth said that 'it was caused by a blow to his face.' 'How can that be,' the man asked incredulously, 'if only the two of us are here?' The boy replied that a witch had done it, but that he had not been able to see her.

The young benandante was thus enveloped in a reputation for magic and mysterious powers by the time that Marchetto tried to get him to come and cure a cousin of his, Giovanni Mantovano, who had been made seriously ill, it appeared, by an act of sorcery. There had been an appeal to the priest of Paderno, but to no avail: his intervention had only aggravated the condition of the patient.

But the boy was nowhere to be found; then Marchetto turned to another benandante, a shepherd named Giovanni who lived in a village near Udine. The latter came to Udine unwillingly, complaining the whole way to the person who had been sent to fetch him. When he arrived at Marchetto's house he absolutely refused to enter. As healers, the benandanti's fame was widespread; their work was sought out and rewarded, and by now they endowed it with an air of self-importance, fully impressed with their own greatness. Marchetto was compelled to descend to the street and with 'blandishments' finally overcame the shepherd's resistance.

The two began to converse. With the arrogance of an educated man for the superstitions of the people, Marchetto asked: 'Is it really true, my good fellow, that you are a benandante?' The shepherd nodded. Then the other promptly inquired concerning that point which interested him most, namely, 'if he had knowledge of witches and of their spells and sorceries' – elements which, once more, seemed to sum up the powers of the benandanti. The shepherd again assented, and Marchetto, pricked by his curiosity, asked him a few questions about the nocturnal reunions; where were they held, how many participated, what did they do, and so forth. Basically, the benandante's replies covered familiar ground. He went out at night in spirit to the field belonging to the Church of San Canziano, together with other benandanti, among whom was an old man, 'who had knowledge of the dead, that is he could see them receiving their punishments.'[34] To these gatherings, 'some rode on hares, others on dogs, still others on sows or hogs, the long-haired kind, and also on other animals.' When they reached the church, 'both men and women danced about, and sometimes ate, and . . . also went with lighted candles to that little church, both inside and out'; meanwhile, the shepherd explained, an angel held a hand over his face and . . . sometimes let himself be seen, and sometimes not.' The witches came from the neighbouring villages: there were twelve at Grazzano, four at Aquileia, eighteen at Ronco and so forth. Earlier he had said that he did not know how many there were in Gorizia because 'they did not go that far away.' Marchetto tired of the conversation and moved on to the point that was really close to his heart: was Mantovano bewitched, or not? The shepherd remained silent: when he was asked again, he stated that he could not say, because if he did 'the witches would beat him.'

'I told him,' Marchetto wrote, 'that I did not believe a word of it, and that this supposed knowledge of his was only a diabolical illusion, and that he did not really know. And he insisted that he did

know, but that he could not talk about it.' Marchetto went on with entreaties and promises, declaring that 'if he knew anything he would have to reveal it so as not to allow so good and so virtuous a youth to die.' But the shepherd would not allow himself to be persuaded, and stubbornly repeated that he feared a beating from the witches. Then Marchetto resorted to threats: 'I went on to tell him that I was man enough to beat him harder than any of the witches, and that I wanted him to reveal what he knew at all costs, if it was indeed true that he knew anything at all about the matter.' Then, with sarcasm, he asked him 'how he had gotten to be, as he said, a benandante, and how his profession originated, and when he began to exercise it.' The shepherd replied that 'it was a year ago that he was summoned one night by name, and he had said: "What is it that you want?" and from that night on he had always been compelled to go, but if he had thought to reply "all right," he would not then have been required to go.'[35] At this point Marchetto could no longer contain himself, and with an indignation mingled perhaps with the wish to startle the shepherd and force him to give the desired answers, he shouted that 'he lied about this, because we were created by God with free will, and no one could compel him if he did not want it, and therefore he should desist from going forth, and reveal it freely if he knew that the excellent Mantovano had been bewitched.'

Unwittingly, Marchetto had accurately defined the gulf that separated the dominant culture from the unreflective, spontaneous culture of the benandanti. What could free will have meant to them? How could they reconcile it successfully with the mysterious need, irrepressible but obscure even to themselves, which impelled them on the nights of the Ember seasons to dream of abandoning their bodies and travel to the field of Josaphat or to a field near Udine to fight against witches? Marchetto's rage almost appears symbolic: 'When he continued to insist that he could not speak, I told him that I wanted him to talk at all costs, because it was he who had got me into that bind.' This drove him to tie the shepherd to a post, grab him by the hair and exclaim that 'he had to be shorn because underneath he might be harbouring some evil.'[36] Here, brutally exposed, was the outrage, sometimes more, sometimes less violent, which Marchetto, as well as the inquisitors, felt towards the benandanti. There was no place in the theological, doctrinal and demonological theories of the dominant culture for the beliefs of the benandanti: they constituted an irrational outgrowth and therefore either had to be made to conform to those theories or be eradicated. At the peak of his exasperation (emotions which still pulsate in the memorandum he submitted to the Holy

Office) Marchetto had yelled at the benandante that 'he considered him to be a real witch, and in no way a benandante; that this term had no meaning, and therefore he had to be a witch.' The shepherd had then burst into tears, begged to be set free, and finally revealed that Mantovano had indeed been the victim of witchcraft, inflicted on him by a witch of Udine, 'rich, old and fat, a neighbour of the aforesaid excellent Mantovano,' who had approached the bed of the patient in the guise of a cat. And after listing the charms that he expected would be hidden in the bed (and which, in fact, Marchetto noted, were found in the morning), the benandante declared that he could say no more. It was learned later that on his way home he told his master that he hadn't divulged 'even half of what he knew', because Marchetto had 'outraged' him.

9

It would appear that the benandanti were becoming bolder: not only were they conscious of their importance as healers, but also with brazen self-confidence, they denounced more and more publicly the witches and warlocks against whom they dreamed they fought at night. They were certain that these denunciations could not be turned against them. After all they weren't witches but benandanti, they didn't attack children but defended them, and they didn't cast spells but broke them.

At the beginning of 1622 two villages near Cividale, Gagliano and Rualis, were thrown into an uproar by a man who had been a benandante for about fifteen years, Lunardo Badau, or Badavin, a native of Gagliano, 'a poor devil who goes about begging.' It was the assistant curate of Ruallis, Don Giovanni Cancianis, who was the first to inform the inquisitor of Aquileia, Fra Domenico Vico of Osimo, in a letter dated 18 February 1622.[37] The document stated that Badau 'has talked and blasphemed and, as has been reported to me, keeps on talking about matters that are of some importance in regard to witchcraft and sorcery, in various homes and with many people.' Badau had claimed that in the village of Ruallis alone there were 'four or five real and true witches, whom he actually named, which disturbs me not a little.' To those who asked Badau how he knew such things, he invariably replied: 'I know because I too go with them to certain places, where there are a great many men and women, including those I have named, and every once in a while we gather in certain places and fight.' The assistant curate then listed the people mentioned by Badau and those who had been miraculously healed in exchange for small rewards, and ended by urging the inquisitor to question Badau himself:

> 'You will have him in your power through cunning and ingenuity, and with flattery and charm, (not, as far as I can see, by threats), and you will be able to examine him expertly; perhaps you will hear such things that prove I may indeed have had good reason to notify you of these matters about which I have spoken.'

The next day, 19 February, it was the turn of Don Giacomo Burlino, curate of the Church of San Pietro delli Volti in Cividale. He wrote to the inquisitor that he had learned 'of certain things, but only through hearsay, about what was being said of a certain boy of Gagliano who talks a lot about witches and claims he is a benandante.' But he knew that someone had already written to the inquisitor on the subject and he did not want to dwell on it; moreover, he did not have much faith in the prophetic faculties of benandanti. 'Various others also are mentioned,' he declared, 'as being either witches or benandanti, as the crazy populace refers to them. When you wish, they can be uncovered, although I believe it will be in vain and cause a great commotion.' Don Burlino showed himself to be less credulous than many inquisitors, but apart from this, his attitude did not differ greatly from theirs. He seemed to use the word 'benandante' with a sort of disgusted contempt, as if in its linguistic barbarity it expressed the worst faults of the 'crazy populace'. There is an echo here of that age-old tradition of satire against the 'villain', thieving, dirty, cunning, cheating, and even superstitious, as we read in a sixteenth-century burlesque: 'The villain does not know the Ave Maria/nor prayer of any kind;/for his devotions/he weaves spells/. . ./The villain does not know how to perform/a single honest act,/he neither knows how to read a text/nor a single commandment/. . ./Night and day/he robs you and goes off to the sabbat . . .'[38]

That same day the assistant curate of Gagliano, Don Leonardo Menis, wrote to the inquisitor to inform him of troubles brewing in his parish. He was referring to accusations being spread about by the same Badau, 'not a witch but a benandante', who 'asserts that there are many witches in these parts and there is gossip of this public nuisance. Something has to be done because it appears that he pretends to know who all the witches are, names them by name, and even knows how long each one has been dedicated to the devil and where they have committed their sorcery.' It would seem that Menis was more concerned about the scandal raised by Badau's disclosures than by the fact that he had so many witches among his parishioners.

But this flood of denunciations was not enough to provoke the intervention of the Holy Office. On 16 June, it was Menis himself who once again presented himself of his own accord before the inquisitor to repeat the accusations he had made by letter four months before. He stated that Badau had claimed that Zannuto Bevilaqua of Fiumano was the 'chief and captain of those warlocks and witches', that several women of Gagliano were witches and had bewitched some children, in other words that Badau was going around creating trouble of every sort. Menis concluded by saying that he had brought these facts to the inquisitor's attention 'to unburden my conscience, for the sake of my honour, and for the salvation of the souls in my care.' And on the same day, 16 June, Don Giovanni Cancianis, vice curate of Ruallis, appeared before the Holy Office to renew his accusations against Badau.[39] Finally the wheels began to turn. According to Cancianis (and what he said was confirmed by the witnesses questioned), Lunardo Badau had become a real threat to the tranquillity of the town. More than once he had publicly declared that Menega Chianton, a woman of Ruallis, was a witch who had devoured eleven children. To prove his charges, he showed his bruised arm and said that 'she beat him and mistreated him'[40] at their nocturnal conventicles. One day when Badau was in Cividale at the shop of a certain Glemon, he ran into Menega, who assailed him instantly: 'Is it true that you are going around saying that I am a witch?' Without hesitation the youth replied: 'Of course it is true, and three others besides you, and you began to perform this office or art three years ago, and you travel as far away as Udine to suck the blood of infants in their swaddling clothes.' And then Menega 'furious at the aforesaid Lunardo, tried to jump on him,' and she would have succeeded if the Glemon woman had not stepped in, saying that she did not want any fighting in her shop. But another witness testified that Badau tried to have the last word: 'If you strike me I am going to accuse you before the law and see you burned.'[41]

These charges created an atmosphere of hostility around Badau: on Christmas night he was obliged to beg hospitality from a woman because the person with whom he had been lodging had driven him away shouting after him that 'they did not want him because he was a benandante'.[42] For his part, the youth lived in real terror of the witches: one night at somebody else's house he began to tremble in the presence of a Slav, 'nor would he say a word that night. He explained the next day that he had not said anything the night before out of fear of the Slav who claimed to be a witch.'[43] This information was furnished by a group of women questioned by the inquisitor's vicar, Fra Bernardino da Genova. Almost all of them had listened to Badau's confidences which were interspersed with childish boasting. He had asserted that he was a benandante, that he went 'in spirit' on the nights of the Ember seasons to certain fields to fight against witches with 'a bundle of fennel which he puts to his mouth and blows on against the witches.' And they in turn were equipped 'with sticks such as are used in ovens.' And he added, 'because we triumphed over the witches there will be a good harvest this year.' He said that he went to these encounters mounted on a hare who travelled so swiftly 'that he could get to Venice in the time it takes to slip one's shoes off.' These tales were received with much disbelief. A woman asked: 'How can a spirit handle sticks and fight?' Badau's reply was 'that it was true and that they really did it.'[44] But as for their fellow villagers who had been accused of witchcraft, all the witnesses agreed in portraying them 'as respectable, devout women, who attend church.'[45] Thus, Badau's public accusations went unheeded. In any case, he was not even questioned.

10

That Lunardo Badau's behaviour was not the result of eccentricity or personal animosity is demonstrated by two sets of depositions from 1623 and 1628–9 regarding another benandante, a peasant of Percoto called Gerolamo Cut (or Cucchiul). On 19 March 1623 a woman of Borgo San Pietro, Elena di Vincenzo, made a long statement in the presence of a notary of Cividale, Francesco Maniaco, clerk of the Holy Office, and of the vice curate Don Giacomo Burlino, with whom we are already acquainted from the letter he wrote to the inquisitor of Aquileia regarding Lunardo Badau. The deposition was made in the home of the witness because she was seriously ill 'and had difficulty passing urine'.[46] It was to cure this very sickness that she had appealed to the benandante Gerolamo Cut. She had been urged to do so by a friend, who assured her that Cut would be able to break the spells worked on her and reveal the name of the sorcerer. His power to do so came to him not because he was a witch, but a benandante. Not at all persuaded, Elena had objected to her friend that her priest would never absolve her from this sin. The other had urged her to push such scruples aside: 'If he refuses absolution you will have to go to other priests who will do it, because I too have been absolved.'[47] Then the benandante had been summoned. He was a man of thirty, medium height, red-headed and light bearded. After attending Mass with the invalid's husband, he had sat down with his hands folded beside the hearth. 'May God forgive me,' he exclaimed, 'and the Madonna di Monte: your daughter-in-law's mother is the one who bewitched you so that you would die and her daughter become mistress. And this is because her daughter, in the market of Cividale, had complained to the aforesaid Domenica Zamparia, her mother, saying: "Mother, you think you have placed me in heaven, instead I am in hell," and the other had replied: "Hush, daughter, you won't have to wait much longer" '. And, even before Elena could tell him from what sort of ailment she suffered, the benandante declared that Zamparia herself, with the connivance of the devil, had placed the invalid's urine in a gourd. They would have to summon the sorceress and reclaim it. Elena hesitated: 'What if she tries to make trouble for me?' The benandante insisted: 'Then I shall go to her house with your husband and get it back, because I am not afraid.' But the husband cut short the discussion, asserting that nothing would be done until the health of the invalid had improved.[48] A week later the benandante returned. Elena was better but in the meantime the sorcery had been repeated. It was essential to confront the person responsible for the illness. But the daughter-in-law of the sick woman refused to go and summon her mother, Domenica Zamparia, who was presumed to be the guilty party. Pointing to the benandante, she said sarcastically: 'If he is a witch he could make her come without having to call her.' Then she went away only to return with her brothers who wanted to beat up Gerolamo Cut; a row broke out which brought Domenica Zamparia to investigate the commotion. Enraged that she had been accused of witchcraft by the benandante, she lit into him, screaming 'various villainies', calling him a witch and trying to get her hands on him. At this point Cut interrupted them with authority, shouting: 'Go out into the courtyard. I can say that you, Domenica, have bewitched this poor woman so that your daughter will become mistress.' Then he swore on the Gospels: 'You have distilled her urine out of a gourd.' The accused and her sons abandoned the scene. The daughter re-entered the house, her hands folded: 'Are you trying to say,' she exploded in the face of the benandante, 'that I too know how to cast spells?' 'Yes, you too know how,' Cut replied solemnly, 'because like mother like daughter, and the knife is no better than the metal it's made of; and even if you do not know as much as she, you know something.' And, after boasting that he had cured a son of the patriarch's clerk and a son of Signor Giambattista of Manzano, and after dispelling Elena's last

qualms by declaring mysteriously that 'he had license from his superiors,' Gerolamo Cut took his leave.[49]

This deposition was not followed up, and Don Giacomo Burlino who had been present complained bitterly about this fact when he denounced Cut anew to the Holy Office three years later. In fact, this is what Burlino wrote from Cividale on 17 January 1626:[50]

> About two (sic) years ago a parishioner of mine who was suffering from an unusual ailment was persuaded by people of little judgment to call for a certain rascal from the village of Percoto. And when he came into the house it was as if the Great Devil himself had entered. He went about accusing this one and that one, turning the father against his children, alienating the husband from his wife; it was practically the same as had happened in another house.

Thus, it seems clear once again that for these country parsons the evil to be uprooted was not represented by the witches, so passionately attacked by the benandanti, but by the benandanti themselves. In these denunciations the benandanti appeared stripped of any sort of magical or at least extraordinary attributes. Their insistence that they attended nocturnal gatherings 'in spirit' mattered little: priests did not believe them (consequently the charges made by the benandanti against the witches they saw in the conventicles were totally ignored) and considered them to be not witches, but 'ruffians', subverters of familial harmony, sowers of discord and scandal. Those who professed themselves benandanti had a choice to make: either to admit that they were witches and participated in the sabbat, or to acknowledge that their accounts of the nocturnal meetings were pure fantasies, and their accusations of witches mere expedients to squeeze out a little money and to spread dissension among peace-loving people. In any case, the discord and disorder provoked by the benandanti with their accusations produced an effect opposite to those encountered thus far: instead of being identified as witches, benandanti were clearly contrasted to them.

'I had the stricken woman make a full account to the clerk of the Inquisition here in Cividale,' Burlino continued in his letter, 'so that the culprit who is like a raging wolf lurking beneath sheep's clothing might be caught. But nothing was done about it and, in fact, he persists in his damned vocation.' Cut had been called to the village of Santa Giustina just a few days before by the father of a sick girl. The benandante had pronounced her the victim of sorcery and then had accused several women, 'with grave danger to their honour and to their souls'. The letter closed with an implicit reminder to the inquisitor of his duties: 'And so since it is the responsibility of Your Most Reverend

Lordship to prevent such misdeeds, I wanted to bring them to your attention . . . so that you may choose to take those measures that you deem appropriate in your wisdom.'

Despite the note of rebuke in Don Burlino's letter (or perhaps precisely because of it) the inquisitor failed to take action. Two years went by. At the beginning of 1628 a new accusation against Gerolamo Cut (resembling the previous ones) reached the inquisitor of Aquileia from the curate of Percoto, Don Mattia Bergamasco. He wrote:

> I accuse before the Holy Office Girolamo Cucchiul, my parishioner, as one who publicly professes to be able to identify the bewitched and heal them, to know who are witches and even their names, without ever having seen them. And he spreads this around with the danger that the relatives of the victims might try to kill a person who may very well be innocent. And he has done this time and again in many places.

Finally, on 21 January the Holy Office decided to investigate Cut, and on 4 February Don Burlino was called as a witness. He confirmed his previous accusations and recalled the case of Elena of Borgo San Pietro (the woman had died despite the efforts of the benandante). But the priest was not satisfied with his own deposition and ten days later he took pen in hand once again to inform the inquisitor that Gerolamo Cut was going around saying that benandanti 'gave help' at night, and that 'priests were powerless' against sorcery.[51] In addition Cut had named a woman of Percoto as a witch and 'the husband of the impugned woman . . . beat him . . . and the rascal taunted him that she really was a witch, and that when she could not bewitch someone, she sucked the blood from her own son, so that he was now in a bad way.' But for unknown reasons the investigation of Cut's case was again interrupted – this time for a year. Depositions made in January 1629 did not contribute anything new: Cut, a 'mean and wretched peasant who could not call anything his own except his reputation of being a benandante and knowing how to recognize witchery' (this, according to Don Mattia Bergamasco whom we have already encountered), was going about the neighbouring villages treating victims of sorcery with superstitious practices of every sort, in exchange for some modest recompense. But what did benandante really mean, the inquisitor asked for the umpteenth time of a peasant from Trivignano who had appeared before him to testify concerning Gerolamo Cut. 'I do not know,' the witness replied, evasively. Then, when pressed:

> 'I really think he is a witch and that he has made some pact with the devil and that he cannot know anything by any other way . . . because he claims to know about witchery and other such things, and I believe that he cannot know these things without the help of the devil or because he belongs to the company of witches.'

From all sides, then, the benandanti were being pressed to abandon their ambiguous and contradictory position – ambiguity and contradiction that stemmed from the popular spontaneous nature of this extraordinary religious survival. (But is it really accurate to call it unquestioningly a 'survival'?) Even in these obscure movements of more or less instinctive responsiveness, there seems to stir, deep down, a desire to simplify: either 'rascals' or witches – the benandanti had to choose between these alternatives.

11

Thus, in the space of a half-century, beliefs connected to the benandanti, and all their ambiguous characteristics, spread throughout the Friuli, with outcroppings beyond the river Isonzo and in Istria.[52] They were beliefs acquired by benandanti in their infancy, generally from their mothers, custodians of this inheritance of traditions and superstitions. For this reason, when they left their native regions, sometimes because they were forced to, these beliefs often became a very tenacious bond which bound and held them. This emerges, almost symbolically, from a group of depositions dated 1629.[53] On 20 May of that year Francesco Brandis, an official of Cividale, wrote to inform the inquisitor of Aquileia that he was holding in the jail of the city a young man of twenty who had been condemned for theft to eighteen months of galley service. The prisoner was about to be transferred to Venice. The letter reported that this person 'has revealed to friends the names of certain witches, the nature of their crimes, the identity of the victims, the time and the method of the witchery, those who died from these causes, etc. He carries on his body the marks of several severe beatings unexpectedly received because he had revealed the sorceries and tried to dispel them.' Brandis obviously placed great faith in these accounts and he urged the inquisitor to intervene before the youth was transferred to Venice with the other convicts, 'so that Your Grace may resolve to institute a trial and put an end to the many evils that have occurred here in this matter.' But Brandis did not reckon on the persistent sluggishness of the Holy Office of Aquileia, as well as its special indifference to the benandanti. The youth went to his fate, and there remained nothing for Brandis to do but write another letter to the inquisitor on 26 May, beseeching him to bring the case to the attention of his colleague in Venice. He enclosed a sheet which described the prisoner's doings in detail. His name was Giacomo Tech, he was of

Cividale, and he had 'spoken up spontaneously and confessed that he is a benandante, in fact captain of the witches' – the writer may have been confused on this point – 'and therefore, even if he was being sent to the galleys, he would still be able to return to these parts, saying that the captain had died only recently and that he had been chosen as his successor.' It did not matter, then, that Tech was a prisoner and was being sent to sea: he was obliged to follow his 'sign' and assume the role of captain of the benandanti entrusted to him. But to fulfil it he would have to return 'in spirit' to the land where he was born and had lived.

In other cases, the influence of the traditions of the ancestral home is less evident but is still significant. In a witchcraft trial held at Parma in 1611, one of the two accused, after undergoing torture, confessed, among other things, that she had participated in the sabbat and surrendered herself to the devil. In her description of the sabbat she introduced a familiar element: 'In that field there were many of us, women and young men, and we fought with canes and played, and then we made it storm.'[54] This jousting with canes – an unusual detail in a witchcraft trial – instantly recalls the battles of the benandanti.[55] But it is not hard to explain the appearance of this element in Parma. The woman speaking was a Friulian, Antonia of Nimis, who had been taken to Reggio as a girl to be a servant in an apothecary's home. Once again, the thing that stands out is the vitality of these beliefs that were impressed upon the minds of the Friulian peasants of this period as an imperishable heritage.

IV THE BENANDANTI AT THE SABBAT

1

This tightly woven fabric of beliefs became unravelled for the first time in the course of a trial against a woman of Latisana, Maria Panzona, the wife of a cooper. She had been arrested towards the end of the year 1618 for stealing handkerchiefs, blouses and other objects preserved as votive offerings and gifts in the Church of Santa Croce. In prison Maria said certain things which aroused the suspicion that she might have healed the sick by diabolical means. This was quickly confirmed: the witnesses interrogated by the judge (the priest of San Giovanni Battista of Latisana had been specially deputised by the Venetian inquisitor for this purpose) unanimously declared that Maria Panzona treated the victims of sorcery with strange mixtures and incantations. When Maria was conducted before the judge on 31 December, she did not hesitate in replying to the customary opening question, whether she knew the reason for her summons: 'I believe that I have been called and brought here to talk about the witches in this area.' Then she proceeded to name them – there were about fifteen of them in all – including a certain Aloysia, nicknamed 'la Tabacca', who 'sucks blood from humans, especially from little children'. She personally had seen her doing this. Maria had been present 'in the form of a black cat and she [Aloysia] in that of a white cat.'[1] So it seems she, Maria Panzona, was a witch too. But when the judge invited her to disclose the crimes which she herself had committed, the woman objected: 'I have never performed spells or charms, because I am a *biandante*, and benandanti are all opposed to witches and warlocks.' And as proof she recalled how she had healed victims of sorcery using concoctions of herbs and an incantation recited three times which went like this:

> 'I mark you against witch, warlock, *belandante* and *malandante*, that they may neither speak nor act until they have counted the threads in the

> linen, the needles on a thorn-bush and the waves in the sea, that they may have nothing to say or do about you nor about any baptized Christian.'

It is striking that a benandante should include *'belandanti'* in an exorcism among their traditional enemies – witches, warlocks and *malandanti*: a contradictory element which becomes more pronounced in Maria Panzona's successive disclosures. 'These witches,' she said, 'are accustomed to go up to the field of Josaphat every three months, and the *belandanti* also go, and I go with them too, and we make this journey on Thursday nights.' Up to this point we are still in the sphere of familiar traditions, associated especially with the benandanti of Latisana. We recall that even the drover Menichino of Latisana, who appeared before the Holy Office in Venice twenty-five years earlier, had asserted that he used to go with benandanti to the field of Josaphat. The same can be said about his statement immediately following: 'the woman seated in majesty on the edge of a well, called the abbess,' who was in that field and to whom all 'pay reverence, bowing their heads'. This was the only allusion in the Friuli to that polymorphous feminine divinity found beyond the Alps at the head of the 'Furious Horde', who was related in so many ways to the myth of the benandanti.[2] But Maria also stated that they were conducted to that field by an animal. She explained, after another question from the judge, that she and her companions were transported 'by cocks and billygoats, who have been changed into these forms, even though I know well,' she added, 'that they are really devils.' And then she elaborated further: 'The one perched on the edge of the well who looks like an abbess is the devil.' This identification was immediate and spontaneous; it was not solicited, as in previous benandanti trials by leading questions from the judges. Thus, it would appear, that the identification of benandanti with witches and warlocks, for which judges and inquisitors had striven for so long, had finally occurred of its own accord. It was a benandante who had recognized that the nocturnal conventicles which she attended were the sabbat, presided over by the devil.

But Maria Panzona's account quickly took a more complicated turn. Witches, she said, consigned their menses to the devil-abbess, who then restored them so that they could be used 'to injure people, make them fall sick, become stunted and even die.' She herself had received 'a certain red substance' from the devil which she had hidden in a wall of her house. It was then promptly brought before her, and Maria recognized it. 'This is a present from the devil, which I use to free bewitched people, especially little children whose blood has been sucked from them. The devil told me it was good for this.' In other words, although she admitted having paid homage to the devil, she did not renounce her own powers as a benandante. It had been the devil himself, in fact, who had suggested to her the means of curing the victims of the witches.

The interrogations resumed on 2 January 1619 with a dramatic confrontation between Maria Panzona and one of the women whom she had accused of witchcraft. The former persisted, but to no avail: 'I saw you two months ago in the valley of Josaphat, and you had been brought there on a cock by the devil and you had a stalk of sorghum.' The other woman denied everything: 'What you say is not true.'[3] A similar scene was repeated in the presence of another alleged witch. When Maria Panzona was interrogated again two days later, she furnished new particulars on the initiation of witches:

> 'Those who want to become witches go forth at night to the sabbat, and there they perform three somersaults, but first they call upon the devil, to whom they all give themselves; they renounce their faith in God three times, and then spit into their hands; after they have rubbed their hands together three times, they are carried off by the devil in spirit, and leave the body behind bloodless and dead, until the devil returns the spirit to it.'

She had been one of those who had done all this, summoned the devil and abjured her faith, about thirty years before (now she was over fifty), instigated by her godfather, Vincenzo dal Bosco del Merlo. Here too there seems to be an absolute correspondence between witches and benandanti, but again Maria introduced a distinction between them: 'All witches renounce their faith, as I said, and surrender themselves to the devil. Many of them, however, do it purely for their own pleasure, and not to injure anyone, as is my case, after I obtained the power and the ability from the devil to heal bewitched people.'[4] It was a subtle distinction, this drawing of a line between true and proper witches and those who gave themselves to the devil 'for their own pleasure': and it is not surprising that in the course of writing on 17 January, to the patriarch of Venice, Francesco Vendramin, to inform him of the case, the parish priest of Latisana should speak of Maria Panzona simply as a witch without going into details, and also should think of the women whom she had accused 'as practically convicted witches'. The priest added that he awaited instructions from the patriarch and the inquisitor 'to root out this diabolical curse'. But in Venice, in view of the tenor of the letter, it was decided to summon Maria Panzona and the two women whom she had denounced as witches, Ursula Tazotta and Aloysia, 'la Tabacca', for trial before the Holy Office.

If all we had available were the records of the Latisana

interrogations we could forthwith place the case of Maria Panzona at the beginning of a new phase in the history of the benandanti. True, Maria did not paint a picture of the traditional sabbat: the conventicles in which she had participated were composed of such archaic elements as the field of Josaphat and the abbess. But the identification of the 'abbess' as the devil, and the abjuration of the faith are decisive facts, much more important than the feeble resistance offered by Maria when she stressed her role as healer of the bewitched, an activity which distinguished her from real witches. All the same, the interrogations in Venice, before the patriarch and the inquisitor, Giandomenico Vignazio, took a very different and unexpected course.

2

The proceedings got underway on 28 February after a preliminary hearing in which Maria, at the request of the judges, confirmed that what she had testified in Latisana was the truth. She was promptly asked to furnish additional details on the central point of her confession: 'How did she abjure her faith and with what words did she do so when she was taken to the sabbat?' The woman launched into her account: the first time, she had been brought to the valley of Josaphat by her godfather, even though he had received two bushels of wheat and two jars of wine from her own father on the condition that he leave her alone. 'But, instead,' said Maria, 'he was around me all the time, saying such things as "if you had come you would have seen so many beautiful things," and I who was just a young girl and foolish, did go.' She went riding on a cock, 'in other words on a spirit which had assumed the form of a cock' (note: a spirit, not a devil, as she had first said in Latisana), 'and we travelled a great distance, into the valley of Josaphat, and the spirit only went, not the body, which remained behind in bed, as if dead.' And at this point the judges voiced their first objection: how could she see the cock carrying off her spirit, if her body remained behind in bed as if dead? This was not a casual question and it reflected, as usual, the impossibility on the part of the judges of accepting the agonizing split in personalities experienced by the benandanti during their lethargies, which they expressed in the physical separation of the spirit from the inanimate body. Maria did not understand: 'How should I know?' was her reply. This was not disrespect on her part, but a simple inability to comprehend. She had believed, and still did – and she said so herself – that the spirit could leave the body, and return to it, but she did not know 'through what power'.

In the valley of Josaphat, she went on, 'there are witches and warlocks who fight for the devils, and there are benandanti who fight for the faith of God: and the benandanti know each other, and they know who the others are with God's help.'[5] She had learned all these things, including the difference between benandanti and witches, from her godfather, Vincenzo dal Bosco del Merlo, himself a benandante, as, for that matter, her father had been also. We can see that Maria did not answer the question put to her, namely, how she had abjured the faith at the gatherings of witches and benandanti. Instead, she emphasized that benandanti fought for God's faith, and could recognize witches through God's power.

At this point, the interrogation was interrupted by an unforeseen event: 'Maria could not continue, she was stricken, and collapsed to the floor in great discomfort.' It was one of those epileptic fits which, by her own admission, constantly plagued her. After she was revived with a drop or two of vinegar and allowed to rest, the judges resumed their questioning. And then, in the words uttered by Maria, there re-emerged all the motifs connected with the myth of the benandanti, uncontaminated by elements of witchcraft.

The first time she went to the sabbat, conducted there by her godfather, she had gone in body and spirit, and she had been 'a young girl'. Her godfather, instead, had been in the form of a butterfly. He cautioned her 'not to speak': 'and he led me,' Maria related, 'to heaven, to the meadow of the Madonna and to hell; and I saw God and the Madonna in heaven with many little angels, and there were roses everywhere; and in hell I saw devils and smaller devils being boiled, and I even saw a godmother of mine.' At other times she went to the field of Josaphat only in spirit. 'Warlocks carry stalks of sorghum, and witches pokers from the ovens,[6] and we benandanti fennel stalks: and the witches fight for the devil and the benandanti fight to defend the faith. . . . And when the witches win, a great famine follows, and when the benandanti win, there is abundance.' In this context, the figure of the abbess crops up again, even if only marginally: 'We go to visit the abbess to inquire how she is, and we ask her what is required to injure people, and I,' Maria went on, 'only spoke with her once. Actually she spoke to me, and asked me what my desire was, whether to do evil or to do good: and when I told her that I wanted to do good, she replied that she did not want to give me anything.' Here, it was not the mysterious abbess who gave benandanti the means of healing the bewitched, but rather, as we saw before, an angel: 'An angel was there

who gave me some powder.' The 'profession' of benandanti thus emerged from these Venetian interrogations once again free of any sort of diabolical compromise or contamination: there was no more talk of a renunciation of the faith; instead it was the benandanti who defended the faith against witches and warlocks.

Just as she had done earlier in Latisana, Maria again denounced the crimes of the witches: 'We know each other when we are of the same school, that is if we were born under the sign where the spirit goes out first in the form of a butterfly . . ., we know one another only if we are of the same company . . . . although we see large numbers of butterflies in that field; all those who belong to one company remain separate from the other companies.'[7] But the Holy Office did not place any weight on her accusations. The two alleged witches who had been brought from Latisana with Maria ('she has been our ruination,' they said[8]) were set free. And when Maria Panzona's interrogations resumed on 11 April, after a long interruption, the judges urged her to reflect carefully about what she had said, since 'so much of it was improbable or downright impossible,' such as, for example, her assertion that she had accompanied her companions to the sabbat as a butterfly and had engaged in battles there. It was an explicit declaration of disbelief: for these Venetian judges the age-old debate over the reality of the sabbat was over. That which needed to be persecuted and condemned was the theological crime, the covenant with the devil, and they hammered home on this point: 'Tell us if you have ever made an express pact with the devil, surrendered your soul to him and abjured your faith in Jesus Christ.'[9] And Maria Panzona stubbornly fought back: 'I have never been a witch, I am a benandante. . . . I have never given my soul to the devil, nor abjured my faith in Jesus Christ.' They confronted her with statements she had made during the Latisana phase of the interrogations. She replied, 'they can say what they wish, and even write it down, but I did not say these things.' At this point she was assigned a lawyer, Jacopo Panfilo, and granted eight days to prepare her defence. But it certainly was not from him that Maria could hope for understanding. On 30 April Panfilo appeared before the Patriarch and the inquisitor general to present his arguments. He had paid several visits to his client in the prison of the Holy Office in the hope 'of making her perceive the errors fixed in her head.' And now, finally, Maria (who according to him was 'a woman of few brains') had promised him 'that she no longer wanted to believe those crazy opinions and fantasies of hers about going to the sabbat as a cat, and all those other lunacies she had held, and so on.' She was willing to pledge 'in the future to always live as a good Christian until her death, and to believe only what is commanded by Holy Mother Church.' She asked to be forgiven and relinquished any further defence.[10] And, in fact, when Maria Panzona reappeared before the judges for her final interrogation on 20 June she did indeed seem to want to pursue humbly the course which her lawyer, with his authority, his learning and his disdainful scepticism, had proposed for her: 'I ask your pardon,' she said, 'for everything that I have said and done, if I have said or done anything to offend you, because I have no brains.' But the judges would not settle for so little. They wanted to know if Maria Panzona had indeed abjured her faith in Christ and worshipped the devil when she had gone to the field of Josaphat, 'because at first she said one thing and then at another time something else.' And Maria, in desperation, pleaded: 'I have never abandoned my faith in Jesus Christ, and I admit no other faith than that of Jesus Christ and of the Blessed Virgin Mary, and what I said in the past is not true, because I had no brains, and if I had had any brains, I would not have said the things I did.' She was nothing but a poor invalid, an epileptic: 'How can you expect me to have any brains left, seeing that I am often attacked by that evil sickness? I have suffered from it for many years and I have been afflicted by it even in your prisons, as the guard can attest, who has often found me lying on the ground.' And, monotonously, she returned to her denials: 'As for me, I cannot tell you anything, I cannot tell you what I may have said, because I have no brains. If you want to put me to death, go ahead. Nothing of what I confessed to you is true, and it is not true that my godfather took me there (the field of Josaphat); and I said these things because I had no brains, and the devil was tempting me.' It was a lie that she had been to the sabbat many times, that she had gone as a cat, none of this was true. Fruitlessly did the judges insist, protest ('this is a subterfuge') and threaten to torture her. Maria denied everything, as well as the allegation that she had been advised to retract matters that she had already confessed. Only after the judges decided that in view of her physical condition she should not be submitted to torture, did the woman revert to her earlier statements and admit that she had indeed been to the field of Josaphat. She had denied it, she said, 'because the person who was sent to be my lawyer told me I should deny everything, and say it was not true.' Now, with the fear of torture behind her, the lawyer's advice forgotten, the temporary incrustations of diabolical elements forgotten, Maria newly confessed her pure faith of the benandante, which no one – neither lawyer nor judges – wanted to acknowledge. 'I have never abjured my faith in Jesus Christ, but I did say that the other witches abjured it . . . (the accused women) are witches, and I know this because I was with them in the form of a cat, and they also were in the form of cats: they to injure and I to protect.'[11] These statements go back decades, rooted in a tenacious, obscure tradition, and are not the hallucinations of a wretched epileptic. This explains the stubborn insistence with which Maria repeated them. Faced with this incomprehensible obstinacy, there was no other recourse for the judges than to terminate the trial. Maria Panzona, pronounced mildly suspect of heresy, was condemned to an imprisonment of three years and to be perpetually banished from Latisana and its territory (under threat of life imprisonment if she did not comply). On 4 July 1619 she made the customary abjuration.

At first glance the serious discrepancy between the confessions in Latisana and those in Venice is inexplicable (and must have seemed so also to the court). The matter is complicated by the fact that in both instances the confessions were not coerced by the judges. It cannot be supposed that the Latisana interrogations, which Maria Panzona herself confirmed as authentic when the Venetian judges read them back to her, could have been falsified. Moreover, they were packed with details, such as that of the 'abbess', present also in the Venetian testimony, which no judge could have invented. The contradiction between the benandanti-witches in the Latisana proceedings, and the traditional benandanti who reappeared in Venice – a contradiction punctiliously underscored by the inquisitors in a sheet attached to the trial records – is indeed real, and Maria Panzona experienced it keenly, if unconsciously. To be sure, the contradiction in her case was still somewhat ephemeral: in the course of the trial the gap was diminished and Maria reverted to being a benandante just like those we have already encountered often – a wavering one, however, unable to explain to the judges who pressed her the reason for her assertions and retractions. But by now the break-up of this complex of myths was under way, a process that would continue on its inexorable course.

3

'When I was in Cividale on some business or other,' a Benedictine of Rosazzo, Don Pietro Martire da Verona, wrote to the inquisitor of Aquileia on 23 April 1623:

there was brought before me a benandante (for that is how this breed of

> people is called) so that I might hear his confession and return him to the straight and narrow path. After I questioned him closely outside confession,[12] I discovered that he was of that breed of witches, and that, therefore, he should be sent to Your Reverence so that you as inquisitor could do what was necessary.

To prevent the possibility of a retraction, he had made the benandante, a young man of Moimacco who was a servant in the home of a nobleman of Cividale, sign a detailed confession of his errors as well as an abjuration (both of which were attached to the letter). He suggested how Giovanni Sion – this was the benandante's name – could be persuaded to come to Udine: 'to free himself from the clutches of the devil he will respond willingly, since he wants to confess at this time of Jubilee and to live like a Christian.' The priest concluded with the hope that the inquisitor might succeed once and for all 'in getting a good hold over this rabble and thus rid the countryside of so great an evil.'

In describing the benandante Giovanni Sion as belonging to that 'breed of witches' Don Pietro Martire was not guilty of one of those misrepresentations to which inquisitors have accustomed us. The statement which he drew up from Sion's words and which the latter reiterated, with only slight differences, at Cividale before the inquisitor's vicar on 29 April, in fact definitively ushered in a new phase in these beliefs. It contained a full-blown, systematic description of the traditional sabbat, the first one that has come down to us from the entire Friuli. Although the benandanti participated in this sabbat, their compromise with the devil was attenuated by their ambiguous and contradictory behaviour. At this point we are still in a transitional phase: but by now the decisive point in the transformation has been reached. Once they avowed their participation in the sabbat, even if there remained indecision and hesitation in their attitude, the benandanti emerged, forced by the choices thrust upon them, from the ambiguous position which had made them both the objects of persecution by the inquisitors (though more in theory than in fact) and of hatred by the witches. Little by little they had become what they had always been expected to be: witches. The identification of benandanti as witches that the inquisitor Fra Felice da Montefalco had skilfully succeeded in extracting from Moduco and Gasparutto by means of some cleverly suggestive questioning, and which had reappeared temporarily in Maria Panzona's confessions, had finally taken hold, half a century later, among the peasants of the Friuli. Sion's 'spontaneous' confession not only represented the decisive step in this assimilation, but it also formed, for the first time in the Friuli, a coherent

popular equivalent to the image of the diabolical sabbat which for decades inquisitors had tried in vain to impose.

For reasons unknown to us Sion was not summoned to Udine. Instead, it was the inquisitor's vicar, Fra Ludovico da Gualdo, who promptly journeyed to Cividale. Giovanni Sion was interrogated there on 29 April.

He began his testimony by saying that he had been urged to go to the sabbat by a witch – a young man, twenty-four years of age, Gerolamo of Villalta, who had been a servant in Moimacco. Three years earlier, on a Thursday during the Ember season of Christmas (in other words, one of the days devoted to the nocturnal gatherings of benandanti), he had offered to lead Sion to a place where he would 'see and enjoy many beautiful things', and also promised 'I will have money and jewellery given to you.' 'Let us go,' Giovanni had instantly replied. Then Gerolamo had taken 'a jar of special oil' and, after stripping, greased his body with it. Suddenly, 'a lion appeared and Gerolamo mounted it.' Giovanni, who had not anointed himself, clambered up on his companion's shoulders. 'In the wink of an eye,' Sion related, 'we found ourselves in Modoletto, in a place called the *Picenale*,[13] and there we saw many people come together, who were dancing and sporting about, gorging themselves with food and drink, and who threw themselves on beds and publicly committed many dishonorable acts.' Even in this description of the sabbat, as it had been so often depicted by inquisitors, and always scornfully repudiated by benandanti, an element appeared, as it had in Maria Panzona's revelations, which suggests the benandanti's unconscious resistance at being identified with witches. Giovanni had already declared that he did not apply Gerolamo of Villalta's diabolical ointment; now he underscored the fact that he had been present at, but had not participated in the orgies of witches and warlocks: 'My companion invited me to climb into those very beds, but out of fear I did not do so, and I always stayed apart with six in my company called benandanti.'

Thus, although the benandanti (whom Sion named one by one), were at the sabbat, they stood aloof precisely because they were benandanti: 'We talked among ourselves, seeing so much gold, silver, necklaces and goblets made of gold, of how we might have carried them off and never have to be poor again; and even though they were offered to us, we did not accept them because we did not trust what they were, suspecting they might not be real.' The pleasures and opulence of the sabbat lured benandanti and witches alike: but deep down in his conscience Giovanni Sion still harboured the ancient hatred for witches, warlocks and their deeds and this moved him to reject intimacy with witches 'out of fear', and the gold and jewels in case 'they might not be real.'

Faithful to the ancient vocation of benandante, Sion denounced a group of witches and warlocks from Cividale, among whom were two women, Lucia and Grisola, whom he accused of several murders. But Sion did not refer to his powers as benandante in his effort to convince Fra Ludovico of the truth of his allegations: he had seen traces of the diabolical ointment used by witches in their sorcery on the limbs of the suspected murder victims. He knew this substance well: 'When I was at those feasts they taught me how I myself should use the oil to bewitch people and cause them to die. I never wanted to do it myself, but I could tell easily when someone had been anointed, and I think that anyone who has not belonged to this profession would not be able to recognize this sign.' Now, even the benandanti's ability to heal had a diabolical origin: 'As a remedy against this witchery they taught me to pick the roots of strawberries, boil them thoroughly and offer them to the patient to drink, as I did to cure the grandson of Signor Bartolomio, my master, who had been bewitched by the housewife Lucia, mentioned above.'

Giovanni had gone to the diabolical assemblies three times in the course of three years. 'Indeed,' he added, 'that guide of mine came every Thursday to tempt me to go to the feasts with him, but I chose not to go.' He had not revealed these sins previously because the devil and Gerolamo had enjoined him to keep the secret, threatening death, if he did not. But now he regretted this: 'On my way to hear the sermon on Good Friday, God inspired me to make a full confession, which I had not done other times.'

At this point the inquisitor asked Giovanni whether he had been branded by the devil or by Gerolamo of Villalta. 'Yes sir', he promptly replied, baring a round scar on his right thigh, 'and this was done to me there at the ball with a branding iron three feet long by the devil in the form of my companion: there was no pain at all.' In Sion's eyes that scar recorded, irrefutably, the *reality* of the diabolical gatherings which he had attended. So when the inquisitor asked him, 'did he consider these things to be true or imaginary, and did he really believe them,' he replied without hesitation: 'My lords, everything that I have said I hold as true and real and in no way an illusion.' We hardly need to recall that all benandanti had asserted that they attended the nocturnal conventicles 'in spirit', 'in a dream'. But now the benandante Giovanni Sion was siding with the theologians and demonologists who sustained the reality of the sabbat, by asserting that the 'celebrations'

in which he participated were true and real, 'and in no way an illusion'.

Sion concluded his testimony in a fit of remorse: 'I no longer want to be involved in these things,' he said, 'I do not believe them, nor do I want to believe in the devil any longer: indeed, when he asked me to deny the most Holy Trinity and the Blessed Virgin, I would not do it; he had a kind of book in which one's allegiance to him is written in blood.' But this mention of the refusal to apostatize, which in a sense completed the description of the sabbat, did not arouse the inquisitor's curiosity, and the benandante was promptly released.[14]

4

Even with its contradictions, Sion's account of the sabbat on the whole closely resembled the picture furnished by all the demonological treatises. This similarity was remarked upon, with a mixture of astonishment and honest intellectual satisfaction, by Don Pietro Martire da Verona. At the beginning of May – only a few days after the first interrogation – the inquisitor's vicar had asked him to have Giovanni Sion sent to Udine. Since Don Pietro did not have anyone who could accompany Sion just then, he had lodged the benandante briefly in his convent. 'We tested him quite thoroughly here in the monastery the last few days,' he wrote to Fra Ludovico da Gualdo on 11 May, 'and during this time he made many willing efforts; and it amazes me more and more how the things which he says occurred resemble what is in the books. He does not omit anything, and what he tells once he tells unchanged all the other times.' To obtain this correspondence with the 'books', it had taken more than a half-century of effort on the part of inquisitors, confessors and preachers (to limit ourselves to the clergy who, indeed, had played a leading role in this endeavour to make popular beliefs conform to the corresponding formulations of the educated classes); now the end of the process had almost been reached.

To be sure, Sion's claim that he had been present at the sabbat not merely in a dream, but in reality and physically, posed new problems for the inquisitors. The interrogations of those whom Sion had accused of being benandanti and co-participants in the sabbat began on 10 May. All, however, unfailingly rejected Sion's charges, while he, in turn, retracted nothing. There were some dramatic moments in their confrontation: addressing Giuseppe of Moimacco, who was continuing to deny that he had been at the sabbat, Giovanni Sion exclaimed: 'Hasn't Gerolamo of Villalta taught you to recite the Pater Noster backwards, as he also did to me? There is no need to deny it because unfortunately it is true, and I would that it was not so.'[15] But neither Giovanni's harangues nor the inquisitor's threats extracted from the accused an admission that they had participated in the sabbat. Even the discovery of two scars – or, as Sion insisted, two diabolical stigmata – on the bodies of two of the three peasants thus confronted, had no effect. The two were imprisoned, while Sion was again freed but with the obligation to keep himself at the disposal of the Inquisition.

From this moment the trial took a new turn. Fra Ludovico da Gualdo began an investigation of one of the witches accused of a murder by Sion – Grisola of Cividale. It came out that many suspected her of having committed crimes and witchery, but nothing more specific than that. Before long, however, the interrogations were halted and the inquisitor, due to the numerous irregularities and lapses in the procedure followed up to that point, decided, with the patriarch's concurrence, to take personal charge of the trial and proceed to Cividale to re-examine the witnesses.

5

On 24 August the benandante Giovanni Sion again stood before the court at Cividale to present testimony. He confirmed what he had told in previous sessions and now added several details which reflected a similar combination of new and old:

> 'I arrived at a beautiful palace and was led to a hall by the above-named Gerolamo. At the head of this room sat the devil, dressed as a captain with a black hat and red plume, a black shock of hair and a black forked beard shaped like twin horns; on his head were two horns similar to a goat's, and his feet were the hooves of an ass, and he held a fork in his hand. I was immediately instructed by Gerolamo that I should reverence him, as I did, by moving only my feet, as we do for the Most Holy Sacrament.'

The devil had asked him: 'My good man, have you come here to serve me?' 'Yes sir,' Giovanni answered. But, he exclaimed, in reply to a question from the inquisitor: 'I took no vow, nor promised, nor swore anything. . . . He did not ask me to abjure either the Most Holy Trinity, or Jesus Christ, or the Most Blessed Virgin, or anything else, but he only asked me to trample on a cross.'

The inquisitor reminded Sion that in his previous deposition he had described being branded by the devil. The benandante remembered, and added other details: 'I was called by that devil, who told me that I should reject the Holy Trinity. But I did not want to, and so he said, "I want to brand you," and he plunged a fork which he held in his hand into a fire on the ground just by his seat, and he branded me on the back of my right leg.' But why had he been branded? Here Sion contradicted himself: in his mind the diabolical connotations of witchcraft and the restraints attached to the myth of the benandanti clashed, mutually cancelling each other. He had just finished saying that the devil had wanted to brand him to make him pay for his refusal to abjure the Trinity; now instead he declared that the mark had been impressed on him 'so that . . . he [Sion] would be his vassal in the future, and obey him.' Carried away by this reply, he also asserted (contradicting himself again) that he had promised himself to the devil for life. But there was no reaction to these statements from the inquisitor; nor did he react during the interrogation the next day when Sion introduced into his description of the sabbat that element which had been almost totally missing up to that point: the vituperation and parody of ecclesiastical ceremonies. The devil, he said, 'urinated and then sprinkled it around as if it was holy water, and each time he made him swear an oath'; also, the devil instructed the witches 'that when they received communion, they should steal the Most Blessed Sacrament and use it to cast spells, and similarly that they should steal holy oil and fry the Host in it for the same purpose.'[16]

The inquisitor released the benandante, for the third time, perhaps intending to resume the interrogation at some later date. Such leniency towards an individual who had confessed his participation in the sabbat, where he had paid homage to the devil, promised himself to him for life and trampled on the cross, is more than a little surprising. Sixteen years before, Maria Panzona's Venetian judges had acted with much greater severity despite their open scepticism about the reality of the nocturnal conventicles. The milder attitude of Sion's judges may have resulted from his avowals of repentance at the beginning of the case, and also from his willingness to cooperate with the Holy Office. In any case these attempts to explain the Inquisition's singular benevolence towards Sion are mere conjectures. In fact, on 29 August 1634, after a series of investigations into the case of Grisola of Cividale and of other women suspected of witchery, the proceedings passed from the Holy Office into the hands of the secular authorities. What had happened? Formally renouncing any intention to pursue the trial, the inquisitor declared that Antonio Diedo, *provveditore* of

Cividale, had appeared before him to request

> 'that he desist from further prosecution, because after due consideration of the merits and nature of the trial, it was ruled that bringing it to a conclusion did not pertain to the tribunal of the Holy Office, in accordance with the laws and decrees of the Most Serene Venetian Republic, and especially pursuant to the instructions he had recently received from the most Serene Prince through his ducal letters.'

Apparently, the doge had intervened vigorously to transfer the conduct of the trial to secular authorities. The inquisitor acquiesced, presumably because he had no choice in the matter, and turned over to the *provveditore*, at his request, a copy of the records of the trial 'of certain women alleged to be witches and sorceresses.' There was no mention of the benandante Giovanni Sion.

What arguments had the *provveditore* of Cividale used to persuade the Holy Office to forsake its jurisdiction over witchcraft proceedings? The inquisitor himself provided an answer: 'Ascertaining that in the aforesaid trial there were neither heresies nor suspicion of heresies, apostasy, nor the suspicion of apostasy, nor the abuse of sacraments and sacramental objects . . . he [the inquisitor] furnished and turned over the trial records to the most illustrious *provveditore*.'[17] This was what the law prescribed on the subject; but, apart from the fact that it was very rarely applied, its appropriateness for the present case is doubtful. Weren't there allusions in Sion's confessions to crimes of apostasy and abuses of sacramental things (not counting the heresy of 'witchcraft' about which the canonists could not agree)?[18] The cautious attitude of Venice in the matter of witchcraft trials and its tendency to withdraw them as quickly as possible from inquisitorial jurisdiction were – as we have said – traditional, and reflected the policy of the *Serenissima* in safeguarding its own judicial autonomy at all costs from any kind of external interference.[19] However, the abdication of its own role by the Holy Office in this instance (even if it was compelled to it) is indeed startling, since it concerned the first case dealing with a full-blown sabbat ever submitted to the inquisitorial tribunal of the dioceses of Aquileia and Concordia. Could the inquisitor have thought Giovanni Sion's statements to be wild fancies beneath condemnation? There must have been talk of this kind if Don Pietro Martire, in dispatching the benandante to Cividale, felt compelled to reassure the inquisitor's vicar: 'Be certain Most Reverend Father that he [Sion] is indeed sound of mind, and whoever says that he is mad speaks falsely.' This theory, which might also explain the decision at one point taken by the inquisitor to remove the trial out of his vicar's hands and resume the interrogation of the witnesses from the beginning, is contradicted, however, by the long investigations of the women whom Sion said he had seen in flesh and blood at the sabbat. So we are faced by a series of contradictions, aggravated by the fact that we do not really know why the inquisitor gave in to the secular authorities.

6

On 15 April 1642, a woman of Basaldella presented herself voluntarily before Fra Ludovico da Gualdo to denounce Michele Soppe, a peasant of Santa Maria la Longa, as a benandante. A few days earlier she had summoned the latter 'to have him see a baby girl of hers, eight months old, who was sick; and when he came he looked at her, and said, after only glancing at her: "From now until Easter I cannot cure her"; and then he went away.' This was the first in a long series of denunciations against Michele Soppe. On 2 June of the same year a peasant of Cussignacco told the inquisitor that Soppe 'always goes around from one village to another making signs over the sick, and plies them with remedies to cure them, and he also reveals who has been bewitched and how, and who the author of the sorcery is.' One of the peasants healed by Michele was telling people that 'if it had not been for the benandante I would be dead.' For his part Michele openly claimed, 'except for me, more than forty whom I have healed would have died.' The peasant concluded his testimony by saying that he was accusing Soppe 'because after a person from Udine was imprisoned as a benandante, I thought it was right to denounce this one too so that these clever swindlers get the punishment they deserve.'

As was the case with the other benandanti, Michele drew considerable hostility because of his accusations. Don Giambattista Giuliano, a priest of Cussignacco, who appeared before the inquisitor on 22 August 1642, lamented, 'He goes about announcing that now this and now that poor woman is a witch, bringing a great loss of reputation and harm to the poor women he has accused, as well as perdition to those women who believe him.' To be rid of this nuisance Giuliano and the curate of Cussignacco had gone to Michele 'to learn from him first how witches cast their spells and then how he cured them.' The benandante had answered them, 'but with confused and difficult words'; then the priest had forbidden him to continue his activities, threatening punishment otherwise. Unperturbed, Michele said that he had been examined by a monk 'who had given him permission to exercise that office,' and he added that 'if he were called he would go, otherwise not.'[20]

Despite these denunciations the Holy Office did not act. Five years passed. On 19 January 1647, a peasant of Tissano, Giambattista Biat, presented himself before the new inquisitor, Fra Giulio Missini da Orvieto. The peasant had a son, Giacomo, who was seriously ill, the victim, he thought, of witchcraft. He turned for help to Michele Soppe who agreed to cure the child for four ducats. 'Since I did not have four ducats to give to Michele,' Biat said, 'I told him that I would work, or have my son work after he was cured, in the house or on the land of Giovanni Terencano of that village; and Giovanni bound himself, in return for our promised labour, to pay Michele his four ducats, if he would wait until the harvest.' But Michele refused to accept this arrangement: 'He wanted half of his payment at once in cash, and would wait for the rest until the harvest.' There was no way to get him to change his mind and, for lack of anything better, Biat had to turn to an exorcist, the priest of the Church of San Giacomo in Udine who declared that the boy was not suffering from natural causes, but had been bewitched. Obviously, the witness hated Soppe: 'I consider him to be a miserable wretch, wicked, and a benandante.' And in reply to a question from the inquisitor, he explained: 'Benandanti are those who go along with witches, so I have heard it said.'[21]

In Giovanni Sion's trial we have seen an awareness take hold in the minds of the benandanti (although not without some resistance) of their similarity to witches; to the people who appealed to the benandanti for a cure for themselves or members of their families, the merging of the two concepts was largely accomplished. The ill-natured behaviour of people of Michele Soppe's stamp – undoubtedly the result of the hardships which filled their miserable lives – could not help hastening the identification of benandanti as witches.

But in their work as healers the benandanti, probably because they were virtually in competition with them, ended up clashing with the exorcists whose activity, especially during the first half of the seventeenth century, knew no pause, as the extraordinary diffusion of such manuals as Girolamo Menghi's eloquently proves.[22] The deposition of Giambattista Biat which we have examined already contained a suggestion of the seemingly parallel functions of benandanti and exorcists (with an expressed preference for the former). The same motif recurred in another deposition dated 15 August 1648. The day before, the inquisitor, Fra Giulio Missini, assisted by the patriarch Marco Gradenigo and other personages, had finally decided to launch a formal inquiry into the case of Michele Soppe. The first to be questioned was Don Francesco Centrino, a priest from Udine. He related that when he had gone to perform exorcisms with the now deceased rector of Santa Maria la Longa, he encountered many individuals who 'gave faith and credence' to Michele Soppe. 'When I saw this,' he asserted, 'I told that man that he must never again show himself nor practise in those ways and forms in my area of jurisdiction, and after this he has never been seen again that I know of; and I admonished my people not to trust him because he is a scoundrel.'[23]

This recital was accompanied by various statements from peasants of Tissano and neighbouring villages who corroborated that Michele Soppe was considered by everyone to be a witch. One man said he personally did not harbour any ill will towards Michele himself, but only 'for these acts of his when he commits these witcheries to the peril of all of us, and in the village they are all disgusted with it.' This prompted the Holy Office to finally attempt to bring a halt to the torrent of denunciations and complaints which had been going on for years. On 21 May 1649, (even so the Inquisition could not overcome its usual slowness in these matters) Michele Soppe was arrested and incarcerated, to be maintained at the expense of the Holy Office 'on account of his poverty'. Meanwhile, the continued questioning of witnesses threw additional light on his personality and activity. Take, for example, the testimony of a peasant of Tissano who was a friend of his:[24]

> 'When we used to come to Udine to go to the offices of the Salt Monopoly at Poscolle with our salt wagons, Michele would leave us there and immediately begin to wander about the city, to see if he could earn a little money, so he told us. And on our way home one time he might say he had made two *lire*, and other times one, or four, or three – sometimes more, sometimes less. And he used to say that he had received it all by virtue of his tongue. I do not know how he really obtained it, but I did see the money he showed me; more I do not know.'

A few days after his arrest Michele began to divulge to the captain of the guard some particulars about witchcraft which he wanted passed on to the inquisitor; finally, on 2 June he asked to appear before the inquisitor himself. But the next day was market day in Udine, and Fra Giulio Missini, presumably to avoid an outburst of popular wrath against the suspect during his transport from prison to the court of the Holy Office, ordered that he be transferred with the utmost secrecy.[25] This small detail reveals a great deal about the place that, little by little, the figure of the benandante had come to assume in the popular mind.

After an extremely brief preamble in which Michele Soppe declared that he supposed he had been arrested under the false accusation that he had bewitched and killed the child of his present master, he began, spontaneously and without the slightest hesitation, to paint a minute picture of the activity of witches:

> 'Witches are to be found everywhere, those who cast spells on people and eat little children. . . . They go here and there into any house they choose without being seen by anyone, and they perform their witchcraft, causing children to be consumed little by little, and finally they cause them to die. . . . There are many witches in the Friuli, more than a hundred, but I cannot say who they are because I do not know their names, although it is true that I see them every Thursday night where the witches gather. . . . I too go to these congregations with the other men who are benandanti like me, and we go to the circular field in the swamps near Malizana, where the devil joins the witches and warlocks in the form of an ass, that is, of an ass with horns, but without the crosses on his shoulders that asses have. In these gatherings we dance and eat, I mean, it seems as if we dance and eat; the witches in the group all go . . . to kiss the devil's arse, after which he gives them the authority to do evil, in other words to perform sorcery, bewitch children and create storms. And they must do these wicked things in accordance with the power that the devil has bestowed on them. For in another congregation they must give an accounting to the devil of the evil they have committed, and if they fail to commit this evil, the devil beats them with thongs, that is, rods with lashes.'

And, after a brief pause, he added solemnly: 'Since I have told you the truth, you will immediately have me put to death.' Fra Giulio Missini urged him to reveal everything, so as to unburden his conscience and not incur divine wrath. But the benandante interrupted him: 'Father, yes of course I will tell the truth, but I do not understand your way of talking because you are not speaking Friulian.'[26]

So, Missini, a native of Orvieto, 'in order to satisfy the aforesaid arraigned peasant and to speak to him in his mother tongue,' immediately found 'an interpreter who was of the Friuli, a religious of upright reputation and good circumstances,' a professed of the Order of Minorite Friars. Even language, then, can be added as in this case, to the social, cultural and mental barriers standing between inquisitors and benandanti. This needs to be kept in mind in assessing the pastoral activity of inquisitors and preachers (who, more often than not, hailed from distant places) among a flock of the faithful largely composed of peasants like Soppe who were still incapable in the mid-seventeenth century of understanding a language that was not the 'mother tongue', namely, Friulian.[27]

Michele Soppe's account sketches a view of the diabolical sabbat containing elements, encrusted like fossils, that can be traced to beliefs which came into the sabbat at a late date, such as, 'the devil . . . in the form of an ass, that is, of an ass with horns, but without the crosses on his shoulders that asses have.' This allusion recalls a statement by a confessed follower of the society of Diana who was tried in Milan at the end of the fourteenth century: 'All kinds of animals, except those donkeys who carry crosses, flock to that society'.[28] But what place did the benandanti occupy in this scheme? Was their transformation into witches complete then?

Actually, the complex of beliefs identified with the benandanti was too deeply engrained in the popular mind to fade away in the course of a few years. Like Maria Panzona and Giovanni Sion, Michele Soppe, without consciously realizing it, tried to safeguard his autonomy as benandante from the diabolical activity of the witches: at the sabbat, he said, the latter approached the devil 'one by one to kiss his arse; but the warlocks who accompany the witches do not, nor do the benandanti who go separately from the witches.' But how did one account for the benandanti's ability to cure the bewitched, by now the only one of their powers that helped to differentiate them with some exactness? Michele tried confusedly to give an explanation: 'Witches and warlocks can make and unmake spells, if they wish, and benandanti too; if they are able to restore the bewitched they do it, and if they cannot, they have to be patient. When the benandanti want to heal someone they find the witch who has cast the spell, beg her to break it and this way they undo it'; he himself had performed this service many times. And, he went on with this attempt to differentiate benandanti from witches, reinterpreting the old beliefs: 'Also, witches recognize each other and are recognized by benandanti because they have a mark under their nose, a cross, which others cannot see. Moreover, during the dance witches and warlocks worship the devil, but benandanti do not.'[29] We can see that the ancient antithesis between witches and benandanti, the former as defenders of the devil's faith, the latter as champions of Christ's faith, still operated weakly, even if the benandanti themselves were not aware of it.

After a minute account of the spells he had broken, spells perpetrated by witches who were well-known to him because he had seen them at the 'congregations', Michele was finally returned to his cell due to the lateness of the hour.

So far we have attempted to trace the gradual development in the convergence of the traits of benandanti and witches, but we have not considered the evolution of witchcraft itself, or rather, of the general attitude towards it, since it's impossible to speak of the development of witchcraft after the stage when the sabbat crystallized and became institutionalized. Between the end of the sixteenth and the first half of the seventeenth century the concept of the sabbat underwent profound changes. The position of a Johann Weyer was no longer an isolated one: the Protestant Johann Godelmann and the Catholic Friedrich von Spee vied with each other in combating the belief in the reality of the sabbat and the flights of witches. Medical advances increasingly lead to the view that witches and the possessed were only frivolous women, victims of hallucinations and melancholy.[30] To be sure, the old attitude towards witchcraft did not die at once: on the contrary, almost everywhere in Europe (and especially in Germany) the first decades of the seventeenth century witnessed a surge in the persecution of witches – persecutions which due to their excesses often ended by swelling the ranks of the sceptics and fuelling the controversies. In any case, even without considering the inhabitants of the countryside, to whom this new, sceptical attitude long remained alien, tenacious resistance was offered by those representing the old view. An example of this position is contained in the deposition of the Dominican Pio Porta, exorcist and prior of San Pietro Martire in Udine. The inquisitor Fra Giulio Missini summoned him on 4 June 1649 to hear his opinion on whether a diabolical element existed in the illness of Giacomo Biat, the youth whom Michele Soppe had refused to treat. Porta seized the opportunity to launch into an emotional and moving speech against the practices of the times:

> 'So varied and so great are the burdens that fall to me daily in this matter of witches and warlocks, that in reality I cannot remember all the details of things I have had to hear as exorcist appointed by the most illustrious and reverend monsignor the patriarch to help the poor bewitched people in this city and diocese. They are so numerous that not two but twenty-one exorcists would not suffice to fill the need.'

He himself, in fact, was occupied with the obligations of his priorate, while the other exorcist, the parish priest of San Giacomo, old and burdened with obligations, had difficulty 'ministering to the needs of the many wretched victims of sorcery in this area'. But these were not the only, nor even the principal causes of Porta's distress. 'And to tell the truth with all due sincerity and respect,' he continued,[31]

'I am not a little amazed that something is not done about these excesses which bring such grievous hurt to this land; and perhaps the reason why a remedy is not found is that there are so many who do not believe in this evil. Although I realize I am less worthy than anyone who exercises this profession, trusting in the help of God, I exert myself to offer proof in the presence of my lords the physicians and of anyone else who desires to be present. I have them feel with their own hands that it is not the frivolity of women nor the whims of monks, but real infirmities, caused by witchcraft alone, which reduce many of these wretches to waste away in their beds with long incurable illnesses; and there are many others as well who through witchery are also possessed and obsessed by the devil. All this, I repeat, I endeavor to demonstrate to any Catholic person.'

Only after he had thus unburdened himself did the exorcist respond to the question. He stated that the youth Biat had been bewitched, and that the author of this sorcery must be the benandante who was then in the prison of the Holy Office, namely Michele.

All these witnesses described Michele Soppe as an insolent and merciless witch. On the other hand, his last master, Domenico Tobia, who was questioned on 16 June 1649, declared that he considered Michele to be 'a good, upright and devout young man'. It was true, Tobia added, that some people claimed he was a benandante (which 'in our Friulian tongue means someone who goes out at night with the witches'): but 'I do not consider him to be such . . . I do not think of him as a man capable of curing anything, in fact I consider him a fool and a clown . . . In my opinion he is stupid and I used to say to those who called him to cure the sick that in my opinion he could not do any of those things, and that he should not be believed, even though everyone said he was a benandante.' And then he painted a picture of Michele Soppe as a pious and God-fearing man:[32]

'When he is not tending the herds and is at home in winter or when it rains, or during such times, he always goes to Mass; he always makes the sign of the cross when the Ave Maria tolls, he recites the Ave Maria, crossing himself first, he rests the oxen from their work at that time, blesses the bread and offers thanks to God after he has eaten; when he goes out to Mass he has a rosary in his hands; in church he is respectful and recites the rosary, and so he performs all the duties of a good Christian.'

9

But Tobias's was the only testimony in Michele's favour. There was a virtual chorus of voices against him: one person said that 'he can do a lot of evil, and perform miracles too, and he can evoke storms when he chooses, even when the sun is shining and the weather is clear; another had heard him boast that he could 'hurt anyone he wanted through the devil's art, and with his witchery make them take sick, wither and die . . . nor could they be succoured by any priest if he did not wish it.'[33] Others talked about Soppe's hard-heartedness when he declined to heal Biat's son: to the women who implored him, and who said 'If you refuse, look to your soul,' he had replied: 'The devil, I do not give a fig about my soul.' He had also spoken brutally to the mother of the invalid: 'Since you will not give me four ducats to have me cure your son, go ahead and buy him four boards to build a box to bury him in.'[34] At this point the transformation of benandanti into witches was practically accomplished. The former were no longer concerned with the protection of children and harvests. Now they were preoccupied exclusively with reaping the fruits of their twofold power, to make and unmake spells. Outsiders had visited Michele and asked him to accompany them to their town to heal some victims of sorcery, but with no luck. 'Good heavens,' he had exclaimed after they left disappointed: 'Anyone who has tricked me once is not going to get away with it again. These strangers wanted me to cure some bewitched people in their village, but I did not want to go, because I once cured the little girl of one of them and he did not pay me; I will not go again, in fact I would like to see that little one returned to that same state of witchery from which I saved her.' Aptly summarizing the consensus of opinion about Michele, a peasant of Tissano declared, 'everyone says that he is a witch and even more than a witch, because not only can he cast spells, he can also break them.'[35]

10

Michele Soppe's first interrogation left a number of points still obscure, a residue of the contradiction relating to belief in the benandanti and witchcraft. It was not clear, in particular, how the benandanti, simply through their participation in the sabbat, had the power, certainly of diabolical origin, to heal the bewitched. In the interrogation of 24 July the inquisitor endeavoured once again to resolve this lingering confusion. Michele offered an explanation he had used on previous occasions: 'I went to look for the witch who had cast a spell on the child; I begged her to lift the spell from her, and she did it for love of me, and when the spell was removed, the child was cured.' The inquisitor did not try to conceal his disbelief. 'Yes father,' Michele insisted, 'all the witches out of love for me removed the spells on people I wanted healed, and no witch has ever refused me.' But how and why, pressed the monk, did the witches obey him? Michele began to weep, and desperately went over the main points of his beliefs for the implacable inquisitor:

> 'I am so bound . . . I am a benandante, and all benandanti ask witches to lift spells from those they wish to cure. When the witches are at their dance they adore the devil but benandanti adore God. Both witches and benandanti go to the devil's ball, but only witches cast spells, the benandanti do not; if the benandanti can get witches to annul the sorcery, good, if not they have to be patient. The witches kiss the devil's arse at the dance and have long conversations with him, but the benandanti do not and hardly speak to him.'

Michele did not know anything more. The contradictions in his account – instantly and accurately discerned by the inquisitor – actually go far beyond him personally, and were typical of the entire laborious passage from the myth of the benandanti to witchcraft. What did benandanti believe? How did they explain the contradictory elements in their nocturnal conventicles? Were they followers of the devil, since they attended the sabbat in a dream; or kindly men, intent only in undoing spells cast by witches and warlocks? In the replies squeezed out of him during the inquisitor's relentless interrogation, Michele Soppe groped for an answer to these questions: What was a benandante? How did a person become one? What means did benandanti use to cure the bewitched?

'Witches tell me immediately as soon as they have done their sorcery and the victim begins to waste away.' Where do they tell him, the inquisitor wanted to know, why do they tell him? 'The devil wants all the witches to tell me and the other benandanti about all the spells they cast,' Michele began to reply. But why did the devil want this? 'I do not know any other reason, except that this is the devil's pleasure,' was Michele's hesitant answer. The interrogation degenerated into bickering over trifles.

In the afternoon, the inquisitor remorselessly repeated his question: did he know how to dispel witchery? Stubbornly, Michele threaded his way (with a slight variation) over his previous course, even though he realized it was a dead end: 'I do not know how to break spells, and I have never done it, and if I have cured the bewitched it is because the same witches who cast the spells removed them out of love for me.' But why did witches obey him? Michele had an inspiration: 'Witches obey me because they are afraid I will betray them and that when they are recognized for what they are the law will see them burned.' But the monk, in a flash, kept him from continuing: was it perhaps permitted to good Christians 'to converse with witches, especially at the sabbat, and to obey them?' (So, the benandanti were not good Christians!) Then a more ancient justification rose from Michele Soppe's memory: 'I was born under that sign, and I am compelled to accompany the witches, I cannot help myself.' What sign was he referring to, asked the inquisitor. Michele replied: 'I do not know what the sign is, but my mother used to tell me that I was born with the caul.' Michele did not remember well; his recollections were mechanical, unconnected to anything real. The monk cut him short: such things were irrelevant – 'they have no bearing on the matter' – and in no way could they coerce man's will.

Unexpectedly Fra Giulio asked the benandante if he thought that those who 'had converse with witches and the devil' in life could hope for the salvation of the soul. 'I believe,' Michele replied, 'that such people if they do not repent and confess themselves cannot go to paradise, but must go to hell.' The monk pointed out that Michele was precisely in this position himself; he had not freed himself of his errors in the confessional, nor had he done penance; what did he think might be in store for him? The benandante replied: 'I think God will have mercy on me, because he suffered on the cross for all of us.' But, God dispenses what is deserved to those who are good and to those who are evil: was he hopeful that he would find salvation while living intimately with the devil? 'No sir,' a bewildered Michele replied.

At this point the inquisitor launched the decisive blow: but for Michele it served as a beacon, pointing a way out of the labyrinth in which he had wandered so long. Had he by any chance concluded a pact with the devil, Fra Giulio asked? For the latter everything had been clear for quite some time; but now it became clear for Michele too. 'Father, yes, I have sworn a compact with the devil and I promised him my soul.' Where, how, when, who were witnesses to it, the judge burst out. And Michele, as if unburdening himself of a great weight:[36]

> 'The place was in the country near Malisana during the dance and conventicle of the witches, in that field where they gather, about two years after I began to go to the ball, in the presence of all the witches and warlocks who were assembled there. It happened like this: the devil asked me if I wanted to give my soul up to him; in exchange he would

grant me all the favours that I desired. At the devil's request I replied that I surrendered my soul to him, as if I promised it out of my own free will. . . . Not only on that occasion . . . but another time still in the same place, with all the witches and warlocks present, a month after the first time, I reaffirmed the promise I had made to the devil of my soul, and promised it anew. Also, at the request of the devil I twice denied Jesus Christ and his holy faith; every time that I went to the witches' ball I kissed the devil's arse, just like all the witches and warlocks, and I did all the things the others did. Also I worshipped the devil whenever the others worshipped him, that is at the ball, one Thursday yes and another no, or sometimes twice yes and twice no. We all kneeled before the devil who was in the shape of an ass, and he turned his backside to us, and we worshipped his arse and the devil's tail, and this praying, with our hands folded, lasted about a quarter of an hour. Moreover, when the devil made me abjure Jesus Christ and his faith he also had me trample on a cross at the same ball in the presence of all the witches and warlocks, just as they all did; and the cross was the size of the palm of a hand, though not a crucifix, and was made from a wood called viburnum. Out of this wood they make crosses for Ascension Day which are carried in procession and then set in the fields as protection against storms.'

With this confession the previously revealed contradictions were resolved: the powers of the benandanti were of diabolical origin, and benandanti were nothing but witches. From the battles waged by the ancient benandanti in defence of Christ's faith, we have arrived at the apostasy, to which the benandante Michele Soppe admitted, of that very same faith. The original myth was even symbolically rejected since the trampled cross was made out of branches of viburnum, in imitation of the crosses which were placed in fields during the processions of the Rogation Days to ward off storms,[37] once a symbol of fertility appropriated by benandanti such as Gasparutto as a weapon in the battles they fought in their dreams against witches.

11

Without need of further urging from Fra Giulio, Michele Soppe, after confessing his apostasy, also asserted that he had killed no less than three children at the devil's orders, among whom was a nephew of his. He described his crimes in morbid detail: he used to enter homes in the guise of a cat 'through the power of the devil', approach the children and suck their blood. 'I took in my mouth the fingers of the hand of that little child who was my nephew, pierced his fingertips with my teeth, sucked the blood which he had in his veins and spit it out as I left the house so it would not be noticed; and I also opened his veins under his left arm on the side of his heart, and I sucked his blood by means of diabolical arts.' Then he confessed that even his cures had occurred through the direct intervention of the devil: 'I healed some of those who had been bewitched,' he affirmed, 'by having the witches who had cast the spells break them themselves; but usually I performed my cures in the way I said, I called the devil, who came instantly each time I called him, although many other times he did not come. Well, the devil comes most of the time, and sometimes I gave him orders and sometimes I beseeched him to do what I wanted, and the devil always obeyed me, did everything that I wanted, and at my say-so the devil broke the spells in those children whom I wanted healed, and they were cured.' But then, once again the old beliefs reappeared unexpectedly, though they were now virtually incomprehensible: 'I called Satan,' related Michele, 'and usually I would be holding a fennel stalk, but occasionally even without the fennel stalk.'[38] The symbol of fertility which the benandanti once had emblazoned on their banners had now become a link between the benandanti themselves and the devil.

12

Michele Soppe's interrogations dragged on for the entire summer without producing any new developments: finally, on 18 October 1649 the defendant was assigned a court-appointed lawyer (Michele was too poor to pay for one himself), who submitted a brief on 12 November requesting that the benandante, a confessed criminal, not be condemned to capital punishment. On 4 December a copy of the trial reached the Congregation of the Holy Office in Rome. Everything, then, was ready for the sentencing. But unexpectedly, an order came from Rome to reopen the proceedings. 'Reverend father,' wrote Cardinal Francesco Barberini to the inquisitor of Aquileia on 11 December 1649, 'Michele Soppe's crimes are extremely serious, but he cannot be sentenced to the maximum penalty unless the crimes of infanticide to which he has confessed are verified.' Meanwhile, he ordered the inquisitor to await further instructions from Rome. These followed without delay. A few days later (18 December) Cardinal Barberini himself explained why the Congregation was dissatisfied with the manner in which the trial against Soppe had been carried out:[39]

Thus Your Reverence will have to conduct delicate judicial investigations to verify them (the crimes of infanticide), by questioning the physicians who treated the children during their illness. They should be diligently examined on the nature of the malady, and whether through the art of their medicine they were able to determine if the illness was or could have been natural, questioning them anew on the entire series of ailments and misfortunes, from the beginning to the end of the sickness. All these opinions should be inserted into the trial records in their entirety, so that if, because of inexperience, the doctors judged that a death had occurred not from a natural disease, but from a *maleficium*, other more skilled physicians, after informing themselves of all aspects of that case, could determine if the infirmity had resulted from natural or supernatural causes, even if they had not personally attended the patients.

These guidelines – both so obvious and yet so far removed from those which had guided Fra Giulio Missini in the proceedings against Soppe – had been influencing the attitude of the Roman Inquisition for some time in regard to witchcraft. The letter of Cardinal Barberini quoted above is nothing more, in fact, than a literal translation (from the words 'will have to conduct delicate') of a passage from the celebrated *Instructio pro formandis processibus in causis strigum sortilegiorum et maleficiorum*. This brief tract, written about 1620, circulated widely in manuscript before it was published in 1655 by Cesare Carena, a theologian of Cremona.[40] Even before this latter date it inspired directives on the subject sent from Rome to the provincial inquisitors, as the letter from Cardinal Barberini to Fra Giulio Missini indicates.[41]

The significance of the break with traditional inquisitorial practice in the matter of witchcraft prosecution represented by the *Instructio* is obvious from the very first words:

> Experience, the mistress of things, openly teaches us that serious errors are committed daily by numerous bishops, vicars and inquisitors in instituting trials against witches, sorceresses and perpetrators of *malefici* to the notable prejudice of justice, as well as of the women being tried. So that in this General Congregation of the Holy Roman and Universal Inquisition against heretical pravity it has long been observed that hardly a single trial can be discovered in this matter that has been correctly and legally instituted.

Written in the circles of the Roman Congregation of the Holy Office, the *Instructio* reflected, not only recent polemics, as much among Catholics as among Protestants, but also the exceedingly mild attitude adopted in witchcraft cases by the Spanish Inquisition.[42] This document did not enter into a general discussion of the reality of witchcraft in its various forms, which was unnecessary, in any case, given its character of practical instruction, but it did wield notable influence in Italy, admonishing judges to exercise extreme caution in such cases. As a direct consequence of Rome's moderating influence witchcraft condemnations virtually disappeared from the Italian peninsula in the second half of the seventeenth century. By the end of that century the Franciscan Sinistrari d'Ameno could write that in Italy, contrary to what was taking place north of the Alps, 'very rarely were crimes of this type turned over to the secular arm by Inquisitors.'[43]

On 12 March, 1650 Cardinal Barberini once again took pen in hand to write to the inquisitor of Aquileia. The trial of Michele Soppe had been discussed anew in the presence of the cardinals of the Holy Office and of Pope Innocent X himself. The decision was unanimous and Barberini emphasized this fact: 'It [the trial] appeared very defective, because almost nothing confessed by him was actually verified in it.'[44] Thus, once again, he urged the judge to question physicians, the families of the children whom Soppe claimed he had murdered and individuals whom he had treated, to ascertain the truth of the facts that had come out in the trial. On 4 March Fra Giulio Missini had already resumed, after a long interruption, the interrogation of witnesses, in compliance with the directives from Rome.

The first to be questioned about Giacomo Biat, the youth whom Michele Soppe had refused to heal (though claiming to be capable of it), were two exorcists active in the city of Udine, one of whom was the monk Pio Porta who, as we have mentioned, argued for the reality of diabolical possession against the claims of physicians and sceptics. Their opinions concurred: the young man had been the victim of witchcraft. The physicians instead were not in agreement. Pietro Diana, seventy years of age, 'a very erudite and learned man', declared, hearkening back to the authority of Galen and Avicenna, that the youth was afflicted 'by miasma or consumption'. He did not rule out, however, that the illness might have had a diabolical origin: on this question he deferred to the exorcists ('About the matter of this illness I wrote as would be appropriate to a physician. But since there are those who believe that sickness has a hidden origin, truly a demoniacal one, judgment is reserved to those who exercise the revered art of the exorcist'); and he affirmed that the devil, 'God permitting,' was capable of achieving such effects. The other physician interrogated, Francesco Casciano, thirty-six years of age, 'public physician of Udine', diagnosed a case of 'emaciation of the entire body'; when the inquisitor inquired if the condition had natural causes or not, he replied sharply: 'The physician only contemplates natural phenomena in the human body, be they diseased or healthy, and considers both to be dependent on natural causes; nor does he acknowledge any supernatural sickness or any dependent on an unnatural cause, just as I cannot state that the child in question suffers from any other ailment than what is natural and due to natural causes, as I have already said.'[45] The import of the two replies differed considerably: and the reason for this great disparity undoubtedly lies in the thirty-four year age difference between the two authorities.

But we are not going to follow the various events in the trial step by step. The questioning of the witnesses produced the information that the parents of the children whom Michele claimed he had killed did not suspect that there had been any witchcraft involved; moreover, there was no field near the swamps of Malizana resembling the one where, in Michele's account, the sabbat had taken place; finally, Michele himself, in the retelling of his own misdeeds at a distance of time, fell into repeated contradictions.

At last, on 12 July 1650, the interrogations ended. The inquisitor asked Michele Soppe (who by now had been a prisoner in Udine for more than a year) whether he wished to have the lawyer who had previously been assigned to him, Giovan Giacomo Pontenuto, review the testimony of the witnesses in his defence. 'What defence do you want me to make,' exclaimed Michele forlornly, 'if there is no one who has helped me, or who has done anything for me?'[46] Thus, two days later, Pontenuto presented a petition to the Holy Office in which 'Michele of Santa Maria la Longa, a confessed benandante declared himself to be repentant of the 'enormities' he had committed and implored the judges to send him 'to a galley of the Most Serene Republic to serve as oarsman, with irons on his feet, for the remainder of his life'. But the request went unheeded. Michele Soppe lingered in prison in Udine awaiting sentence for another four months. Evidently, new instructions from Rome were expected, and they arrived on 29 October 1650. Soppe's case had again been discussed in the presence of the pope and the cardinals of the Congregation of the Holy Office, and these were the conclusions communicated by Barberini to the inquisitor of Aquileia: 'Have this Michele examined by specialists to determine if he is mentally deficient, at least in the matter of the alleged witchcraft. If he is judged to be of sound mind, subject him to light torture to discover his intent. If he keeps to his position, have him abjure *de vehementi* and sentence him to prison at your discretion. This is the way to end the trial.'[47] But the judges in Udine did not have time to reach a verdict. The termination of this case, which in the eyes of Barberini and his Roman colleagues had certainly dragged on much too long, came about differently. All this time Michele Soppe must have been in poor health. In February, he complained to the inquisitor because his daily allowance had been reduced to 18 *soldi*. 'It is not possible,' he wrote on that occasion, 'to live on such a small

subsistence in these times of famine'; therefore he had asked to be provided 'with a small serving of soup', in addition to his ration of bread and wine. It may be that his death, which came in prison on 20 November 1650, was caused by the suffering he had endured in confinement. Two days before he had prepared a will, in which he requested that his clothing (a 'vestment of greenish linen', a 'shirt', a few pairs of 'cotton socks', and so on) be distributed among the poorest prisoners, and that Masses be celebrated with the little bit of money remaining to him.

In the final analysis, the fate of the benandanti was a strange one. Having been virtually ignored as benandanti, they became transformed into witches too late to be persecuted: by now the mental climate had undergone a profound change. Michele Soppe was an unknowing victim of this transformation, which we are able to retrace bit by bit, in its almost inevitable progress, as it was lived by different individuals in different ways.

13

At this point we must take a step back. On 8 January 1647 – that is, two years before Michele Soppe's trial – a young peasant of Zuiano, Bastiano Menos, presented himself of his own accord before Don Pietro Martire da Verona in the Church of the Madonna del Soccorso, claiming that he was a benandante and had been going out for a year 'in spirit to the parade'.[48] He had not discovered that he was one, until he was called by the captain of the benandanti, Michele of Santa Maria la Longa, who lived in Tissano. This Michele was none other than Michele Soppe. Bastiano was a benandante of the older mould, so to speak. Don Pietro Martire asked him, as was now customary, what this word 'benandante' meant, and he replied, significantly: 'We must keep God's faith,' and added that he was 'under that sign because he had been born with the caul.' He knew the witches of his 'state' which was that of Santa Caterina near the Cormor, and he named them. He had threatened them with death many times, first 'with the spirit' and 'later with both the spirit and the body . . . and this was the reason the witches break spells for him.' By these means he had brought many people back to health, 'and his captain [Michele Soppe] has earned more than a hundred ducats in this way; he is called to give help almost weekly.'

Certain similarities with Michele Soppe's accounts, of an external character – real and not imaginary – emerge from this confession. Menos actually asserted that he served as Michele's subordinate, aiding him in his role as healer. And yet there was a profound difference between the two: Menos declared that he fought witches and kept 'God's faith', whereas Michele, from his very first appearance before the Holy Office, said that he participated in the witches' ball in the presence of the devil.

On 16 February 1647 Menos was summoned by the inquisitor, who had been opportunely alerted by Don Pietro Martire da Verona. This time the youth's account was much more rambling:

> 'I am a benandante, and I have gone out with the other benandanti called by their captain, whose name is Michel of Santa Maria della Lunga . . ., I went with him and with the other benandanti twice a week, every Wednesday and Thursday night for the space of a whole year, to a place called the field of Santa Chaterina on the way to the Cormor, a mile and a half from Udine, on the other side of the water, where we remained for an hour, or an hour and a half approximately. On one side were the benandanti and on the other the witches. The witches had staves in their hands, like those for scraping ovens, and we benandanti had stalks of fennel or elder. Our captain went ahead and stayed a while with the witches. I do not know if he spoke with them or what he did; then he returned to us, and many times combat ensued between the benandanti and the witches, but sometimes not, and then everyone went back home.'

Bastiano declared that he knew only two people in the ranks of the benandanti: Michele, who was the captain, and Domenico Miol of Basaldella, nicknamed Totolo, destined to inherit the duties of captain at Michele's death. Instead, Bastiano was acquainted with many of the witches against whom he fought, and, in general, declared that he knew how to recognize witches because they had, invisible to all except benandanti, a small cross under their noses (remember that the same thing had been said by Michele Soppe).

At this juncture the questioning of Bastiano Menos was interrupted: the youth was let go, under obligation to return the next day. But more than two years passed before he reappeared: he finally presented himself on 10 July 1649, begging forgiveness for failing to keep his word: 'Many times,' he said, after he had obtained an interpreter to translate for him, 'Monsignor Canon Mierlo urged me to return to obedience, and he told me this on behalf of Your Reverence; and I kept becoming more fearful and afraid. I was frightened because I am an ignorant peasant.' But then, 'so as to stop living in this confusion,' he had finally decided to appear before the Holy Office. He confirmed the story he had told in his previous deposition and added a few details about the ceremony of initiation: 'One night the aforesaid

Michele called me by name and said, ''Bastiano, you must come with me''; and I, who was an ignorant youth, told him ''yes''; and he mounted a cock, and he made me get on a hare, both animals being in attendance outside . . . and on these creatures, as though flying swiftly over the land, we reached the field of Santa Chaterina.' But this time the inquisitor was not in a mood to accept Menos's tales calmly: meanwhile the trial against Soppe had begun, and he suspected that Bastiano too was a sort of witch-benandante. For that reason he asked 'whether in the sabbat he had seen a cross, images of the saints, oppressed children, or anything else.' 'I did not see anything,' Menos replied; and he also denied having committed any act 'in contempt of God or divine law' during the nocturnal gatherings. He explained that 'when I used to go to the field with the witches I did not know it was a sin, but later I learned that it was a sin because I was told so.' Then the inquisitor, after cautioning him 'of the evil he had perpetrated and of the danger to his soul from this grievous offence against God,' decided to accord him the greatest possible mercy 'on account of his simplicity, ignorance and fear': he absolved him from excommunication and imposed a series of salutary penances.

The same day in which this sentence was pronounced (19 July 1649) Menos was summoned to testify in the case of Michele Soppe, who by this time had been incarcerated for several months. Nothing new came out of his deposition; only, that the first night after he had testified before the Holy Office, Michele Soppe had come to call him, as usual. But by this time Bastiano had become convinced of the error of his ways and had not wanted to go. Michele had shrugged: 'If you don't want to come I won't call you anymore; forget it.'[49]

A few days later, on 26 July, in the course of an exhausting interrogation ('I am all sweaty,' he said at one point, 'I cannot stop sweating because of the great mental effort'), Michele Soppe revealed the names of the benandanti who had gone with him to the witches' ball. Among them he listed (without benefit of any prompting, or even hints, on the part of the inquisitor) Bastiano Menos and Domenico Miol of Basaldella. On this point there is absolute agreement with Menos's confession, and it cannot be supposed that it was the result of recent exchanges between the two benandanti, since we know Michele had been in prison for some time. We therefore have to suppose that the two had been in contact prior to the arrest.

Michele verified that it was he who had introduced Bastiano Menos to the nocturnal gatherings:

> 'This Bastiano used to come with me to a pasture where his master's animals grazed; he became friendly, and I asked him in the pasture if he

> wanted to come with me and the witches to the dance; he said yes, he would come. I repeated this a second time when we were at the pasture; he told me that he would come, and then I said to him, "I shall come to call you at night, don't be afraid, we shall go together." And so I did: the following Thursday I mounted my goat and went to find Bastiano who was in bed; I called him by name and said to him: "Bastiano, do you want to come with me to the dance of the witches?" And he replied, "Yes, I do." I had another goat with me, and Bastiano mounted it, and together we rode off to the dance of the witches in Santa Catarina's field beyond the Cormor, on the road between Udine and Codroipo.'

Up to this point there are many significant similarities between the accounts of Soppe and Menos: the appearance of Michele, the exhortations to his friend, the journey mounted on animals (true, Menos did not speak of goats, but of a hare and a cock), the place of meeting. However, the two accounts diverge after this: Michele had by now crossed the line which separated benandanti from witches, and the ancient traditions had become foreign to him. He said that Bastiano Menos, whom he had persuaded to attend the witches' dance, 'adored the devil, kissed the devil's arse, and I do not know if he did anything else besides participate in the fighting of the witches.' And he explained what he meant for the benefit of the inquisitor who did not know what this fighting was about: 'The witches battle with marshy stalks, which are water reeds, and the warlocks with branches of fennel, but they do not hurt each other much.'[50] We can see that Michele Soppe did not identify the individuals fighting against the witches armed with fennel as benandanti, and he even described them vaguely as 'witches'. This is eloquent testimony of the disintegration which was taking place within the myth.

Menos had accused Domenico Miol of being a benandante, in fact of being Michele Soppe's successor in the role of captain. From 1647 on Domenico too had frequently been denounced as a benandante. He was born with the caul, and would identify witches and heal victims of sorcery in exchange for a little money.[51] But it was not until the summer of 1649 that the inquisitor, visibly struck by the similarities and connections in the confessions of Michele Soppe and Bastiano Menos (whose interrogations he ordered copied and inserted into the record of Miol's trial), resolved to confront head-on the case of Domenico Miol. On 2 August, in a specially summoned congregation of the Holy Office, it was voted unanimously, but only after lengthy discussion, to order Miol's arrest. Now that the ambiguity surrounding the benandanti had vanished, the inquisitors of Aquileia were much more diligent and concerned. Miol admitted that he had healed victims of witchcraft, but by means of prayers, nothing else, and obstinately denied that he had

ever attended the nocturnal gatherings. On 24 November he was thereby pronounced 'lightly' suspect of heresy and apostasy because of his calling as benandante ('which in correct language', the sentence fussily specified, 'means companion of warlocks and witches'). He was then condemned to make a solemn abjuration; in the event of his relapse, he would have to serve for three years on the galleys of the Republic. In spite of Miol's reluctance to talk, it is clear that the reciprocal accusations of complicity made by these benandanti and the relationships by which they themselves claimed to be bound, were not invented. They were objective, real associations, of a sectarian type. As we see by comparing the confessions of Michele and Bastiano Menos, each benandante relived in a different way, presumably during the course of their mysterious fainting spells, the traditional beliefs, which by now were in the process of disintegration. Thus a problem which seemed to have been answered in the negative crops up again: that of the *reality* of at least some of the benandanti's gatherings – a reality which in the accounts of the participants certainly appeared inextricably interwoven with elements of pure fantasy. But how to prove that these conventicles did take place in some cases? As with the analogous problem of the reality of the witches' covens, none of the evidence suffices. In a way, we can understand the demonologists who, in the face of the extraordinary number of 'eyewitnesses' decided that the reality of the sabbat was a proven fact. But for us, these witnesses are worthless since they all moved in a precise sphere of beliefs and expectations, which inevitably conditioned their attitudes, and their very perception of things. Can we find evidence from outside this sphere, a spectator who might have looked upon these events with a clear eye unblurred by prejudices?

Possibly it is just this sort of evidence that is found in a deposition made before the Holy Office of Aquileia by a woman of Gradisca.[52] The very late date – 1668 – is not, as we shall see at once, accidental. This woman, Caterina Sochietti, had taken into her home, 'as an act of charity to ward off possible trouble', a sister-in-law, a little girl of eight called Angiola, who had seemed 'very licentious' to her. Four days after she was brought to Gradisca from Udine (where she had lived) the child told a strange tale to one of the servants of the house: 'Would you like to come with me to nuptials where you will eat sweets, where there are handsome gentlemen and ladies dancing, and the tallest of these gentlemen plays the violin so softly as to put one to sleep, and said he wanted to give me a beautiful ring?' When Caterina Sochietti heard about this story she summoned the child and asked for an explanation. Angiola told how her mother used to oil her wrists, and then take her to 'a man, where there were many other men and ladies dancing, and also some girls,' whom she knew. 'That tall gentleman,' she explained, 'plays the violin for that company, where there is eating, but mostly dancing': and in this company 'she remained below with a little brother of hers eating candies,' while her mother 'was upstairs with the tall gentleman'. One day at one of these gatherings the girl met a lace worker named Valentino Cao, who said to her: 'So, you are here too! Where is your mother?' And Angiola replied: 'She is upstairs chatting with the gentleman.' Then Valentino said, 'Now I am going to find her too,' and after a little while he returned with the mother. Another time (these are still Angiola's stories, as reported to the inquisitor by Caterina Sochietti) a handsome youth came up to her who also was a member of the company. He took her by the hand and led her 'to that tall gentleman, who asked: "Who does this girl belong to?" The young man replied: "She is Pacciotta's daughter." The tall gentleman then said: "What do you want with her?" and he replied, "I want her for my lover, if you will give her to me." "I want her for myself, retorted the gentleman." ' Then the youth led her to a room and, the girl went on, 'he kissed me and fondled me, and my mother was there too, laughing, and then we went out again to the ball.'

Unlike her contemporaries, the girl did not say that she had gone to the sabbat or that 'the tall gentleman' was the devil; and yet all the elements of the sabbat were there. The only thing missing in this bare and objective description, almost photographic in its impassibility, are the embellishments, the beliefs which usually enriched the accounts of witches' conventicles. These beliefs were dying out and the girl plainly was unaware of them: she limited herself to recording with a detached eye, a *fact*, or rather, a series of separate acts which she did not know how to connect or interpret.[53] With the disintegration of the myths and fantastic trappings of witchcraft, we discover, almost with a sense of disappointment, a shabby and downright banal reality – a gathering of people, with dancing and sexual promiscuity. In a number of cases the sabbat must really have been like this, or, more accurately, also like this.[54] Although it isn't possible to extend this conclusion by simple analogy to encompass the benandanti, there's no doubt that it lends plausibility to the hypothesis that meetings of a sectarian type took place among them, resembling or at least not very different from those described.

14

We have seen how the belief in diabolical witchcraft finally succeeded in establishing itself in the Friuli in these decades, combining with and super-imposing itself on older traditions, especially those of the benandanti. In this regard, witchcraft, in a strict sense, has appeared to us to be extraneous to the popular myths considered thus far: extraneous not only because it was disseminated by inquisitors, preachers and exorcists, but also because it was much further removed from the mentality of the Friulian peasants than were the benandanti, protectors of the harvests, defenders of grains and vineyards, enemies of spell-casting witches. But it would be hasty to conclude from this that diabolical witchcraft was, always and everywhere, experienced artificially like a myth imposed from outside, without ties to the desires, fears and aspirations of its adherents.[55] For example, in 1532, a young Modenese witch, after telling the inquisitors that she had participated in the sabbat, proceeded to urinate on the saints' relics given to her by the monks of San Domenico after her abjuration. Pointing to a crucifix she declared: 'I do not choose to believe in him . . . and I want to believe in my own [lord], who dresses in gold and has a golden staff' – 'her lord', to whom 'she prayed.' All of this testifies to a rudimentary but none the less vital sort of religiosity.[56] It matters little that the image of a richly attired devil may have had erudite rather than popular origins. The opulence and pleasures of the sabbat were too great a lure for miserable peasants. Orsolina la Rossa, another witch tried by the Modenese Inquisition in 1539, was well aware of this. To the judge who wished to know why so many men and women flocked to the diabolical gatherings and could not seem to overcome this vice, she replied: 'It is because of the carnal pleasure they take with the devil, both men and women, and for no other reason.'[57] A similar requital for the despair of a miserable existence was sought by Sestilia Torsi, a woman who belonged to one of Udine's first families. In 1639 she declared to the inquisitor, Fra Ludovico da Gualdo, that out of desperation 'because she had not married' she invoked the devil 'to sport dishonestly with him', and continued calling him thirty years in succession with such names as 'god and my love, powerful, great, happy, and even with amorous terms'; and she had been brought 'to the festivities outside in the country with the witches, dancing, feasting and dissipating with them.'[58] But sometimes the internal reasons for the espousal of witchcraft were more complex, as we find in a Friulian trial of this period.

On 30 January 1648, a poorly clad young woman, Menega,

daughter of Camillo of Minons, appeared before the inquisitor, Fra Giulio Missini. A monk who served as her confessor had previously described her to the inquisitor as a witch, manically obsessed from the age of seven. This was her story: 'My step-father does not want me in his house, although my mother does, so that I exist on alms and go about begging. It is true that once I found a master . . . , but because of the way the devil bothered me the master did not want to keep me, and so I still have to beg and I cannot work.' Menega had struck up a friendship with two women of Faedis, Giacoma and Sabbata – two witches, she said, who persuaded her to surrender herself to the devil:[59]

> 'Lady Giacoma and Lady Sabbata instructed me and raised me in witchcraft, told me not to obey my father and mother, that I should curse those who begot me and brought me up, and that if I should remain with them they would do all the good that was possible for me, as if I was their own daughter, and that I should abjure the faith of Jesus Christ. They threatened that if I did not do it they would kill me, and I would never know the majesty of God; also I was to curse the water created by God and God himself who created it, and I cursed the fire that it might never blaze again . . . what's more, Sabbata had me take one of my sisters, a child of my mother, not my real father, and this sister was so small she was still nursing, she had me take her, crush her underfoot and suffocate her. Lady Sabbata used to come to my house whenever my mother went into the woods, and she got me to pinch the creature hard, and then made me suck with my lips the lips of the little creature, and then she gave her something black to drink called the devil's urine, and also she had me stuff the little one's mouth with ashes because of the great hate I felt for her. . . . Finally, she had me kill her, but after the creature was dead and my mother returned home, I confessed the truth to her, and my mother, to cover up for me so that my step-father would not kill me, made an excuse that the other children had overturned the cradle and that little creature had died. And so my step-father chased me out of the house and I wander about lost, begging for charity.'

Clearly Menega found that maternal comfort and that protection in the two witches which she had not experienced in her own family, neither in her mother preoccupied with her new children, nor in her step-father who hated her or simply neglected her. The witches took the place of her family and legitimized her feelings of intolerance and revolt against her real family, sentiments she could not express, and which she ascribed to convenient inventions called Lady Sabbata and Lady Giacoma. Menega felt a blasphemous aversion towards a world in which she had been so unhappy, towards a God who had created a world that was beautiful and hospitable for others but not for her; and she transferred these sentiments to the two witches who exhorted her against her will to curse God, water and fire. Consequently, it was one of the two witches who urged her to vent her repressed hatred for the half-sister who had robbed her of her mother's undivided affection – a hatred which for an instant her own words ingenuously betrayed: 'She had me stuff the little one's mouth with ashes because of the great hate I felt for her.' This is an exceptionally clear case, but who knows how often belief in witchcraft may have helped to alleviate suffering and inner wounds such as Menega's.[60]

15

But let us return to the benandanti who, incidentally, made a fleeting and colourless appearance even in Menega's confessions (the girl related that she had gone to the witches' balls and there profaned the sacraments in the company of her two protectresses and of five benandanti). The assimilation of benandanti with witches creates a new problem, one which obviously had not existed in connection with the older benandanti: that of the sincerity of their disclosures. The earlier accounts differed substantially in concept from the notions of the inquisitors, and, in fact, preceded them. So the possibility that they had been elicited by fear of torture or of the stake, can be excluded. The weapon of suggestive questioning was employed by inquisitors not to draw forth these tales, but rather to turn them in a desired direction. Except for this last case, quite easy to recognize, the accounts of the benandanti could be accepted as direct expressions of their mentality and beliefs. But with the transformation of the benandanti into witches the elements of the case change. This transformation was indeed 'spontaneous' in the sense that it was determined by profound impulses (not even perceived by the individuals who were affected) and not by distinct and conscious calculation. Nevertheless, frequently this 'spontaneity' was channelled and diverted by the opportune intervention of the inquisitors. So for the first time, we are confronted with the problem of the benandanti's *sincerity*. Michele Soppe may have been sincere when, at the end of Fra Giulio Missini's deft interrogation, he confessed that he had abjured the faith in the presence of the devil. This does not alter the fact, however, that without the impetus of the inquisitor's questioning, that confession – which itself could be logically and theologically dependent on preceding confessions (themselves, for that matter, also partially influenced in the sense we have just mentioned) – probably would never have occurred. Thus the content of the benandanti's assertions came to depend more and more on the intervention of inquisitors: and the importance of this intervention is obvious in those instances where it is suddenly lacking. This is clearly demonstrated by the events in a trial which took place at Portogruaro in these very years.[61]

On 23 December 1644, Olivo Caldo, a peasant of Ligugnana, who made signs over the sick and was reputed to be a benandante, was arrested at the order of Archbishop Benedetto Cappello, bishop and lord of the city of Concordia. From Olivo's very first utterance what was by now the typical picture for this period began to emerge, a confused muddle where remnants of ancient myths were intertwined with elements drawn from diabolical witchcraft. He related: 'Fate decreed that I should be born a *biandante*[62] with a caul about me, that I wander about and that my spirit go forth while the body remains behind. . . . Benandanti are summoned when they are between thirty and forty years of age.' Witches called them out: every Thursday the latter journeyed 'to the valley of Josaphat in the centre of the world', where they encountered 'many men, women and people of authority, and it lasted an hour, a half-hour.' They went 'on a billy-goat which they led home, and the spirit mounted, but the body remained where it was.' In these gatherings they made 'all the noise that can be made of every possible kind.' At this point the archbishop interrupted Olivo to ask 'if orders were given that this person or that one be harmed.' This was the first of several solicitations made during the trial. Olivo readily adjusted himself to it: 'Yes, sir they do indeed command that as much harm as possible be done to everyone, and from one Thursday to the next they must give an account of the evil they have committed and what has been commanded of them.'

In the following interrogation (on 31 December) a lively exchange broke out between the judge and the defendant. Significantly enough, it concerned the soul's departure from the body. The archbishop asked Olivo 'how he imagined that the soul could go off and leave the body behind.' The benandante did not seem to perceive the difficulty: 'The soul which is in the body goes and the body remains, and then it returns to the body.' 'You must tell the truth,' retorted the judge, 'about this separation of soul and body which is not possible and therefore is a lie.' Olivo again deferred to his interlocutor's will, and limited himself to stating in a general sort of way, 'I was carried on a billy-goat.' But who led the animal? The desired answer came punctually: 'The devil.'

Olivo described the devil, who had appeared to him in the guise of 'a rich and handsome man', who displayed 'things of every kind, goods and real money'. Sticking to the path ordained for him by the judge, the benandante asserted that the devil had asked for the gift of his soul, but that he had refused it. The judge admonished him to reflect closely on what he was saying. Olivo corrected himself: 'I dreamt that I promised it to him.' What did he dream he had promised? 'My soul.'[63] Thus, piece by piece, the usual mosaic fell into place: Olivo Caldo had abjured God and the Christian faith, had gone out at night in the company of witches 'to do witchery and counter-witchery', had paid homage to the devil and caused the death of four children by his spells.[64] What stands out in this picture is the mention – obviously not the result of suggestion by the judge – of battles between witches armed with wooden staves and benandanti armed with stalks of fennel.[65]

Olivo Caldo's replies seemed dictated by terror. This became obvious when he tried to hang himself in his cell on 2 January 1645. Saved in the nick of time, he resumed the tales of his witchery, continually adding fuller and more elaborate details. But the falseness of these self-accusations became apparent after the questioning of the parents of the children whom Olivo claimed he had killed with his evil deeds. Finally, during the interrogation of 12 February, it dawned on the judges that when they suggested things to Olivo

> 'he alternately accepted and denied them all and they tested him to see if he maintained the same opinion about them; and now it could be seen clearly . . . that he admitted everything that was asked of him; and so it was determined that the defendant, as was obvious from the records of the trial, had been inconsistent and vacillating during all his interrogations, and had always agreed with whatever was being suggested to him. Therefore it was decided, in view of his weakness and foolishness, not to go on, but refer everything to the Congregation.'

Thus, the tribunal of the Holy Office assembled on the predetermined day, and in the presence of the bishop, the mayor of Portogruaro and other personages, the bishop's vicar described a private conversation he had had with Olivo Caldo. The latter

> 'had declared in a serious and reasonable tone that everything he said during the trial was false, and that he had lied out of fear and dread of the law, and that he really thought that in this way he might more easily and quickly free himself from the toils of justice. He claimed, moreover, that he was neither a benandante nor a witch, had never talked with the devil, nor even seen him; that he did not know what the valley of Josaphat was, nor what was done there, since he had not been to that place; that he had never made anyone die or suffer an injury; that everything he said he had heard others say, and did not know anything himself; that his real fault consisted of having once made a sign over some people who came to him, and that he was instantly sought out for this; and he used to perform this service because he was poor and unable to earn a living.'

The next day all this was confirmed by Olivo himself. His only offence was that of having made signs over the sick (even the ancient stipulation that only the victims of witchcraft should be cured was gone): 'And I used to make my signs,' he said, 'at random, and if they worked, good, and if they failed I did not give it any thought,' and he heard it said by many that people born like himself with the caul 'have this ability to make signs' and are called benandanti.

When the judges saw that he stuck firmly to his last confession, even after they had threatened him with torture, they pronounced Olivo Caldo 'to be "lightly" suspect of apostasy from the holy faith of Christ and true cult of God,' and they prescribed the usual penances and banished him for five years from the diocese of Concordia.[66]

It is impossible to ascertain whether Olivo Caldo did or did not believe that he went to the valley of Josaphat in a dream to fight witches and warlocks, as his distant predecessor Menichino of Latisana had done, and whether his last confession was sincere or once again dictated by fear. What stands out clearly, however, is the intrinsic weakness of the myth of the benandanti, at this point in the final throes of its distorted and spurious state, now identical with witchcraft. It was enough, in fact, for the judges to ease their grip, allowing certain elements which had emerged in the course of the trial to come up momentarily for discussion – elements that the benandante had laboriously put together step by step following the interrogator's leads – for the entire edifice of Olivo's confessions to crumble. The absolute lack of roots and autonomy of this complex of beliefs is apparent here, even if we take into account Olivo Caldo's justified fear, and the more so when we recall the earlier trials. The spread of a different, increasingly sceptical and at the same time more rationalistic attitude towards witchcraft and magical phenomena in general, necessarily brought with it also the break-up and passing of the myth of the benandanti. It was simply a result of that principle, becoming common among people of good sense, which Olivo Caldo himself expressed when he replied to a friend who claimed to never have been the victim of witches or warlocks, and to not believe in their existence: 'Do you know why you were not bewitched? Because you did not believe in it.'

With the trial of Olivo Caldo, the story of the benandanti, in theory, comes to an end. But only in theory: in reality, the denunciations and the trials were to persist, even if in a progressively more desultory way, while repeating, unchanged, the old familiar motifs.

In addition to the trials of the benandanti-witches examined above, denunciations continued to pour into the Holy Office of Aquileia against benandanti professing to be healers: one, for example, concerned a Giacomo *'marangone'*, or carpenter, from Gemona, accused in 1636 and 1642, who treated the sick with blessed bread, garlic, salt, fennel and 'a bit of viburnum, of the kind that is carried along with the crosses'.[67] Then too, along with this activity as healers, the hostility of the benandanti against witches persisted: in 1639 it was reported to the inquisitor of Aquileia that a benandante, Menigo, also a carpenter, meeting a certain Caterina on the road, threatened to accuse her as a witch and denounce her misdeeds and complain about the blows he had received from her in the nocturnal battles.[68] Accusations of this type continued to stir up unrest in the villages. On 27 July 1642, Ludovico Frattina, priest of Camino di Codroipo, in a letter to the inquisitor, reported the activities of a herder named Giacomo, a notorious benandante, charged with having incriminated as witches several women of Camino and neighbouring villages. Giacomo was intending to interrogate one of these women to ascertain her guilt: 'And since she claims to be innocent,' the letter ran, 'she would like to accuse him of impugning her honour, and she could have him punished for the sake of justice, and this would serve to silence the grumbling of the people about these matters.'[69]

But if the benandanti created problems and worry for the clergy, they often threw the witches themselves into a state of downright terror. Bartolomea Golizza, a poor peasant of Fara, appeared before the Holy Office on 16 April 1648 to admit that she had bewitched people, attended the sabbat during 'the Ember seasons of the year and at other times too', where she had seen 'the devil in the shape of a ram, who then transformed himself into a fine gentleman with a large plumed hat, wholly dressed in black velvet, with long sleeves also made of velvet. . . . Now, however, I want to stop being a witch, and I want to be converted and become a good Christian, so that they will not try to hurt me, or hand me over to the law, as they have threatened to do and as the children I meet on the street always remind me will happen.' These 'children' were benandanti: 'They know the four of us who are witches, because they have been with us at our gatherings.'

And since the benandanti had seen these witches in the shapes of cats, bewitching a cow, they had denounced them to a certain Father Basilio, and, the woman added, 'to that Father Basilio I confessed everything.'[70]

The accusations against the benandanti-healers, generally rather thread-bare and lacking in real interest, were not followed up by the Holy Office.[71] It is noteworthy, however, that they were still highlighted with a question – what did 'benandante' mean? – which reflected the perplexity of the judges about a term which to the very end they considered to be foreign, as well as changeable and variable in meaning: 'By benandante is meant one who does neither good nor evil, can detect witchery and dispel it, and knows who the witches are'; 'by benandante is meant a man who knows how to bring relief for the injuries caused by witchcraft and can recognize them; he himself must not commit them, but must know how to cure them'; 'by benandante I mean a person who goes along with the witches and by warlocks I mean the same thing.'[72] But the old beliefs were practically spent. We are tempted to give a symbolic meaning to the gesture of a young woman of Talmasone, arraigned by the Holy Office in May 1666 for having accused several women of being witches: she handed over to the inquisitor the caul in which she had been born and which she wore on her person. 'Whoever is born with this,' she said, 'can easily know who the benandanti are,' (benandanti and not witches!), 'and since I have it on I leave it to you, Reverend Father, so that you may see that I do not believe it to be true; and if I happen to know that the women mentioned above are suspected to be witches, it is because I heard it rumoured about, but not because of the caul, nor because I was born with it.'[73]

There is evidence that belief in the benandanti existed even in Dalmatia in this very period. As we have said, it is impossible to decide, on the basis of the fragmentary sources available, if the diffusion of these ideas had begun in an earlier period. Our references are fleeting indeed. A few women from the island of Arbe, tried as witches in 1661, after describing the devastation they had wrought on wheat fields and vineyards at the instigation of the devil, declared that a certain Bortolo Passavin 'is a good spirit and . . . chases away the bad weather.'[74] This bit of evidence takes on further meaning in light of beliefs preserved in the Balkan peninsula – belief in the *Kerstniki*, for example, individuals mysteriously associated with such arboreal and vegetal deities as the *Vile* (and thus also called *viljenaci*), who arm themselves with sticks and fight against witches on the eve of the feast of St John.[75] These are ancient beliefs: in a number of witchcraft trials held at Ragusa in the second half of the seventeenth century the defendants declared that they were *'villenize'* and that they had learned the remedies for curing the victims of spells from the 'Vile'.[76] This is undoubtedly a tradition parallel to the Friulian one of the benandanti.

17

The trials of the benandanti-witches had an equally long existence, continuing, now in a fixed pattern, for a few more decades. But it cannot be said that the old beliefs had become totally extinct. In 1640 a youth of Udine, Titone delle Tranquille, responded to the inquisitor's customary question, that he did not know for a fact what benandanti were, but 'from what people say, it would seem that if it were not for these benandanti the witches would gather up, or, to put it better, would destroy all the harvests.' It may well be that this allusion to older and less suspect traditions was simply a ruse, since Titone himself had been accused of being a benandante from several quarters and barely succeeded in fending off the allegations of the judge.[77] Eight years later, a peasant woman of Monfalcone, Giovanna Summagotta, considered 'weak-minded' and 'sort of crazy' by her fellow villagers, was accused because she had told her neighbours that she was a benandante and went 'to the ball of the witches', where she saw and promised to show 'so many beautiful things and so many people, tables spread for eating, feasts, balls, amusements'. She was placed on trial, partly at the urging of Alessandro Zorzi, the mayor of Monfalcone, who confided that 'through her other witches can be discovered.' But Summagotta denied everything and in turn accused a certain Pasqualina, who had spoken to her of her sufferings as a benandante: 'You were blessed to have been born at a fortunate moment without signs, for if you had been born as I was, you would be as troubled as I.' Then Pasqualina went on to describe the nocturnal gatherings in which she participated, where 'on one side are the benandanti, on another the goblins, and on still another the witches who also do battle.'[78] Traces of the old distinction between benandanti and witches can be detected even where the association between them was virtually complete. In 1648, a child of nine called Mattia, a benandante, managed to throw the village of Fanna into turmoil with his boasts. 'Wrestling in the pasture with other children of his age, he was bested by them; and so he said to them: "You may be stronger than I,

but I know more than you'' ':[79] and he had asserted, later confirming everything before the Holy Office, that one Thursday night he had been awakened by his grand-mother who slept by him and had been taken to the sabbat, his grand-mother mounted on 'a big red-hued billy-goat with horns as long as this' and he on 'a shoot of rye' – obviously a relic from the original characterization of the benandanti as protectors of the harvests. At the sabbat he had seen the devil, and many people adoring him, dancing obscenely and stamping on the cross: 'But I,' Mattia had exclaimed to the inquisitor questioning him, 'never ate with the others, didn't adore the devil or trample on the cross; in fact I paid homage to the cross and it grieved me that others trampled on it.'[80] A similar maze of old and new motifs reappeared in a deposition of 1661 against Bastian Magnossi of Grizzano: he treated victims of spells, but he wanted to be paid well because 'at night he had to go and fight witches and benandanti, more than four-hundred miles away at Benevento,' adding that 'if it were not for the benandanti . . . we would not have any crops to live on, because they protect us from the witches.'[81] For a few benandanti the inevitable decline into witchcraft manifested itself as a dramatic inner temptation: a young peasant, Andrea Cattaro, from a hamlet near Concordia, born with a caul and a benandante from the age of twelve, was called by the witches and transported to the sabbat, where he had seen the devil and 'many other smaller devils'. But on the journey he had also spotted an angel, his guardian angel, in fact: 'He called to me and begged me not to go, and that I should accompany him instead; the witches chimed in that I should not follow him, because they said that angel was a rogue, a ruffian, a wretch.' Andrea had hesitated, but at the prospect of surrendering his soul to the devil, 'after a long struggle', he declared that he wanted his soul to be with God and the Madonna: 'and when that was said everything vanished.'[82]

The proceedings against Andrea Cattaro, begun in 1676, were not concluded. Even this series of trials broke down through incredulity and lack of interest. A few years before, on 6 July 1668, Fra Raimondo Galatini, vicar of Rosazzo, had written to the inquisitor of Aquileia to inform him that various peasants of the area (as well as a priest, it seems) had confessed to being *'bellandanti'* and 'of having attended the gathering of the witches, making a compact with the devil and abjuring the faith, abusing the sacraments by falsifying confessions and receiving communion, and the other things that witches ordinarily do at their conventicles in Modoleto.' Fra Raimondo went on to say that judicial action had been initiated against them: but now 'this trial will not be pursued, for reasons I do not know, to the great detriment of the

Christian religion and injury to the poor creatures who suffer from these accursed people.'[83] But, obviously, his complaints no longer interested anyone. 

APPENDIX

To illustrate the kind of source material on which the present research is based, the records of the trial against Paolo Gasparutto and Battista Moduco are included here. In a few cases, as already noted in the course of the book, obvious errors have been corrected.

(ACAU, *S. Uffizio*, 'Ab anno 1574 usque ad annum 1578 incl. a n. 57 usque ad 76 incl.' proc. n. 64.)

In the city of Cividale, on 21 March 1575. Trial for heresy against certain witches, completed on 26 November 1581.

Monday 21 November 1575

Before the most reverend lord Iacobo Maracco, etc., vicar general of Aquileia and apostolic commissioner, and the reverend father, master Giulio d'Assisi, inquisitor against heretical pravity in the diocese of Aquileia, in Cividale, in the convent of San Francesco, there appeared the venerable priest Bartolomeo Sgabarizza, rector of the parish church of Brazzano, who was received as a witness. After he took an oath from the hands of the aforementioned reverend vicar, having been cautioned, examined and interrogated, he stated:

I heard that in Brazzano a child, the son of M. Piero Rotaro, was sick from an unknown ailment, and that to learn about this ailment a certain *madonna* Aquilina had been consulted who was reputed to know if a person was bewitched. And the answer came in letters from the noble M. Raimondo Raimondi, M. Piero's father-in-law, that the child was under a spell cast by a woman who supposedly ate meat on Fridays, as I read in M. Raimondo's letter. I was astonished to learn this and in the course of discussing all the possibilities in the case with M. Piero, he told me that it was said that in Iassico there lived a certain Paolo de Gasparutto who claimed that he roamed about at night with witches and goblins, and that it was possible to bewitch children. I begged M. Piero to summon the aforesaid Paolo, and to inquire diligently of him what might serve in the present case. And he promptly had Paolo come and when he was there he questioned him on the doorstep of his shop. Since I was passing by I went up to them and asked: 'What are you two discussing here?' And M. Piero replied that they were talking about his little boy, and was asking Paolo if there was any way to heal him. And I turned to Paolo and inquired, well, what was his opinion about these spells; and he replied that this little boy had been possessed by witches, but at the time of the witchery the vagabonds were about and they snatched him from the witches' hands, and if they had not done so he would have died. At this point I interrupted, saying, 'Do you by any chance have some way to cure this child?' And he said that he did not have anything else besides what he had already taught M. Piero, namely to weigh him for three Thursdays, and that if the child gained in weight the second Thursday he would be cured, but if he decreased, he would die. Since I wanted to learn more I asked him how and when they did such things. He told me that on Thursdays during the Ember Days of the year they were forced to go with these witches to many places, such as Cormons, in front of the church at Iassico, and even into the countryside about Verona. When I asked him what they did in these places, he said that they fought, played, leaped about and rode various animals, and did different things among themselves; and the women beat the men who were with them with sorghum stalks, while the men only had bunches of fennel, and for this reason he begged me not to sow sorghum in my field and whenever he finds any growing he pulls it up, and he curses whoever plants it. And when I said that I wanted to sow it, he began to swear. Because this all seemed very strange to me I came to Cividale to talk with you sir, or with the father inquisitor. And since I chanced upon this Paolo here in Cividale I brought him to the father inquisitor in San Francesco, to whom he admitted all these things, and also, as he had told me before, that when the witches, warlocks and vagabonds return from these games all hot and tired, and pass in front of houses, where they find clear, clean water in pails they drink it, if not they also go into the cellars and overturn all the wine, and he urged me always to keep clean water in the house. When I said that I did not believe these stories, he invited me to accompany him and he would show them to me. And he told me all the above things in the presence of M. Piero [Rotaro] and repeated them before the father inquisitor.

Questioned, he said:

He told me that there were some of these people in Brazzano, Iassico, Cormons, Gorizia and Cividale, but he did not want to say who they were.

Questioned again, he said:

After the father inquisitor and I had promised to go with him so that we might get him to talk, he said that he would go twice before Easter, and even if the father inquisitor was in Cividale and I in Brazzano, he would arrange it for us to be together, and having promised, one was then obliged to go. Once we were there we were to say nothing, even if we were to see certain wild dancing, otherwise we would be compelled to remain there, and he also told me that he had been badly beaten by the witches for having spoken about these things; and some of these who are good, called vagabonds, and in their own words benandanti[1] prevent evil, and some of them commit it.

Questioned as to the time, he said:

It was last week.

And about the place and the witnesses, as above.

Questioned, he said:

Today I left the above mentioned child who was dying.

Thursday 7 April 1575

Before the most reverend lord, Iacobo Maracco, etc., vicar general of Aquileia and commissioner, etc., and the above named reverend father, master Giulio, in the presence and with the participation of the most illustrious lord, Giovanni Baduario, *provveditore* of the city of Cividale, on the lower level of the palace of the most reverend *provveditore* of Udine, there again appeared the priest Bartolomeo Sgabarizza as a witness. After taking an oath at the hands of the most reverend vicar, cautioned, examined and interrogated anew about the aforementioned matters, and after his earlier testimony was read back to him as a reminder, he declared:

What I stated in that deposition of mine before your lordship and the reverend father inquisitor is true and I hereby ratify and confirm it anew.

And he also added:

On the second day of the celebration of Easter I went to say Mass at Iassico, a village attached and subject to my church of Brazzano, to which Paolo Gasparutto belongs. It is customary on the day that one goes to celebrate Mass to prepare a meal for the priest, and since Paolo is one of the commissioners, he too came to eat with me in the home of his colleague, the chief administrator in the parish, whose name is Simon di Natale. During the meal I spoke about matters appropriate to the season, that is, guarding against sin and pursuing good and holy works. But Paolo interrupted this discussion to say: 'My father, this would have been the night to conduct the father inquisitor to that place you know about,' and so he went on to tell me that the night before he had been to the customary games with his companions. They crossed several great bodies of water in a boat and at the river Iudri one of his companions became afraid because a fierce wind had come up, and the waters were rough, and he remained behind the others, and he [Paolo] had stopped to give him courage. The boat reached shore and he had crossed safely, and then they were in the countryside not far away, and they jousted and busied themselves with their usual pastimes. And so I brought him home with me, and treated him kindly so as to draw other details out of him, if I could. He confirmed everything contained in my first deposition, adding that he had discussed with his companion that I might promise to accompany him to see those jousts and pleasures, and that his companion had replied that this would please him very much. And I, to get him to talk, dealt gently with him and asked him: 'Dear friend, tell me who this companion of yours is and where he is.' He replied that he lived ten miles from Brazzano, but he would not tell me his name.

He said:

I also asked him what games took place in these fields, and he told me what I stated in my first deposition.

Questioned again, he said:

The child about whom I spoke in my first deposition who was the cause of this discussion died a few days ago from this malady.

Questioned, he said:

I asked Paolo Gasparutto if he had been one of those who had snatched that child out of the witches' hands, and he replied: 'It suffices that he was taken away by the witches called vagabonds,' and he would not say more, neither about himself nor about the others.

Questioned, he said:

It is openly rumoured about Brazzano and other neighbouring places that this Paolo is one of the benandanti witches, as they say, and this reputation is based on his own words, because he freely admits to anyone with whom he has occasion to speak, even taking an oath on it, that he goes to those entertainments.

Interrogated about who could be questioned for the truth, he replied that Pietro Rotaro, the aforementioned Simone the administrator, and others in the village of Iassico could be questioned. Gasparutto has confessed these things in the presence of M. Pietro and Simone the administrator.

Questioned again, he said:

I could not get any other details out of him, but even without talking he did say that if I wanted to go with him I would see them, but I never promised him I would go; I exhorted him to seek out the father inquisitor and he promised to come Saturday next to lead him to these games.

Master Pietro Rotaro of Brazzano, witness received as above, sworn, cautioned and interrogated under the oath previously taken, stated:

A few weeks ago, a child of mine, a little boy of four months fell sick, and suspecting that he had been bewitched, as it was rumoured about by certain women, I went looking for Paolo of Iassico, called Gasparutto, who is known to go about with these witches and to be one of the benandanti. I asked him to provide me with some remedy for the little child if he had been bewitched. And he came to see him and no sooner had he seen him but he said that a spell had been cast on him by the witches and that he had been rescued from their hands by the benandanti. And when I asked him for a remedy he told me that if we weighed him in the morning and he had gained in weight he would be cured, and he made me weigh him then, saying that the illness would not proceed further; but my little boy died three days later, without our learning the reason.

Questioned again, he said:

The aforementioned Paolo has admitted many times, even just yesterday to me, and to Father Bartolomeo, that he goes about with these witches, but he belongs to those who oppose the evil, called benandanti. They go out to one country region or another, perhaps to Gradisca or even as far away as Verona, and they appear together jousting and playing games; and the men and women who are the evil-doers carry and use sorghum stalks which grow in the fields, and the men and women who are benandanti use fennel stalks; and they go now one day and now another, but always on Thursdays, and when they make their great displays they go to the biggest farms, and they have days fixed for this; and when the warlocks and witches set out it is to do evil, and they must be pursued by the benandanti to thwart them, and also to stop them from entering the houses, because if they do not find clear water in the pails they go into the cellars and spoil the wine with certain things, throwing filth in the bungholes.

He stated, questioned again:

The above named Paolo said that when they go to these games some may travel on horseback, others on a hare or a cat, on one animal or another, but he would not name the men and women who attended.

He stated, questioned again:

He [Paolo] told me that when he goes to these games his body stayed in bed and the spirit went forth, and that while he was out if someone approached the bed where the body lay and called to it, it would not answer, nor could he get it to move even if he should try for a hundred years, but if he did not look at it and called it, it would respond at once; and when they err, or speak with someone, their bodies are beaten, and they are found all black and blue, and he has been beaten and mistreated because he spoke with others. He told me that he would be mistreated for fifteen days for having told me these things, and if I did not believe him, that I should promise to go with him, and I would see them for myself.

He also stated:

He said that for any who wait twenty-four hours before returning, and who might say or do something, the spirit would remain separated from the body, and after it was buried the spirit would wander forever and be called *malandante*.

Questioned again, he said:

In Udine in the quarter of Grazzano there is a woman called Aquilina who is reputed to know when a person has been bewitched if she is brought something that had been worn by the stricken person. M. Raimondo de Raimondi, my father-in-law, went to this woman a few days ago, and brought her a quilt which had been over my child; and she told him that he had come to her too late, and therefore she could not help him and the boy would die. My father-in-law told me this after the child's death, excusing himself that he had not wanted to tell me so as not to worry me, although he had written to me that he had been to visit that woman and she had given him good hope. I believe I have that letter at home and if I find it I will send it.

Questioned, he said:

Signor Belforte Mintino of Cividale told me a short while ago that Battista Moduco, an official of the magnificent commune, confessed here in the square to him, and to signor Troiano d'Attimis and other gentlemen that he is one of the benandanti, and that he goes about in their company.

Adding also:

This Paolo told me that these *malandanti* eat children.

Interrogated about witnesses, he mentioned himself and the aforementioned priest Bartolomeo; concerning the place and time, he stated in Brazzano in the shop of the above named Pietro. And so forth, etc.

In general, he stated that it was public knowledge in Iassico and other neighbouring places.

The noble Belforte Mintino called as witness, sworn, cautioned, examined and interrogated as above, stated:

I do not know anything for a fact of the things about which your lordships are questioning me, except that signor Troiano d'Attimis, my brother-in-law, told me that the official Battista Moduco said to him a short while ago in the square that he too belonged to those benandanti and went out at night, and especially Thursdays.

And the rest, etc. About generalities, etc.

The nobleman, Troiano de Attimis, citizen of Cividale, called as a witness, sworn, cautioned, examined and interrogated as above, said:

Finding myself a short while ago in the square with signor Belforte, my brother-in-law, and the gentlemen Cornelio Gallo and Ettore Lavarello, signor Belforte stated that he had heard that some of these witches were in Brazzano, and that there was one even in Cividale, not far from us, and we left at once. When I saw the official Battista Moduco, I called him and asked him: 'And you, are you one of those witches?' He told me that he is a benandante, and that at night, especially on Thursdays, he goes with the others, and they congregate in certain places to perform marriages, to dance and eat and drink; and on their way home the evil-doers go into the cellars to drink, and then urinate in the casks. If the benandanti did not go along the wine would be spilt. And he told other tall tales like these which I did not believe, and so I did not question him further.

About generalities, etc. Magnassuto of the magnificent commune reported that the aforesaid witnesses were sworn and ready to testify.

27 June 1580

Done in Cividale in the palace of the illustrious *provveditore* in the customary hall of audiences before the above mentioned illustrious assistant, and before the reverend father inquisitor, master Felice Montefalco, inquisitor general for the entire patriarchate of Aquileia and Concordia, as well as his reverend commissioner, master Bonaventura Vivaruccio.[2] There appeared Paolo who, as above, sworn, cautioned, examined, and interrogated, replied:

I do not know the reason why I have been summoned and commanded by the officer of your illustrious signory.

Questioned about the place, he replied:

I am a native of the village of Iassico.

Questioned about his father, he replied:

I do not have a father, he is dead.

Questioned about his father's name, he replied:

Hieronimo Gasparutto, and my mother Maddalena of Gradisca, and she too is dead.

Questioned, he replied:

I have gone to confession and received communion every year from my priest.

Questioned, he replied:

I do not know if there is anyone in our village who is a Lutheran and leads an evil life.

Interrogated if he had heard about or knew personally anyone who was a witch or a benandante, he replied:

Of witches I do not know any, nor even of benandanti.

And when he had said this, laughingly he added:
Father, no. I really do not know.
Questioned, he replied:
I am not a benandante, that is not my calling.
Questioned, he replied:
I do not know whether any child in our village has been bewitched.
Questioned, he replied:
M. Pietro Ruota called for me, saying: 'Come a moment to see what my little boy has.'
Questioned, he replied:
And I went to see the child and told him I did not know anything about it.
Questioned, he replied:
I have never spoken with our priest about being a witch or a benandante.
Questioned, he replied:
I spoke with the previous inquisitor and with our priest about benandanti.
Questioned, he replied laughingly:
I talked with the last father inquisitor and told him that I dreamt I fought with the witches.
Questioned, he replied:
I have not invited anyone to the games to which the benandanti go.
Interrogated whether when he was called by M. Piero he went to eat or drink in the shop of the aforesaid M. Pietro Ruota and when the priest arrived they spoke about matters concerning the benandanti, he replied:
No, sir.
Questioned: have you ever spoken with that M. Piero about benandanti in his shop in the presence of the priest? he replied:
No, sir.
Questioned: did you ever promise the priest or the father inquisitor to take them to the games of the benandanti? Laughingly, he replied:
No, sir.
Questioned: why did you laugh? he replied:
Because these are not things to inquire about, because they are against the will of God.
Questioned: why is it against God's will to ask about these things? he replied:
Because you are asking about things that I know nothing about.
Questioned: have you ever told the priest Bartolomeo that at night you go into the countryside around Verona and Vicenza and that you fight, going with the benandanti? he replied:
No, father.
Questioned: did you say to the father inquisitor and to the priest Bartolomeo 'promise me that, whether you like it or not, you will come with me at night?' he replied:
No, father, not that I can remember (and while saying this he closed his eyes).
Questioned: how can it be that you assert you do not perform this art when, at the time that monsignor Maracco was here, you said to the last father inquisitor, 'tonight is the time to go to these games?' he replied:
I do not know that I said these things and I do not remember.
Questioned: did you ever yell at the priest Bartolomeo not to plant canes in his field? he replied:
No, sir.
Questioned: have you ever told the last father inquisitor and the priest Bartolomeo that when the witches and benandanti return from their games slack and weary, if they do not find clear water in the houses, they go into the cellars, and they urinate and spoil the wine? he replied:
No, father. And then he added, laughing: 'Oh, what a world.'

Questioned: did you ever promise the priest Bartolomeo to take him to these games? he replied:

No, father.

Questioned: have you ever told anyone you were of the benandanti? he replied:

No father.

Questioned: have you ever been beaten by the devils for having said and revealed the things the benandanti do? he replied:

No, father.

Questioned: do you have any enemies? he replied:

No, father.

Then, cautioned to tell the truth, and exhorted by the reverend father inquisitor to be truthful, because if he did so, he would be received and treated with mercy, interrogated, he responded:

Father, I cannot say anything else, because this is all I know.

Having heard this the reverend father inquisitor decreed that he be placed in custody so that he might be led to find humility, and reconsider better, etc.

The same day as above

Held in the same place, in the presence and with the participation of those above. There appeared the official Battista Moduco, nicknamed *Gamba Secura*, cited, cautioned, sworn, examined and interrogated, he testified as follows. Interrogated, he replied:

Father, no I do not know why I was summoned here.

Questioned, he replied:

I came because I was called by the official.

Questioned, he replied:

I have confessed myself and taken communion every year, confession from priest Martino and communion from priest Iacomo, who resides here in Cividale.

Questioned, he replied:

I was born in Trevignano, but I have lived thirty years continuously in Cividale.

Questioned, he replied:

My father was from Trevignano and was called Iacomo Moduco, and my mother was called Maria of Gonars.

Questioned, he replied:

Father, I have not heard about nor know anyone who is a heretic.

Questioned, he replied:

I have not known anyone who is a heretic, nor had any dealings with them.

Questioned, he replied:

Of witches I do not know if there are any; and of benandanti I do not know of any others besides myself.

Questioned: what does this word 'benandante' mean? he replied:

Benandanti I call those who pay me well, I go willingly.

Questioned, he replied:

I have spoken with the illustrious one (*clarissimo*) and with others about being a benandante.

Questioned, he replied:

I cannot speak about the others because I do not want to go against divine will.

Questioned, he replied:

I am a benandante because I go with the others to fight four times a year, that is during the Ember Days, at night; I go invisibly in spirit and the body remains behind; we go forth in the service of Christ, and the witches of the devil; we fight each other, we with bundles of fennel and they with sorghum stalks. And if we are the victors, that year there is abundance, but if we lose there is famine.

Questioned: how long have you been involved in this, and are you now? he replied:

It is eight years and more that I have not participated. One enters at the age of twenty, and is freed at forty, if he so wishes.

Questioned: how does one enter this company of the benandanti? he replied:

All those who have been born with the caul belong to it, and when they reach the age of twenty they are summoned by means of a drum the same as soldiers, and they are obliged to respond.

Questioned: how can it be that we know so many gentlemen who are born with the caul, and nevertheless are not vagabonds? he replied:

I am saying everybody born with the caul must go.

Cautioned to tell the truth about the way one entered in this profession, he replied:

Nothing else happens, except that the spirit leaves the body and goes wandering.

Questioned: who is it that comes to summon you, God, or an angel, a man, or a devil? he replied:

He is a man just like us, who is placed above us all and beats a drum, and calls us.

Questioned: are there many of you who go? he replied:

We are a great multitude, and at times we are five-thousand and more.

Questioned: do you know one another? he replied:

Some who belong to the village know one another, and others do not.

Questioned: who placed that being above you? he replied:

I do not know, but we believe he is sent by God, because we fight for the faith of Christ.

Questioned about the name of that captain, he replied:

I cannot say.

Questioned, he replied:

He is head of the company until he reaches the age of forty, or until he renounces it.

Questioned, he replied:

This man who is captain is from Cologne.

Questioned about his stature and his age, he replied:

He is a man of twenty-eight, very tall, red-bearded, pale complexioned, of noble birth, and he has a wife.

Questioned about the captain's insignia, he replied:

It is white, and the flag, that is the cross-bar that he carries above him, is black.

Questioned, he replied:

Our standard bearer carries a banner of white silk stuff, gilded, with a lion.

Questioned, he replied:

The banner of the witches is of red silk with four black devils, gilded.

Questioned, he replied:

The captain of the witches had a black beard, he is big and tall, of the German nation.

Questioned about the places, he replied:

Sometimes we go to fight in a large field in the territory of Azzano, other times in a field near Cuniano, and other times still on German soil, in certain meadows near Cirghinis.

Questioned, he replied:

We all go on foot, and we benandanti fight with bundles of fennel, and the witches with stalks of sorghum.

Questioned: do you eat fennel and garlic? he replied:

Yes, father we do, because they serve against the witches.

Questioned, he replied:

There are no women among us, but it is true that there are women benandanti, and women go against women.

Questioned, he replied:

In the fighting that we do, one time we fight over the wheat and all the other grains, another time over the livestock, and at other times over the vineyards. And so, on four occasions we fight over all the fruits of the earth and for those things won by the benandanti that year there is abundance.

Questioned, he replied:

I cannot say the names of my companions because I would be beaten by the entire company.

Questioned: tell me the names of your enemies, of the witches, that is, he replied:

Sir, I cannot do it.

Questioned: if you say that you fight for God, I want you to tell me the names of these witches, he replied:

I cannot name nor accuse anyone, whether he be friend or foe.

Repeatedly admonished and asked to give the names of the witches, he replied:

I cannot say them.

Questioned: for what reason can't you tell me this?' he replied:

Because we have a life-long edict not to reveal secrets about one side or the other.

Questioned, he replied:

This commandment was made by the captains of each side, whom we are obliged to obey.

Questioned: this is just a dodge; since you assert that you are no longer one of them, you cannot be obliged to obey them. So, tell me who these witches are, he replied:

The woman who used to be the wife of Paulo Tirlicher of Mersio in Slavonia near Santo Leonardo, and another named Piero di Cecho of Zuz from Prestento, thirty-six years of age.

Questioned, he replied:

This woman has dried up the milk of animals, putting some things over the covers and roofs of houses, such as certain pieces of wood tied with ropes, and I think that if she isn't dead she could still be found today.

Having heard these things the reverend father inquisitor dismissed him, so that he might reconsider, etc.

Tuesday 28 June 1580, in the morning, held in the same place, in the presence and with the participation of the above

After the aforementioned Paolo was led from prison, sworn, admonished, examined and interrogated under oath, he testified as follows.

Questioned: have you thought better about speaking the truth than before, he replied:

Yes, father, and I will tell it rightly.

Questioned: are you of the benandanti? he replied:

Yes, father.

Questioned: how long have you been in this company? he replied:

Ten years.

Questioned: are you still in this company? he replied:

For four years I have not been in it.

Questioned: what did you have to do to enter this company, and what age were you? he replied:

I was twenty-eight and when I entered it was because I was summoned by the captain of the benandanti of Verona.

Questioned: what time of the year were you called? he replied:

During the Ember Days of Saint Matthias.

Questioned: why didn't you tell me this yesterday? he replied:

Because I was afraid of the witches, who would have attacked me in bed and killed me.

Questioned: the first time that you went did you know that you were going with benandanti, he replied:

Yes, father, because I had been warned first by a benandante of Vicenza, Battista Vicentino by name.

Questioned about his family name, he replied:

I don't know it.

Questioned whether that man had a father, he replied:

No, sir.

Questioned about his age, he replied:

At that time Battista was thirty-five years of age, tall in stature, with a round black beard, well-built, a peasant, but I do not know what village he was from.

Questioned: when that man came to warn you, what time of the year was it? he replied:

It was the month of December, during the Ember season of Christmas, on Thursday about the fourth hour of the night, at first sleep.

Questioned: what did he say when he came to warn you? he replied:

He told me that the captain of the benandanti was summoning me to come out and fight for the crops. And I answered him, 'I do want to come, for the sake of the crops.'

Questioned: when he spoke to you were you awake or asleep? he replied:

When Battista appeared before me I was sleeping.

Questioned: if you were asleep, how did you answer him and how did you hear his voice? he replied:

My spirit replied to him.

Questioned: when you went forth, did you go with your body? he replied:

No, father, but with the spirit, and if by chance while we are out someone should come with a light, and look for a long time at the body, the spirit would never re-enter it until there was no one left around to see it that night; and if the body, seeming to be dead, should be buried, the spirit would have to wander around the world until the hour fixed for that body to die; and if the body wasn't buried, the spirit would not re-enter that body that day until the following night, provided no one had looked at it.

Questioned: before you were called, that is the day before by this Battista, had you known this Battista? he replied:

No, father, but they know who is a benandante.

Questioned: how do they know who is a benandante? he replied:

The captain of the benandanti knows it.

Questioned: how many are you in your company? he replied:

We are only six.

Questioned: what weapons do you use to fight? he replied:

We fight with viburnum branches, that is, with the staff which we carry behind the crosses in the processions of the Rogation Days; and we have a banner of white silk, all gilded, and the witches have one that is yellow, with four devils on it.

Questioned: where did you go to fight? he replied:

In the countryside around Verona and Gradisca.

Questioned: how do you know where you are supposed to go? he replied:

During the Ember Days preceding, the benandanti and the witches challenge each other, and they name the place.

Questioned: have you ever promised to take anyone to these games? he replied:

Yes, the last father inquisitor; and if he had come along, you would not be questioning me now.

Questioned: do you go other times than these four? he replied:

No, father.

Questioned: how can this be if you told father Bartolomeo the second day of Easter in the month of April, 1575, when he was eating with you in your village, that you had been out the night before? he replied:

Tell father Bartolomeo that it isn't true.
Questioned: who is your captain? he replied:
He is a person from Verona, I do not know his name, and I believe he is a peasant, of average height, a plump man with a red beard, about thirty years old.
Questioned: how did he become captain? he replied:
I don't know.
Questioned: who are your companions here? he replied:
They are from beyond Vicenza and Verona and I do not know their names.
Questioned: fighting with those witches, didn't you get to know any? he replied:
One is called Stefano of Gorizia, a peasant, short in stature, about forty years of age, with a thick black beard; the other is called Martino Spizzica from the village of Chians in the territory of Capo d'Istria, about three miles from the village of Risan, a man with a gray beard, big chested, he could have been about thirty-nine years of age at the time.
After hearing these words, the reverend father inquisitor dismissed him, ordering him to reappear in twenty days in the monastery of our order, San Francesco, in Udine, in the chamber which served as the customary residence of the aforementioned father inquisitor.

24 September 1580

Held in the convent of San Francesco in the chamber of the reverend father inquisitor.
Papinus, an officer of the illustrious *provveditore* of the city of Cividale, reported that he had personally cited Paolo, son of the deceased Gasparutto of the village of Iassico and the aforementioned Paolo appeared, together with the above named Papino in the monastery of San Francesco, as above, before the reverend father inquisitor, etc. Then the reverend father inquisitor ordered that he be imprisoned and it was so done.

Monday 26 September 1580

Held in the palace of the illustrious *provveditore* of the city of Cividale, Giovanni Baduario, in the customary audience chamber, before the reverend father inquisitor, master Felice da Montefalco apostolic general for the entire patriarchate of Aquileia and the city of Concordia and of its dioceses, in the presence of the aforementioned illustrious *provveditore* and of his most excellent vicar, Paolo Patavino.
Led from his cell was Paolo, son of the deceased Gasparutto, of the village of Iassico and arraigned, sworn, examined, interrogated under oath, he testified as follows. Questioned, he replied:
I did not come to Udine as I had promised because I was sick the whole month of July.
Questioned, he replied:
I have come to think that I should tell the truth.
Questioned: who led you to enter the company of these benandanti? he replied:
The angel of God.
Questioned: when did this angel appear before you? he replied:
At night, in my house, perhaps during the fourth hour of the night, at first sleep.
Questioned: how did it appear? he replied:
An angel appeared before me, all made of gold, like those on altars, and he called me, and my spirit went out.
Questioned, he said:
He called me by name, saying: 'Paolo, I will send you forth as a benandante, and you will have to fight for the crops.'

Questioned, he said:

I answered him: 'I will go, I am obedient.'

Questioned: what did he promise you, women, food, dancing, and what else? he said:

He did not promise me anything, but those others do dance and leap about, and I saw them because we fought them.

Questioned: where did your spirit go when the angel summoned you? he replied:

It came out because in the body it cannot speak.

Questioned: who told you that your spirit had to come out if it was to speak to the angel? he replied:

The angel himself told me.

Questioned: how many times have you seen this angel? he replied:

Every time that I went out, because he always came with me.

Questioned: when he appears before you or takes his leave, does this angel frighten you? he replied:

He never frightens us, but when the company breaks up, he gives a benediction.

Questioned: doesn't this angel ask to be adored? he replied:

Yes, we adore him just as we adore our Lord Jesus Christ in church, and it isn't many angels but one only who leads the company.

Questioned: when he appears before you, does he show himself seated? he replied:

We all appear at once and he stays in person by our flag.

It was asked of him: does this angel conduct you where that other one is seated on that beautiful throne? he replied:

But he is not of our company, God forbid that we should get involved with that false enemy!

Then he added: it is the witches that have the beautiful thrones.

It was asked of him: did you ever see witches by that beautiful throne? he replied, gesturing with his arms:

No, sir, we did nothing but fight!

Questioned: which is the more beautiful angel, yours or the one on the beautiful throne? he replied:

Didn't I tell you that I have not seen those thrones?

Adding: our angel is beautiful and white; theirs is black and is the devil.

Questioned: who was the first benandante sent by the angel to call you? he replied:

It was Battista of Vicenza, as I stated on another occasion.

Questioned: when that angel appeared before you, were you married, and was your wife in bed? he replied:

I was not married then, and this happened more than four years before I married.

Questioned: how old were you at that time? he replied:

Twenty-four or maybe twenty.

Questioned: have you ever told your wife that you went out? he replied:

No, father. (And with an immediate change of expression): so that she would not be afraid.

It was asked of him: if this is a good thing and the will of God, why did you think she might be afraid? he replied:

I did not want to reveal all my secrets to my wife.

It was asked of him: you have told me that women go to fight women; why didn't you tell it or reveal it to her, and get her to do it herself since you say it is a good thing? he replied:

I cannot teach this art to anyone when our Lord God has chosen not to teach it himself.

Questioned: have you ever been beaten? he replied:

Yes, father, when I told these things to our priest, the aforesaid father Bartolomeo, and got two whacks across the shoulders.

Questioned whether the marks could be seen on the body? he replied:

My whole body ached, but I could not see if there were marks.

Questioned: how long were you ill? he replied:

Six or eight days.

Questioned: who was it who gave them to you? he replied:

A witch, whom I only know by sight.

Questioned: how did you decide that he was a witch? he replied:

Because we fought with him.

Questioned: who are the people in your company? he replied:

One is Battista of Vicenza, as I said before; I do not know the others.

After hearing the above, the reverend father inquisitor ordered that the aforesaid Paolo be returned to his cell.

1 October 1580

Held in the palace of the illustrious *provveditore* in the chamber of audiences before the reverend father inquisitor of Aquileia, in the presence of the illustrious *provveditore* Giovanni Baduaro, his most excellent vicar, etc.

There appeared the woman Maria, wife of Paolo of Iassico, sworn, admonished, examined and interrogated under oath, she testified as follows:

Questioned, she replied:

No, sir, I do not know why I have been called here.

Questioned, she replied:

Yes, sir, I have gone to confession and received communion from father Gasparo.

Questioned again, she replied:

I have been married to Paolo de Gasparutto of the village of Iassico for eight years.

Questioned, she replied:

In the time that I have been married I never noticed any of the things that you ask about my husband, whether he went out in spirit and was a benandante. However, one night, about the fourth hour before daylight, I had to get up, and because I was afraid I called to my husband Paolo so that he would get up too, and even though I called him perhaps ten times and shook him, I could not manage to wake him, and he lay face up. So I went off without having him rise from bed, and when I returned I saw that he was awake, saying: 'These benandanti assert that when their spirit leaves the body it has the appearance of a mouse, and also when it returns, and that if the body should be rolled over while it is without its spirit, it would remain dead, and its spirit could never return to it.'

Questioned, she replied:

It could have been about four years ago that what I mentioned above happened, and it was winter but I do not remember what day, but it wasn't during the Ember Days.

Questioned, she replied:

I heard from Pietro Rotaro who used to be a miller, that one day in his mill he saw a person who might have been Paolo my husband. He was like a dead man, and he did not wake even when he was turned over and over, and a little later he saw a mouse circling his body, and I do not know if it entered his mouth.

Questioned about different things, she said she did not know anything else, and so was dismissed for the present; and although she cried and wailed considerably at first, she was never seen emitting tears.

Sunday 2 October 1580

Held as above, but in the hall, in the presence of the above mentioned.

There appeared Battista Moduco, led first from his cell in the convent of San Francesco in Cividale, cautioned, examined and interrogated, he testified as follows. Questioned, he replied:

Ever since I heard from that friend of mine who is in prison that an angel appeared to him, I have come to think that this is a diabolical thing, because our Lord God does not send angels to lead spirits out of bodies, but only to provide them with good inspiration.

And questioned again, he replied:

A certain invisible thing appeared to me in my sleep which had the form of a man, and I thought I was asleep but I was not, and it seemed to me that he was from Trivigniano, and because I had about my neck that caul with which I was born, I thought I heard him say: 'You must come with me because you have something of mine'; and so I told him that if I had to go, I would, but that I did not want to depart from God; and since he said this was God's work, I went at age twenty-two, or twenty-three.

Questioned again, he said:

Yes, sir I always wore that caul about my neck, but I lost it, and after that I never went again.

Questioned, he said:

Those who have the caul and do not wear it, do not go out.

Questioned, he said:

The one who appeared seemed to be a certain Zan de Micon of Trivignano, who is dead now.

Questioned, he said:

It was a Thursday night in the Ember season of Christmas.

Questioned, he said:

No, sir I did not know that he was going to come to me that night, nor that he was a benandante, and I had never talked to him before about such things.

And he added of his own accord:

I have never said anything, except after I stopped going forth because he told me: 'Don't say anything, otherwise you will be beaten.'

It was asked of him: do you know if anyone has ever been beaten for this? he replied:

Yes sir, and I among them, because once I wanted to just say a little word and was beaten and left for dead.

It was asked of him: who beat you? he replied:

Those who used to come with me, perhaps ten people from that village of Trivignano, who now are all dead.

Questioned, he said:

Yes sir, there were witches in that village, including a certain Seraphino who is dead now.

It was asked of him: did you see what the witches did when they went out? he replied:

No sir, except the Ember Days when they fought with us: but they also go out on Thursdays.

Questioned, he said:

On Thursdays the witches are always hurting this or that person; I do not know if they are called by anyone.

Questioned, he said:

The witches do reverence and pray to their masters who go about with great solemnity in black dress and with chains around their necks, and who insist on being kneeled to.

It was asked of him: do you benandanti kneel before your captain? he replied:

No, sir, we only pay our respects to him with our caps, like soldiers to their captain.

It was asked of him: after they have knelt, do the witches play other games? he replied:

Sir, this I have not seen because they go hither and yon.

It was asked of him: when did you see the witches kneel down, and where? he replied:

In the field of Mazzone, after we had fought, when they were setting out in every direction.

It was asked of him: how could you make yourself believe that these were God's works? Men do not have the power either to render themselves invisible or to lead the spirit away, nor are God's works carried out in secrecy. He replied:

That one begged me so much, saying: 'Dear Battista, get up,' and it seemed as if I was both sleeping and not sleeping. Since he was older than me, I allowed myself to be persuaded, thinking it was proper.

Questioned, he said:

Yes sir, now I do believe that this was a diabolical work, after that other one told me of that angel of his, which I mentioned before.

Questioned, he said: the first time I was summoned that person led me to the field of Mazzone and the captain took me by the hand and said: 'Will you be a good servant?' and I replied, yes.

Questioned, he said:

He did not promise me anything, but did say that I was carrying out one of God's works, and that when I died I would go to heaven.

Questioned, he said:

The captain had a white insignia as I said before, and he did not have a cross, not even over his clothing, which was black.

Afterwards he added: they were of black cloth with gold.

It was asked of him: what difference was there between your captain and the one of the witches? he replied:

Ours was somewhat pale of face, and the other one swarthy.

Questioned, he said:

There we did not mention Christ by name, nor the Madonna, nor any saint specifically, nor did I ever see anyone cross himself or make the sign of the cross; but in truth they did talk of God and the saints in general, saying: 'May God and the saints be with us,' but without naming anyone.

Questioned, he said:

There were no horses while we fought, except for some belonging to certain gentlemen of each band mounted on certain four-footed animals, black and white and red, of I don't know what kind, who stood watching.

Questioned, he said:

Those of the witches were on one side and ours opposite, but they didn't bother with one another.

Questioned, he said:

Yes, I did indeed know some benandanti, but I didn't know any of those gentlemen, because they came now in one way, now in another. But we benandanti and witches always came the same way.

Questioned, he said:

While waiting for the company we did not do anything, we neither ate nor drank; but on our way home, I wish I had a *scudo* for every time we drank in the wine cellars, entering through the cracks, and getting on the casks. We drank with a pipe, as did the witches; but after they had drunk, they pissed in the casks.

Questioned, he said:

Dear sir, have I not told you that simply because I said a couple of things I was beaten terribly, so my sides were all black and blue and also my back and arms? And this is why I never told it to the confessor.

After these facts were heard, he was returned to his cell, so that he might reflect better, etc.

Monday 3 October 1580

Held as above before the reverend father inquisitor of Aquileia, master Felice Montefalco, in the presence of the illustrious *provveditore*, Giovanni Baduario,[3] and the magnificent and excellent vicar.

Conducted from the prison assigned to him, Paolo Gasparutto of the village of Iassico, examined and interrogated, testified as follows:

Questioned, he replied:

I believe that the apparition of that angel was really the devil tempting me, since you have told me that he can transform himself into an angel.

Questioned, he replied:

About a year before the angel appeared to me, my mother gave me the caul in which I had been born, saying that she had it baptized with me, and had nine Masses said over it, and had it blessed with certain prayers and scriptural readings; and she told me that I was born a benandante, and that when I grew up I would go forth at night, and that I must wear it on my person, and that I would go with the benandanti to fight the witches.

Questioned, he replied:

My mother did not go forth and she was not a benandante.

Questioned, he said:

From the time I received the caul until the angel came to me, nothing was said to me, nor was I taught anything.

Questioned, he replied:

When that angel, which I believe is the devil, called me, he did not promise me anything, but told me that he would summon me through a benandante called Battista of Vicenza, whom he did indeed send.

Questioned, he said:

I did not know this Battista, whom I had never seen, but when he came he said: 'I am Battista of Vicenza.'

Questioned, he replied:

We went out by the door, even though it was locked tight.

Questioned: in what way can you tell when children have been bewitched? he replied:

It can be determined because they do not leave any flesh on the body, and they leave them with nothing, and they remain dried up and withered, nothing but skin and bones.

It was asked of him: what remedy was it that you used for the child of that man of Brazzano? he replied:

I told him to weigh him three Thursdays.

Questioned, he replied:

The remedy is this, that while the child is weighed on the scale, the captain of the benandanti uses the scale to torment the witch that has caused the injury, even to the point of killing him.

Questioned, he replied:

The child died because they were late in weighing it.

And he added:

When the child gains in weight on the three Thursdays he is weighed, the witch withers and dies, and if the child withers, it is the witch that lives.

Questioned, he replied:

While I was a benandante I could call upon one to accompany me, and every benandante can do this: but first he is asked to swear that he will disclose nothing, because if he said something, it would bring harm to him and to his companion.

Questioned: who would harm them? he replied:

Those witches.

This testimony having been received, the reverend father inquisitor, with the concurrence of the illustrious *provveditore* and of the most excellent Paolo Pradiola, vicar of his magnificence, released him for the present, on condition that he reappear when summoned, etc.

Led from the prison assigned to him was the official Battista Moduco, alias *Gamba Secura*, and examined, cautioned and interrogated he testified as follows. Questioned, he replied:

I have already said that I could not go without the caul which my mother gave me. She told me that I was born with it and that she had it baptized with me and had some Masses said over it, and that I must wear it, and over that caul I too had more than thirty Masses and benedictions said when I was in Rome with the former Signor Mario Savorgnano.

And questioned, he said:

Yes, indeed, Sir, the priest who blessed it knew, and he used to place it under the altar cloth while he said Mass.

Questioned, he said:

I had it blessed by a monk in that church named for the Madonna near the gate to enter Rome.

And questioned, he said:

It was one monk only who said the Masses, which I don't know if they were thirty or thirty-two, and he held the caul in his hand and I gave him a golden *scudo* as an act of courtesy.

Having received this testimony the reverend father inquisitor as above dismissed him for the present, with the concurrence of the aforementioned and with the same injunction to reflect better, etc.

25 November 1581

Leonardo Colloredo, public crier of Cividale, reported under oath that he had been assigned to go to the village of Iassico and summon Paolo, son of the deceased Gasparutto, of the village of Iassico, to appear on Sunday before the father inquisitor to hear his sentence read in the Church of San Francesco in Cividale, on 26 November 1581. Similarly, Colloredo reported that he had summoned Battista Moduco to appear on Sunday, 26 November 1581 to hear his sentence read in the same Church of San Francesco in Cividale.

(ACAU, S. *Uffizio*, 'Sententiarum contra reos S. Officii liber primus'.)

In the name of Christ, amen.

We, brother Felice da Montefalco, doctor in sacred theology and inquisitor general against heretical pravity for the entire patriarchate of Aquileia and diocese of Concordia, especially delegated by the Holy Apostolic See.

Since you, Battista Moduco, public crier in the city of Cividale, diocese of Aquileia, was denounced to us by individuals worthy of belief as a suspect of heretical pravity, and that you had been so infected for many years, to the great detriment of your soul, therefore, we upon whom falls the responsibility, in view of the office that we fill, to instill the holy Catholic faith in the hearts of men and eradicate heretical pravity from their minds, desiring (as we were and are obliged) to become better informed about these matters, and determine whether the disturbance which has come to our ears is supported by some measure of truth, and, if it did possess truth, to supply a wholesome and opportune remedy, began to make inquiries, examining witnesses, summoning you, and in the most suitable way that we could, interrogate you under oath about the things of which you were accused, and pursuing all and each individually, which we did, as justice demands, and as we are obliged to do by the laws of the Church.

Therefore, since we wanted to bring your trial to a fitting conclusion and examine clearly what had been uncovered, and whether you walked in the shadows or in the light, and whether you were infected by the stain of heresy or not, to study the merits of the trial we have solemnly convoked before us experts in both canon and civil law, in the presence of the illustrious Giovanni Baduario, worthy *provveditore* of the city of Cividale, in the venerable convent of San Francesco in that city, fully aware that in the eyes of canon law, sound is the judgment which is confirmed by the opinions of many. And after having received and digested the advice, and after having seen and diligently pondered the evidence of the trial, and after having weighed each and every element on a single scale, we came to the determination that you, by your own confession pronounced before us under oath, have been caught up in numerous perversities and heresies, and first of all:

That for twenty-two years you abided in these errors and heresies, since you confessed that you were with the benandanti for that length of time, and that you entered in the Ember season of December, that your mother gave you the cloth or caul with which you were born, saying that she had it baptized with you and also had Masses said over it, and that you had to carry it with you, because you were going with the benandanti. You also stated that you had the caul the night that man of Trivignano whom you knew, but not as a benandante, appeared to you. And he told you that you had to go with him, because you had something of his, and you responded that you would go with him if you were obliged to do so, and, indeed, you did journey forth with that man time and again for twenty-two years.

Moreover, we heard from your own mouth that when you were in Rome, without the slightest fear of God, you had twenty Masses celebrated over that caul and numerous prayers and scriptural readings performed by a priest.

In addition, you dared to say many times, and dared to assert it before us, that all those born with the caul belong to that society, and when they reach age twenty they are obliged to join that society.

That the days when you went forth were the Ember seasons of the year, at night, between Thursdays and Fridays; that the places where you were accustomed to go to do battle were the great field situated near Azzano, and sometimes in the countryside about Conegliano, and sometimes even in German lands in a field near a place called Circnis [Cirghinis], and that the first time you went it was to the great field.

It is also our understanding that you said that when you went to these places weddings were performed, with leaping about, drinking and eating, and that there was fighting with spears of fennel.

Furthermore, so great was your audacity and so small your fear of God, that you dared to affirm before us that to reveal the names of the witches and benandanti was to go against divine will; and you also declared that you believed and firmly held that these impious games were permitted by God, and that you fought for God. Similarly, you asserted that you seriously believed that the captain, under whom you went to these games, had been placed there by God.

In addition, so great was your perseverance and credulity in committing evil, that you believed and firmly held, that not only were these the works of God, but that indeed after death you would enter heaven because of them.

You also said with your own mouth that in these games and combats of yours, the standard-bearer of the benandanti carried a banner of white silk gilded with a lion depicted, and that one of the witches carried a red silk banner, gilded, depicting four black devils.

That on the return from these games you entered wine cellars to drink and commit other things.

Moreover, you dared to believe and affirm that the spirit and the soul could leave the body at will and return to go to these battles. And what is a sign of your enormous error and wickedness is that you received the most sacred sacrament of the Eucharist without ever having confessed these great wickednesses and errors of yours.

But since the merciful and compassionate God occasionally permits some to fall into heresy and error, not only so that Catholic and educated men may become exercised in praise of the holy, but also so that the fallen henceforth be made more humble and take up the works of penitence, therefore, after having diligently discussed the merits of the trial, as indicated above, we have ascertained that in following our frequent instructions and those of other virtuous men, you have returned, adhering to a healthier opinion, to the bosom of Holy Mother Church and to its unity, salubriously fleeing the aforesaid heresies and detesting the errors, and acknowledging the irrefutable truth of the faith of the Holy Church, impressing it within the very viscera of your body. Consequently, we have admitted you (and we admit you) as a warning to publicly abjure the aforementioned heresies and any other, according to the following formula. After the abjuration we shall absolve you from the sentence of greater excommunication by which you became bound after your fall into heresy; and in reconciling you to Holy Mother Church, we restore the sacraments to you, provided that with a true heart and unfeigned faith you return to the unity of the Church, just as we believe and hope you have done.

Proceed then with the following abjuration:

I, Battista Moduco, official of Cividale in the Friuli in the diocese of Aquileia, here in the presence of you the father inquisitor against heretical pravity for the entire diocese of Aquileia and Concordia, with the sacred Gospels before me, and with my hands laid on them, I promise to believe with my heart and confess with my tongue that holy, Catholic and apostolic faith which Holy Mother Church believes, confesses, proclaims and observes. Consequently, I abjure, revoke, detest and disown every heresy of whatever kind it might be, and sect raised up against the Holy, Roman and Apostolic Church.

Moreover, I promise to believe with my heart, and confess with my tongue having committed evil in staying with the benandanti for twenty-two years and having believed and declared that it was a work of God, and that those who opposed it opposed God.

Equally, I confess to having committed evil during the Ember Days when I went out with the other benandanti and witches to fight for the crops and the wine.

I confess and believe that our spirit and soul cannot leave the body nor return to it at will. I also declare and admit that I grievously sinned by never unburdening myself of these errors in confession. Likewise, I abjure and detest the wrong I did wearing the caul in which I was born and having Masses celebrated over it, a thing detested by Holy Mother Church.

Similarly, I abjure and detest having gone in those places I mentioned, to those games and nuptials and to the combats with fennel stalks.

Similarly, I abjure and detest having spoken badly and against Holy Mother Church that whoever reveals the names of these witches and benandanti acts against the will of God, and that these games are God's, and the fighting is for God.

I also abjure and detest the wrong I did in having believed and affirmed that the captain under whom I served had been placed there by God.

Similarly, I abjure and detest my persistence and opinion in believing that not only were those works of God but that after my death I would go to heaven because of them.

I also abjure and detest having said that in those games and combats the standard bearer of the benandanti carried an insignia of white silk, gilded, with a lion, and the one of the witches an insignia of red silk with four black devils on it, gilded.

Similarly, I abjure and detest having affirmed that I believe and hold for true that the soul can leave the body and return at pleasure when it goes to these games.

Finally, I detest and abjure any and every possible evil act and heresy that I have committed against Holy Mother Church, which with all my spirit and affection I approach and kneel before, beseeching pardon from the most exalted creator.

Moreover, I swear and promise that in the future I shall not hold or believe any heresy, nor have familiarity with any, nor teach them to others, but if I learn that someone is infected with heresy or belongs to the witches, or to the witches and benandanti, I will reveal this information to you the father inquisitor or to your successors.

I also promise and swear to fulfil to the best of my ability any penance imposed upon me or that you will impose on me; nor shall I flee nor absent myself, but whenever I shall be called I will respond as quickly as possible and so God help me, and these holy Gospels. But if in the future I should fall again into the above abjured things (may God forbid), I want to be immediately considered relapsed, and I oblige and bind myself now and in the future to the punishments reserved to the relapsed, provided that they be legitimately proved in court or confessed by me.

Truly, since it is most unworthy to avenge injuries against temporal lords, while calmly tolerating injuries against the Lord of the heavens and creator of all things, since it is so much more serious to offend the eternal than the temporal majesty; therefore, in order that he who shows mercy towards sinners also show mercy towards you, so that you may be an example to others and crimes not remain unpunished, and that you may come to act more cautiously in the future and be rendered less disposed and in fact more hesitant about commiting the aforesaid and any other illicit acts,

We, father Felice Montefalco, the above named inquisitor general and judge over cases of the faith, in session as a tribunal, for the purpose of passing judgment, according to judicial custom, together with the authority of the reverend lord the bishop of Cattaro, patriarchal vicar and suffragan, with the counsel of the aforesaid lord *provveditore* and of others who are expert in sacred theology and both [canon and civil] laws, with the sacrosanct Gospels before us, as if our judgment emanated from the countenance of God and our eyes discern what is just, having only God before them and the inviolable truth of the orthodox faith, you, Battista Moduco, are arraigned in our presence, to make the aforesaid abjuration in this place at this day and hour, and to hear the definitive sentence or penance to be imposed, as follows:

First:

We condemn you to a term of six months in a prison which we shall assign to you, which you will not leave without our express permission, obtained in writing.

Second, on every Friday of the Ember Days you will fast and beseech God to forgive you the sins which you committed on those days, and you will observe this for two continuous years.

Third, three times a year, at the Resurrection, at the Assumption of the Blessed Virgin Mary in the month of August and at the Nativity of our Lord, for five years you will confess your sins and receive the most sacred sacrament of the Eucharist, bringing or sending an attestation from your priest to the Holy Office that this was fulfilled.

Fourth, you are and will be obliged to send to the Holy Office of the Inquisition all the wrappings or cauls in which your children were or will be born, without burning these cauls by fire.

Moreover, as salutary penances on individual holy days for a period of three years you will recite the Rosary, praying to God to forgive the sins and errors you have committed.

We reserve to ourselves the authority to reduce these penalties or absolve you, in whole or in part, as we may deem best.

Sunday 26 November 1581

The aforesaid sentence was moved, given and in writing judicially promulgated by the above named reverend father, Felice da Montefalco, inquisitor, etc., seated as a court; forthwith, after the sermon uttered in the presence of all the people, also performed was the above written abjuration by the aforesaid Battista Moduco before his reverend lordship in the venerable church of the convent of San Francesco in the city of Cividale by the altar of St Anthony.

Read by me, Antonio Masetto, notary of Cividale, functioning as secretary, with a large multitude as before present and listening.

The same day.

The above named Battista Moduco, humbly praying and beseeching the reverend father inquisitor named above to permit the said Battista to provide for his family, remitted the punishment or penance of six months in prison, in accordance with the provision contained in the sentence, on condition that for the fifteen days following, Battista not leave nor escape from the territory of this city. With this transacted, only the above penalty of imprisonment was for the time being remitted.

In the presence of the reverend father, master Bonaventura Tivarutio, and the most excellent lord, Giulio Delaiolo, honorable vicar to the illustrious *provveditore* of the city.

In the name of Christ, amen.

We, father Felice Montefalco, doctor of sacred theology and inquisitor against heretical pravity for the entire patriarchate of Aquileia and diocese of Concordia, specially delegated by the Holy Apostolic See.

Since it came to our attention that you, Paolo, son of the deceased Gasparutto, of the village of Iassico in the diocese of Aquileia, was denounced to us by individuals worthy of belief as a suspect of heretical pravity, and that you had been so infected for many years, to the great detriment of your soul, a denunciation which struck us sharply in the heart, therefore, we, upon whom falls the responsibility, in view of the office that we fill, to instill the holy Catholic faith in the hearts of men and eradicate heretical pravity from their minds, desiring (as we were and are obliged) to become better informed about these matters, and determine whether the disturbance which has come to our ears is supported by some measure of truth, and, if it did possess truth, to supply a wholesome and opportune remedy, began to make inquiries, examining witnesses, summoning you, and in the most suitable way that we could, interrogate you under oath about the things of which you were accused, and pursuing all and each individually, which we did, as justice demands, and as we are obliged to do by the laws of the Church.

Therefore, since we wanted to bring your trial to a fitting conclusion and examine clearly what had been uncovered, and whether you walked in the shadows or in the light, and whether you were infected by the stain of heresy or not, to study the merits of the trial we have solemnly convoked before us experts in both canon and civil law, in the presence of the illustrious Giovanni Baduario, worthy *provveditore* of the city of Cividale, in the venerable convent of San Francesco in that city, fully aware that in the eyes of canon law, sound is the judgment which is confirmed by the opinions of many. And after having received and digested the advice, and after having seen and diligently pondered the evidence of the trial, and after having weighed each and every element on a single scale, we came to the determination that you, by your own confession pronounced before us under oath, have been caught up in numerous perversities and heresies, and first of all:

For ten continuous years you abided among witches, called by you benandanti, believed in your heart, and time and again confirmed with your mouth that this was one of God's works. Indeed, most execrable of all, you affirmed and firmly believed and said that whoever went against this sect acted against the will of God. And you dared to affirm this before our tribunal and, a matter of no small interest, not only did you follow this diabolical sect during all the years you dedicated yourself to these works, but you also urged others to accompany you, and once they had promised, they were compelled in the future, whether they wanted to or not, to attend your spectacles and crimes. And you taught those who came that they must not name the holy name of God nor of his saints, or they would have to remain there. Moreover, you confessed to us out of your own mouth that when you were twenty-eight, during the Ember Days in the month of December, in the night following Thursday at about the fourth hour, a devil appeared before you in the form of an angel who called you by your own name and said: 'Paolo, you must go to fight for and sustain the crops against the witches.' You promised him to go and the angel promised to send you a man of Vicenza who would summon you and lead you. And he came precisely in the month of December, on a Thursday, at the fourth hour of the night, and spoke to you, saying: 'The captain calls you forth to battle.' Thus, repeatedly, you went to these diabolical pastimes, led by the devil and by the captain from Verona, and gave yourself over to these works. And what is impious and most execrable, you committed idolatry every time you attended a spectacle of this kind and adored the aforesaid evil angel in the same way that our Lord Jesus Christ must and ought to be adored in churches and other places.

The localities to which you used to go were the country places around Gradisca, Verona, Cormons near Iassico, in all the Ember seasons of the year on the night following Thursday. In these places, as it appears to us from the trial, you and your companions played, leaped about and rode various animals. And it was always during the Ember Days that you were accustomed to fight for the harvests, one time for the corn and the wheat, a second for all the small crops, a third for the wine and a fourth for the animals. The arms which you were accustomed to bear in these games and battles were either stalks of fennel or sticks commonly called viburnum.

On the way back, thirsty, you and your companions entered homes and cellars, and did many evil things while drinking.

We have also learned from you that you held and firmly believed, when you were conversing with the evil angel and attending those games, that the spirit can leave the body and return at its pleasure. You also tenaciously asserted this falsehood, that while you were involved in this wantonness, if someone should draw near with a candle or a light where your body lay to observe it and never took his eyes from it and cried out as loudly as he could, it [the body] would never answer, but if this someone moved his eyes and then called, it would respond immediately.

Moreover, you said that if a person looked at your body lying in bed the whole night long, your spirit would not return to the body, neither the next day nor the one after that, except at night. And if during that time your body was placed in a grave, your spirit would have to wander vagabond about the world until the day and hour fixed by God for its death.

Similarly you asserted that if you should reveal to anyone the names of your companions and what they did during these activities, you would be beaten at night by your accomplices, as in fact you affirm happened to you.

We also gathered from you that the year before the angel appeared to you, your mother gave you the membrane or caul with which you were born, saying: 'I had this caul baptized with you and nine Masses celebrated over it, as well as benedictions, prayers and scripture recited. Therefore, accept it and wear it, because you are destined to become a benandante when it will be time.'

Finally, while you were performing all these diabolical things, you received the most sacred Eucharist and confession, but you chose not to reveal these crimes to your confessor, which is the most obvious sign of your impiety and perdition.

But since the merciful and compassionate God occasionally permits some to fall into heresy and error, not only so that Catholic and educated men may become exercised in praise of the holy, but also so that the fallen henceforth be made more humble and take up the works of penitence, therefore, after having diligently discussed the merits of the trial, as indicated above, we have ascertained that in following our frequent instructions and those of other virtuous men, you have returned, adhering to a healthier opinion, to the bosom of Holy Mother Church and to its unity, salubriously fleeing the aforesaid heresies and detesting the errors, and acknowledging the irrefutable truth of the faith of the holy Church, impressing it within the very viscera of your body. Consequently, we have admitted you (and we admit you) as a warning to publicly abjure the aforementioned heresies and any other, according to the following formula. After the abjuration we shall absolve you from the sentence of greater excommunication by which you became bound after your fall into heresy; and in reconciling you to Holy Mother Church, we restore the sacraments to you, provided that with a true heart and unfeigned faith you return to the unity of the Church, just as we believe and hope you have done.

Proceed then with the following abjuration:

I, Paolo Gasparutto of Iassico in the diocese of Aquileia, in the presence of you the father inquisitor against heretical pravity for the entire aforesaid diocese and that of Concordia, specially delegated by the Holy Apostolic See, with the sacred Gospels before me, and with my hands laid on them, I promise to believe with my heart and confess with my tongue that holy Catholic and apostolic faith which the Holy Roman Church believes, confesses, proclaims and observes. Consequently, I abjure, revoke, detest and disown every heresy of whatever kind it might be, and sect raised up against the Holy, Roman and Apostolic Church.

Moreover, I promise to believe with my heart, and confess with my tongue having committed evil in staying with the benandanti for ten years and having believed and declared that it was a work of God, and that those who opposed it opposed God.

Likewise, I confess having done wrong in getting others to come to see these spectacles.

Similarly, I detest and abjure that honour and adoration which I displayed in my adoration of the angel.

I also confess having done a great wrong during the Ember Days of the year going out with the other benandanti and witches to fight for the crops and wines.

I also confess and believe that our spirit and soul cannot leave and return to the body at will.

In addition I confess that souls (even though the body is placed in a grave) do not and cannot go wandering about the world.

I also admit that I was wrong in never confessing these errors of mine.

I abjure and detest whatever sort of heresy is or shall be condemned by the Holy, Roman and Apostolic Mother Church.

Moreover, I swear and promise that in the future I shall not fall again into the aforesaid heresy, nor in others, and will not believe them, draw near to them, nor teach them to others; and if I learn that someone is infected with heresy or belongs to the witches, or to the witches and benandanti, I will reveal this information to you the father inquisitor or to your successors.

I also promise and swear to fulfil to the best of my ability any penance imposed upon me or that you will impose upon me.

I also swear and promise that I shall not flee nor absent myself, but whenever I shall be called by you or by your successors, I shall present myself as quickly as possible, and so God help me, and these holy Gospels. But if in the future I should fall again into the above abjured things (may God forbid), I want to be immediately considered relapsed, and I oblige and bind myself now and in the future to the punishments reserved to the relapsed, provided that they be legitimately proved in court or confessed by me.

Truly, since it is seriously unworthy to avenge injuries against temporal lords, while calmly tolerating injuries against the Lord of the heavens and creator of all things, since it is so much more serious to offend the eternal than the temporal majesty; therefore, in order that he who shows mercy towards sinners also show mercy towards you and so that you may be an example to others and crimes not remain unpunished, and that you may come to act more cautiously in the future and be rendered less disposed and in fact more hesitant about committing the aforesaid and any other illicit acts.

We, father Felice Montefalco, the above named inquisitor general and judge over cases of the faith, in session as a tribunal for the purpose of passing judgment, according to judicial custom, together with the authority of the reverend lord the bishop of Cattaro, patriarchal vicar and suffragan, with the counsel of the aforesaid lord *provveditore* and of others who are expert in sacred theology and both [canon and civil] laws, with the sacrosanct Gospels before us, as if our judgment emanated from the countenance of God and our eyes discern what is just, having only God before them and the inviolable truth of the orthodox faith, you, Paolo Gasparutto, are arraigned in our presence, to make the aforesaid abjuration in this place at this day and hour, and to hear the definitive sentence or penance to be imposed, as follows:

First:

We condemn you to a term of six months in a prison which we shall assign to you, which you will not leave without our express permission, obtained in writing.

Second, on every Friday of the Ember Days you will fast and beseech God to forgive you the sins which you committed on those days, and you will observe this for two continuous years.

Third, three times a year, at the Resurrection, at the Assumption of the Blessed Virgin Mary in the month of August and at the Nativity of our Lord, for five years you will confess your sins and receive the most sacred sacrament of the Eucharist, bringing or sending an attestation from your priest to the Holy Office that this was fulfilled.

Fourth, you are and will be obliged to send to the Holy Office of the Inquisition all the wrappings or cauls in which your children were or will be born, without burning these cauls by fire.

Fifth, in the Rogation processions before the Ascension of our Lord, it will be prohibited to you and to your domestics to carry viburnum branches, nor are you to keep said viburnum in any form in your home.

Moreover, as salutary penances on individual holy days for a period of three years you will recite the Rosary, praying to God to forgive the sins and errors you have committed.

We reserve to ourselves the authority to reduce these penalties or absolve you, in whole or in part, as we may deem best.

Sunday 26 November 1581

The aforesaid sentence was moved, given and in writing judicially promulgated by the above named reverend father, Felice da Montefalco, inquisitor, etc., seated as a court; forthwith, after the sermon uttered in the presence of all the people, also performed was the above written abjuration by the aforesaid Paolo Gasparutto[4] before his reverend lordship in the venerable church of the convent of San Francesco in the city of Cividale by the altar of St Anthony.

Read by me, Antonio Masetto, notary of Cividale, functioning as secretary, with a large multitude as before present and listening.

The same day

The above named Paolo Gasparutto,[5] humbly praying and beseeching the reverend father inquisitor named above, so that the said Paolo might be able to return to his home, and provide for his family and children, remitted the punishment or penance of six months in prison, in accordance with the provision contained in the sentence, on condition that for fifteen days following, Paolo not leave nor escape from the territory of this city and the village of Iassico. With this transacted, only the above penalty of imprisonment was for the time being remitted.

In the presence of the reverend father, master Bonaventura Tivarutio, a fellow brother in the above named minorite convent, and the most excellent lord, Giulio Delaiolo, honorable vicar to the illustrious *provveditore* of the city.

NOTES

Abbreviations used in notes

ACAU	Archivio della Curia Arcivescovile, Udine
ACVB	Archivio della Curia Vescovile, Bergamo
ASCB	Archivio Storico Civico, Brescia
ASCM	Archivio Storico Civico, Milan
ASL	Archivio di Stato, Lucca
ASM	Archivio di Stato, Modena
ASP	Archivio di Stato, Parma
ASV	Archivio di Stato, Venice
BCAU	Biblioteca della Curia Arcivescovile, Udine
BCB	Biblioteca Comunale, Bologna (Archiginnasio)
HAD	Historijski Arhiv Dubrovnik
TCLD	Trinity College Library, Dublin

Preface to the English Edition

1 E.W. Monter, 'Trois historiens actuels de la sorcellerie', *Bibliothèque d'Humanisme et Renaissance*, 31 (1969) 205–7. See also by the same author the anthology *European Witchcraft* (New York, 1969) pp. 158–64 for a discussion of and excerpts from the *Benandanti*.

2 E.W. Monter, 'The Historiography of European Witchcraft: Progress and Prospects', *The Journal of Interdisciplinary History*, 2 (1972) 443–4.

3 M. Murray, *The Witch-Cult in Western Europe* (Oxford, 1921; reprint 1962).

4 See above, pp. 20–2 and *passim*.

5 J.B. Russell, *Witchcraft in the Middle Ages* (Ithaca, 1972) pp. 41–2; H.C. Erik Midelfort, 'Were there really witches?' in R.M. Kingdon, ed., *Transition and Revolution: Problems and Issues of European Renaissance and Reformation History* (Minneapolis, 1974) pp. 203–4.

6 N. Cohn, *Europe's Inner Demons: An Enquiry Inspired by the Great Witch-Hunt* (London, 1975) p. 223.

7 P. Burke, *Popular Culture in Early Modern Europe* (London, 1978) p. 78.

8 W.E. Peuckert, *Geheimkulte* (Heidelberg, 1951) pp. 266 ff. Peuckert (who does not 1972) p. 116.

9 M. Eliade, 'Some Observations on European Witchcraft', *History of Religions*, 14 (1975) pp. 153–8. But on this problem (and others connected to it), see now the important book by H.-P. Duerr, *Traumzeit: Ueber die Grenze zwischen Wildnis und Zivilisation* (Frankfort a.M., 1978).

1 J. Hansen, *Zauberwahn, Inquisition und Hexenprozess im Mittelalter und die Enstehung der grossen Hexenverfolgung* (Munich & Leipzig, 1900; reprint, 1964); *Quellen und Untersuchungen zur Geschichte des Hexenwahns und der Hexenverfolgung im Mittelalter* (Bonn, 1901). Hansen developed and documented what had been an intuition of S. Riezler (*Geschichte der Hexenprozesse in Bayern*, Stuttgart, 1896).

2 M. Tejado Fernandez, *Aspectos de la vida social en Cartagena de Indias durante el Seiscientos* (Seville, 1954) pp. 106 ff., 127 ff., 142 f.

3 F. Byloff, *Hexenglaube und Hexenverfolgung in den österreischen Alpen ländern* (Berlin & Leipzig, 1934).

4 Girolamo Tartarotti, *Del congresso notturno delle lammie libri tre* (Rovereto, 1749).

5 Jules Michelet, *La sorcière*, ed. originale publiée avec notes et variantes par L. Refort, 2 vols (Paris, 1952–6); *The Sorceress: a Study in Middle Age Superstition* (London, 1905).

6 M. Murray *The Witch-Cult in Western Europe* (Oxford, 1921; 2nd ed. 1962, with a preface by S. Runciman). In her later works on the subject, Murray contented herself to reiterate, in a still more rigid and unacceptable form, the thesis proposed in this first book.

7 See, for example, the review by W.R. Halliday, in *Folklore*, 33 (1922) pp. 224–30.

8 W.E. Peuckert, *Geheimkulte* (Heidelberg, 1951) pp. 266 ff. Peuckert (who does not cite Murray) introduced this thesis in his customary racist antithesis between the virile Germans dedicated to the hunt and to war, and the effeminate Mediterraneans, tied to agriculture and vegetation, to 'demonstrate' that witchcraft originated with the latter.

9 J. Marx, *L'Inquisition en Dauphiné* (Paris, 1914) pp. 29 ff. (Bibliothèque de l'Ecole des Hautes-Etudes, fasc. 206.)

10 L. Weiser-Aall, in *Handwörterbuch des deutschen Aberglaubens*, eds, E. Hoffmann-Krayer and H. Bächtold-Stäubli, III, coll. 1828, 1849–51.

11 The question of the connection to comparable beliefs in the classical world (one recalls Apuleius's description in the *Golden Ass* of the witch who oiled herself before setting out to a rendezvous) has not yet been dealt with satisfactorily.

12 A. Mayer, *Erdmutter und Hexe: Eine Untersuchung zur Geschichte des Hexenglaubens und zur Vorgeschichte der Hexenprozesse* (Munich & Freising, 1936). This work came to my attention through A. Runeberg, 'Witches, demons and fertility magic', *Societas Scientiarum Fennica: Commentationes humanarum litterarum* (Helsingfors, 1947) XIV[4], 84 n.

13 Because of my ignorance of Swedish I have been unable to utilize D. Strömbäck, *Sejd* (Lund, 1935). To judge from references made to it by W.E. Peuckert and A. Runeberg, the book would appear to furnish interesting observations on this point.

14 The connection witches-shamans is advanced hesitantly by Peuckert (*Geheimkulte*, p. 126) and, more forcefully, by E. Stiglmayr, *Die Religion in Geschichte und Gegenwart*, 3rd ed. (Tübingen, 1959) III, coll. 307–8.

15 See G. Marcotti, *Donne e monache. Curiosità* (Florence, 1884), pp. 290–1; E. Fabris Bellavitis, in *Giornale di Udine e del Veneto Orientale*, a. XXIV, 2 August, 1890; V. Ostermann, *La vita in Friuli*, 2nd ed. by G. Vidossi (Udine, 1940) *passim*; A. Lazzarini, *Leggende friulane* (Udine, 1915) p. 14. See also the entries for 'belandànt, benandànt', in *Il Nuovo Pirona, vocabolario friulano* (Udine, 1935), and 'benandante' in E. Rosamani, *Vocabolario giuliano* (Bologna, 1958). Battistella (*Il Sant'Officio, e la Riforma religiosa in Friuli*, Udine, 1895, p. 102) referred to 'madmen and swindlers, so-called *benandanti*'.

Text

I THE NIGHT BATTLES

1

1 ACAU, *S. Uffizio*, 'Ab anno 1574 usque ad annum 1578 incl. a n. 57 usque ad 76 incl', trial n. 64, f.lr. On the Friulian Inquisition see the old study by A. Battistella, *Il Sant' Officio e la Riforma religiosa in Friuli* (Udine, 1895). On the religious situation in the Friuli during the sixteenth century, see works by P. Paschini, especially his 'Eresia e Riforma cattolica al confine orientale d' Italia', *Lateranum*, n.s., a. 17, n. 1–4, Rome, 1951. The wealth of material that pertains to the Holy Office of Aquileia and Concordia is preserved in the archive of the Curia Arcivescovile in Udine. Battistella, who was unable to use this *fondo* in the course of writing his book, provides only little summary information about it. The trials, which constitute by far the most exhaustive part of the collection, are numbered and arranged in chronological order. The bundles in which they are enclosed (approximately a hundred) are not numbered consecutively. There is an eighteenth-century manuscript inventory of the first thousand trials, entitled 'Novus liber causarum S. Officii Aquileiae, regestum scilicet denunciatorum, sponte comparitorum, atque per sententiam, vel aliter expeditorum, ab anno 1551 usque ad annum 1647 inclusive . . .'. preserved in the Biblioteca Comunale, Udine (MS 916: cf. A. Battistella, *Il Sant' Officio*, p. 7). This register was used by Battistella and, for the trials against magic and superstitious practices, by V. Ostermann (*La vita in Friuli*, 2nd ed. by G. Vidossi [Udine, 1940], *passim*) and, to a lesser degree, by G. Marcotti (*Donne e monache. Curiosità* [Florence, 1884]). An inventory of the post-1647 trials exists in the archive of the Curia Arcivescovile in Udine. After the first thousand trials the numbering begins again from 1. To avoid confusion I have uses this numbering adding *bis* (trial no 1 *bis*, 2 *bis*, etc.). (There are now two published inventories of the two series of trials described above: *1000 processi dell' Inquisizione in Friuli* [Udine, 1976] 'Regione Autonoma Friuli – Venezia Giulia. Quaderni del Centro Regionale di Catalogazione dei beni culturali, 4]; and *I processi dell' Inquisizione in Friuli dal 1648 al 1798* [Udine, 1978] 'Regione Autonoma Friuli – Venezia Giulia. Quaderni del Centro Regionale di Catalogazione dei beni culturali, 7]. Both catalogues were prepared by Luigi De Biasio and Maria Rosa Facile).

Maracco had become vicar general in 1557: about him see P. Paschini, 'Eresia', p. 40, n. 17 and by the same author, *I vicari generali nella diocesi di Aquileia e poi di Udine* (Vittorio Veneto, 1958) pp. 23–5.

2 'Goblins' is a translation of *Sbilfoni*. cf. Sbilfons, 'folletti' in *Il Nuovo Pirona, vocabolario friulano* (Udine, 1935) *sub voce*.

3 ACAU, *S. Uffizio*, 'Ab anno 1574 . . .', trial n. 64, f. 1 v. We call Ember Days the three days of fasting prescribed by the ecclesiastical calendar in the first week of Lent (Ember season of spring); in the Octave of Pentecost (Ember season of summer); in the third week of September (Ember season of autumn); and in the third week of Advent (Ember season of winter).

4 ACAU, *S. Uffizio*, 'Ab anno 1574 . . .', trial n. 64, f. 2 r. The form 'benandante' seems to be the oldest. Subsequently, apart from a few occasional variants such as 'buono andante' (see above, p. 76), 'bellandante' (*belandant*) also begins to be used, at first considered incorrect and thus almost always changed to 'benandante': see 'Ab anno 1621 usque ad annum 1629 incl. a n. 805 usque ad 848 incl.', trial n. 815 (year 1622). The note 'and in their own words benandanti', is a marginal addition in the same hand. It may have been inserted by the witness during the rereading of the interrogation.

5 ACAU, 'Sententiarum contra reos S. Officii liber primus', f. 97 r.
6 The river Iudrio, a tributary of the Natisone.
7 ACAU, S. *Uffizio*, 'Ab anno 1574 . . .', trial n. 64, f. 2 v.
8 *Ibid*., f. 3 r.
9 *Ibid*., ff. 3 r–v.
10 *Ibid*., f. 4 r.

2

11 On the persecution of witchcraft, and the attitude towards it of judges and inquisitors, see the previously cited works by J. Hansen.
12 M. Del Rio, summing up an age-old judgment, defines the crime committed by witches who participated at the sabbat, 'crimen enormissimum, gravissimum, atrocissimum, quia in eo concurrunt circumstantiae criminum enormissimorum, apostasiae, haeresis, sacrilegii, blasphemiae, homicidii, immo et parricidii saepe, et concubitus contra naturam cum creatura spirituali, et odii in Deum, quibus nihil potest esse atrocius' (*Disquisitionum magicarum libri sex*, [Venice, 1652] pp. 493–4). The 1st ed. dates from 1599–1600.

3

13 See also *Annales Minorum* t. 23, 2nd ed. (Ad Claras Aquas, 1934) p. 107.
14 ACAU, S. *Uffizio*, 'Ab anno 1574 . . .', trial n. 64, f. 4 v. On heretical infiltrations into the diocese of Aquileia in this period, besides P. Paschini, 'Eresia', pp, 55–83, see also *'Purliliarum comitis Bartholomei Visitatio Diocesis Aquilegis 1570* (BCU, MS. 1039).
15 ACAU, S. *Uffizio*, 'Ab anno 1574 . . .', trial n. 64, ff. 4 v – 5 r.

4

16 *Ibid*., f. 5 v.
17 *Ibid*., ff. 5 v-6 r.
18 *Ibid*., ff. 6 r-v.

5

19 *Ibid*., ff. 6 v-7 r.
20 *Ibid*., ff. 7 r-v.
21 On the processions of the Rogation days, see V. Ostermann, *La vita in Friuli*, I. pp. 129 ff.

6

22 ACAU, S. *Uffizio*, 'Ab anno 1574 . . .', trial n. 64, f. 8 r.
23 See above, pp. 87 and 103.
24 ACAU, S. *Uffizio*, 'Ab anno 1574 . . .', trial n. 64, ff. 8 r-v.
25 *Ibid*., f. 8 v.

7

26 *Ibid.*, f. 9 v. Needless to say, Gasparutto's influence on Moduco on this occasion does not explain the general agreement between the confessions of the two benandanti.
27 ACAU, *S. Uffizio*, 'Ab anno 1574 . . .', trial n. 64, ff. 9 v-10 r.
28 See above, p. 6.
29 ACAU, *S. Uffizio*, 'Ab anno 1574 . . .', trial n. 64, f. 11 r.

8

30 The *provveditore* of Cividale, taking courage from an authorization issued by the Council of Ten, did not recognize that heresy cases – in the case in question, 'a trial instituted against a benandante' – in which citizens of Cividale were implicated, should be judged in Udine, in the presence of the governor (*luogotenente*) of the *Patria* of the Friuli. This is the gist of the letter written to the Patriarch on 11 January 1581 by the vicar general, Paolo Bisanzio (cf. P. Paschini, *I Vicari generali*, pp. 26–7). The patriarch insisted: and on 18 February Bisanzio again cautioned the *provveditore* of Cividale that it was inconvenient 'in similar cases for the patriarch to have to go wandering about the *Patria* on similar errands dismembering this tribunal, and introducing new tribunals in it'. (BCAU, MS. 105: '*Bisanzio: Lettere* dal 1577 sino al 1585', eighteenth-century copy, ff. 93 r-94 r-v, 95 v). But it was the *provveditore* who got his way: in vain did the patriarch, from Rome, alert the Venetian inquisitors (on 29 February 1581) that, following the example of Cividale, the more distant provinces such as Carnia and Cadore would end demanding the creation of their own separate seats of the Holy Office (ASV, *S. Uffizio*, b. 162). Similarly without effect was Bisanzio's letter of 8 March to the Venetian inquisitors in which he asserted that if the tribunal of the Holy Office were to be moved about the diocese from place to place, it would be deprived of the 'secrecy' necessary in such cases (BCAU, MS. 105: '*Bisanzio: Lettere*,' ff. 98 v-99 r). A Ventura (*Nobiltà e popolo nella società veneta del '400 e '500* [Bari, 1964], pp. 190–1) alludes to the persistent rivalry between Cividale and Udine.
31 The tendency of ecclesiastical authorities to treat magic and witchcraft as 'heresy' developed slowly. In a bull dated 13 December 1258, Alexander IV affirmed that inquisitors against heretical pravity could not sit in judgment over crimes 'de divinationibus et sortilegiis', except when 'manifeste haeresim saperent' (J. Hansen, *Quellen und Untersuchungen zur Geschichte des Hexenwahns und der Hexenverfolgung im Mittelalter* (Bonn, 1901) p. 1. It was a relatively loose formulation, and, therefore, incapable of curbing a trend already set in motion, connected as well to the ever-increasing spread of magico–superstitious practices. Two centuries later, Nicholas V in a bull dated 1 August 1451 addressed to Hugo Lenoir, the inquisitor general of France, exhorted him to pursue and punish 'sacrilegos et divinatores, etiam si haeresim non sapiant manifeste' (*Ibid.*, p. 19). This gave inquisitors the possibility of arrogating to themselves cases involving simple superstition, as in fact occurred in many instances. (The decisive element consisted, clearly, in the relations existing between inquisitor and secular judges in various places: thus, in Paris, for example, it is the latter who at the end of the fourteenth century succeed in winning jurisdiction over witchcraft trials: see J. Hansen, *Zauberwahn, Inquisition und Hexenprozess im Mittelalter und die Enstehung der grossen Hexenverfolgung* [Munich & Leipzig, 1900] p. 363, n. 3). Later, witches' confessions regarding the sabbat, adoration of the devil and the profanation of the sacraments were catalogued under the rubric 'haeresis fascinariorum' (N. Jacquier) or 'haeresis strigatus' (B. Spina). See the abjuration pronounced on 8 February 1579 by Gioannina, an inhabitant of Cendre in the diocese of Como: 'I abjure, deny and renounce this heretical, idolatrous and apostate sect of the witches, into which I fell and in which I persevered for several

years . . . I also reject, abjure and renounce that heresy which holds and asserts that the devil must be worshipped and that offerings have to be made to him, as I have done. . . . In addition, I abjure that perfidious and apostate heresy which holds and asserts that we must renounce the faith . . .' (TCLD, MS. 1225, ser. II, vol. 2, ff. 35 r-v). When this was not possible implicit apostasy and heresy were hypothesized, as in the case, for example, of the *inquisitio* drawn up in the course of the trial against the Modenese witch Anastasia la Frappona (1519), cited by this writer in the *Annali della Scuola Normale Superiore di Pisa, Lettere, storia, e filosofia*, ser. II, vol. 30 (1961) 282n. This was the sense in which even Bartolomeo Spina expressed himself authoritatively against G.F. Ponzinibio in the *Quaestio de strigibus* (Rome, 1576) pp. 177–8 (the treatise was written *c.* 1520–5). But on this point agreement was anything but obvious, as the doubts of Francesco Pegna demonstrate (see his notes to Bernardo da Como's *Lucerna inquisitorum haereticae pravitatis* [Venice, 1596] pp. 46–7, 49, 51), not to mention opponents, such as Alciato. In Rome itself, within the Congregation of the Holy Office, a tendency began to form which favoured leaving to secular judges cases involving non-heretical superstitious practices. Thus, on 21 December 1602, Cardinal Camillo Borghese, the future Paul V, speaking for the entire Congregation issued an annoyed rebuff to the vicar of the Bolognese inquisitor, who contended that 'cases involving superstition, spells and sorcery do not belong to the jurisdiction of his Lordship, but must be consigned to the Holy Office.' The Bolognese official was invited to refrain 'from these innovations, since he must know very well that bishops are not obliged to communicate trials to inquisitors in such cases except when they concern obvious heresy' (BCB, MS. B. 1862, letter n. 84). This was a hearkening back, in effect, to the message in Alexander IV's bull: a first step towards that ever more openly sceptical and 'rationalist' attitude which was gaining ground in the circles of the Roman Congregation of the Holy Office and would find expression, some decades later, in the *Instructio pro formandis processibus in causis strigum, sortilegiorum et maleficiorum*. On this document, see above, pp. 126–7. On the problem in general, see Henry Charles Lea, *A History of the Inquisition of Spain*, 4 vols, (New York, 1907) IV, pp. 184–91.

32 Sentence against Moduco: 'tanta fuit audatia tua et parvus timor Dei, ut ausus sis coram nobis affirmare quod propallare nomen strigonum et benandantum est ire contra divinam voluntatem; et ulterius affirmasti te credere et firmiter tenere hos scelestos ludos a Deo esse permissos, et vos pro Deo proeliari. Item affirmasti te firmiter tenere quod ille capitaneus, sub quo ibas ad similia spectacula, fuisset a Deo positus. Ulterius tanta fuit perseverantia tua et credulitas in mala committendo, quod credebas et firmiter tenebas quod non solum opera ista Dei erant, verum quod mortuus pro illis paradisum introisses. . . . Et quod est signum ingentis fallatiae et sceleris tui, accepisti sacratissimum Eucaristiae sacramentum sine eo quod unquam confessus fuisti haec tam magna scelera et errata tua' (ACAU, 'Sententiarum contra reos S. Officii liber primus', ff. 90 v-91 r). Sentence against Gasparutto: 'et quod impium ac nephandissimum est, idolatriam commisisti quoties ad huiusmodi spectacula adibas, angelum supradictum malum adorabas, sicuti Dominus noster Jesus Christus in ecclesiis ac aliis in locis adorari solet, ac debet' (*Ibid.*, f. 94 v).
A copy of the two sentences – not of the abjurations – sent to the Roman Congregation of the Holy Office is preserved in TCLD, MS. 1226, Ser. II, vol. 3 ff. 328 r-330 v. The discrepancies between the original and the copy are minimal and of little importance. The sentences are translated above (pp. 147–71).

33 ACAU, *S. Uffizio*, 'Ab anno 1574 . . .', trial n. 64, f. 1 v.

34 Such public, detailed and prolix abjurations as Gasparutto's and Moduco's undoubtedly contributed to spread the very beliefs that were being suppressed. Thus, Cardinal Arigoni, on 18 February 1612, wrote to the inquisitor of Bologna to look out 'in preparing sentences not to describe the superstitions and magical practices, abuses of sacraments, sacred and sacramental things that are encountered in their

trials and confessions, so that people present at the abjurations will not have the opportunities to learn them' (BCB, MS. B. 1864, letter 48).

9

35 Sentence against Gasparutto: 'dicebas, quod si quis contra hanc sectam inibat, contra Dei voluntatem faciebat . . .' (ACAU, 'Sententiarum . . . liber primus', f. 94 v). In addition to 'sect' and 'society', the inquisitors and the benandanti themselves spoke of 'art' and 'profession'.

36 It was said of a woman suspected of witchcraft, in a trial held at Feltre in 1588, that 'she had a caul that had been blessed, which her husband wore, and that it had power against enemies so that her husband could not be hurt by them, and she could have gotten 25 ducats for it, but she had neither wanted to give it away nor sell it' (ASV, *S. Uffizio*, b. 61, trial against Elena Cumana). The same belief is evidenced in later Friulian trials: for example, on 25 December 1647, two women of Udine were tried by the Holy Office for having placed a caul (*'una camisiutta'*) under the altar of a church so as to have Masses celebrated over it and then sent it to a young man who was off to war, so as to guarantee his safety (ACAU, *S. Uffizio*, 'Anno integro 1647 explicit pm millenarium a n. 983 usque ad 1000', n. 1000). But the powers of the *'camisiutta'* had other applications as well: in a trial of Piacenza in 1611 it was said that a Friulian lawyer, Giovanni Bertuzzi di Nimis, had secured the amniotic membrane in which a son of his had been born 'and with that caul he won all his cases' (ASP, section VI, 119, MS. 38, ff. 59 v-60 r: the passage is not cited by A. Barilli 'Un processo di streghe nel castello di Gragnano Piacentino,' *Bollettino Storico Piacentino*, 36 [1941], 16–24, who examines this trial from another point of view). The amniotic membrane was also used by witches to prepare so-called 'virgin paper' which was used in casting spells of various sorts: see P. Grillando, *De Sortilegiis* (Frankfort a.M., 1592), pp. 33–34. In general, on all these beliefs, see the entries, 'Nachgeburt' and 'Glückshaube' in *'Handwörterbuch des deutschen Aberglaubens*; T.R. Forbes, 'The Social History of the Caul,' *The Yale Journal of Biology and Medicine*, 25 (1953), 495–508, with full bibliography.

37 S. Bernardino da Siena, *Opera omnia* (Florence, 1950) I, 116. See also T. Zachariae, 'Abergläubische Meinungen und Gebräuche des Mittelalters in den Predigten Bernardinos von Siena', *Zeitschrift des Vereins für Volkskunde*, 22 (1912) pp. 234–5.

38 The testimony offered before the Venetian Inquisition on 17 May 1591 by the Capuchin Fra Pietro Veneto, ruler of the monastery of Santa Caterina di Roveredo, probably reflects, somewhat imprecisely, beliefs concerning the benandanti (he had just preached in Latisana and had heard confessions from women suspected of witchcraft): 'and it's the opinion of some, that people born with the caul are compelled to go to the sabbat' (ASV, *S. Uffizio*, b. 68, trials of Latisana). For their survival in Friulian folklore, see E. Fabris Bellavitis in the *Giornale di Udine e del Veneto Orientale* a. 24, 2 August 1890 and V. Ostermann, *La vita in Friuli*, II, pp. 298–9. For survivals in Istria, see R.M. Cossar, 'Usanze, riti e superstizioni del popolo di Montona nell' Istria', *Il Folklore italiano*, 9 (1934) p. 62 ('Concerning the origin of witches, the old Istrian saying tells us: "the witch was born with the caul" '); and by the same author, 'Tradizioni popolari di Momiano d'Istria', *Archivio per la raccolta e lo studio delle tradizioni popolari italiane*, 15 (1940) p. 179 (where the *'Cheznichi'* are discussed, who correspond, as we shall see, to the benandanti). For similar beliefs in Romagna (whoever is born with the 'veil' draws all the evils) see M. Placucci, in the *Archivio per lo studio delle tradizioni popolari*, 3 (1884) p. 325 and L. De Nardis in *Il Folklore italiano*, 4 (1929) p. 175.

38 ASM, *Inquisizione* b. 2, libro 5, f. 46 v.

39 A. Tostado, *Super Genesim Commentaria* (Venice, 1507), f. 125 r (passage noted by J. Hansen, *Quellen*, p. 109 n; in *Zauberwahn*, p. 305, the same author underscores how Tostado's commentary to the famous *Canon Episcopi* was instead intended to sustain the *reality* of the diabolical sabbat). Even the most convinced believers in the physical flight of witches and in the reality of the sabbat did not fail to note the gravity of facts analogous to those cited, and sought to introduce them forcefully in their interpretative scheme, supposing the direct intervention of the devil who on these occasions substituted himself for the witch. See, for example, B. Spina, *Quaestio*, p. 85.

40 On Della Porta's experiment, see most recently G. Bonomo, *Caccia alle streghe* (Palermo, 1959), pp. 393–7. In that same period a similar experiment was carried out by the Spanish physician Andres a Laguna, who described it in a commentary upon Dioscorides published at Antwerp in 1555: see H. Friedenwald, 'Andres a Laguna, a pioneer in his views on witchcraft', *Bulletin of the History of Medicine*, 7 (1939) pp. 1037–48. In modern times the effects of the magical ointments were tried on themselves by the physician O. Snell (*Hexenprozesse und Geistesstörung. Psychiatrische Untersuchungen* [Munich, 1891] pp. 80–1) and the folklorist W.E. Peuckert (see J. Dahl, *Nachtfranen und Gastelweiber. Eine Naturgeschichte der Hexe* [Ebenhausen bei München, 1960], p. 26). The results were anything but decisive: Snell, convinced that the witches' accounts were due to hysteria or mental disorders, got a simple headache out of the ointment; Peuckert, a champion of the reality of the sabbat and of the nocturnal reunions, experienced, instead, according to him, hallucinations that resembled perfectly those described in witchcraft trials.

41 ASV, *S. Uffizio*, b. 68 (trials of Latisana). See also above, p. 76.

42. ACAU, *S. Uffizio*, 'Ab anno 1621 . . . ,' trial n. 832, unnumbered leaves.

43 I am pleased to thank A. Frugoni for this interpretation of the passage cited.

44 ASV, *S. Uffizio*, b. 72 (Maria Panzona), ff. 38 r, 46 r. See also above, pp. 103, 105. As far as witches are concerned, cases in which epilepsy has been verified are rare. Extremely significant evidence is found in a Lucchese trial of 1571. About the accused, Polissena of San Macario (later burned as a witch), a witness testifies that one day 'standing by a bed, she let herself fall backward, and remained extended and immobile on the bed, so that she appeared to be dead; and the women who were around her thinking some accident had befallen her applied vinegar to her, and my mother, who had received a recipe from me for making vapours under the noses of people who have fainted, so that if they are not dead they revive, seeing that that woman was not coming to, made the vapour by burning a piece of a man's shirt before her, just as I had told her . . . and when this was done Polissena opened her eyes and began to make an ugly noise like a bellowing so loudly and with her eyes convulsed, that everybody fled out of fear and left her alone, *because we suspected she was a witch* . . . my mother told me that the next day Polissena said to her: "When I am in the state that I was in last night don't bother with me, because you do me more harm than good." ' And another witness confirmed: 'Polissena used to tell me that *she* succumbed to the *malvitio* [that is epilepsy]' (ASL, *Cause Delegate*, n. 175, ff. 190 v-8 r-v; the leaves of the trial succeed each other without order. The italics are mine). F. Riegler (*Hexenprozesse, mit besonderer Berücksichtigung des Landes Steiermark* [Graz, 1926] pp. 58–9) supposes affected by epilepsy, an old woman of Feldbach who, in the course of a witchcraft trial (1673–5), is revealed to have been a victim of sudden prostrations, remaining unconscious for long stretches. But her falling once occurred during the Ember Days: this evidence, perhaps, should be joined to others that document the diffusion in German areas of the beliefs we are examining here (See Chapter II). On the question, see, despite its general qualities, S.R. Burstein, 'Aspects of the Psychopathology of Old Age Revealed in Witchcraft Cases of the

Sixteenth and Seventeenth Centuries', *The British Medical Bulletin*, 6 (1949) pp. 63–72.

45 For a similar interpretation of a phenomenon of this type, see E. De Martino, *La terra del rimorso* (Milan, 1961) pp. 43–58. The present investigation owes a great deal to De Martino's works, especially his *Il mondo magico*.

11

46 ASL, *Cause Delegate*, n. 175, f. 215 r. The italics are mine.

47 *Ibid.*, f. 224 r. The italics are mine.

48 On judicial torture, see P. Fiorelli, *La tortura giudiziaria nel diritto comune*, 2 vols, (Milan, 1953–4). On witchcraft trials, see especially II, pp. 228–34.

49 ASL, *Cause Delegate*, n. 175, f. 196 r, see also f. 226 r. For similar beliefs in the Balkan peninsula, see F.S. Krauss, *Volksglaube und religiöser Brauch der Südslaven* (Münster i. w., 1890) p. 112.

50 ASL, *Cause Delegate*, n. 175, f. 196 r.

51 ACAU, *S. Uffizio*, 'Ab anno 1574 . . .', trial n. 64, f. 3 v.

52 ASL, *Cause Delegate*, n. 25, f. 176 v. A section of this trial, but not the passages cited here, has been published, with a few errors in transcription by L. Fumi, 'Usi e costumi lucchesi', *Atti della R. Accademia Lucchese*, 33 (1907) pp. 3–152.

53 ACAU, *S. Uffizio*, 'Ab anno 1574 . . .', trial n. 64. f. 9 v. A little later Gasparutto's wife added: 'I heard from Pietro Rotaro who used to be a miller, that one day in his mill he saw a person who might have been Paolo my husband. He was like a dead man, and he did not wake even when he was turned over and over, and a little later he saw a mouse circling his body' (*Ibid.*).

54 See W. Mannhardt, *Wald – und Feldkulte*, 2nd ed. by W. Heuschkel, vol. I, *Der Baumkultus der Germanen und ihrer Nachbarstämme. Mythologische Untersuchungen* (Berlin, 1904) p. 24. For a similar belief in Hesse, see K.H. Spielmann, *Die Hexenprozesse in Kurhessen*, 2nd ed., (Marburg, 1932) pp. 47–8. In a Modenese trial of 1599 in which a certain Polissena Canobbio was accused of witchcraft, her going to the sabbat was described thusly: 'the aforesaid *madonna* Polissena . . . undressed and oiled herself . . . dressed herself again, lay down her full length face up, and instantly it was as if she was dead . . . a little more than a quarter of an hour later all three of us saw a tiny mouse approach the body of the above mentioned *madonna* Polissena, saw her open her mouth and the mouse enter her mouth, and we also saw her immediately come to life and raise herself, laughing and saying that she had been in the servant's room . . .' (ASM, *Inquisizione*, b. 8, trial against Claudia of Correggio, unnumbered leaves). Subsequently, the accuser, Claudia of Correggio, confessed that she had made up everything to revenge herself on Polissena, her former mistress: nevertheless, the deposition, since it documents the most common notions of the period regarding witchcraft, retains all its interest. In general, see also J. Frazer, *The Golden Bough; a Study in Magic and Religion*, 3rd ed., 12 vols, (London, 1911–15; Italian translation, *Il ramo d'Oro* [Rome, 1925], I, 305).

55 ACAU, *S. Uffizio*, 'Anno eodem 1648 completo a numero eodem 27 usque ad 40', trial n. 28 *bis*.

56 ACAU, *S. Uffizio*, 'Ab anno 1621 . . .', trial n. 832.

57 See Giberti's *Breve ricordo*, recently republished and commented by A. Prosperi, 'Note in margine a un opuscolo di Gian Matteo Giberti', *Critica Storica*, 4 (1965) esp. p. 394: 'Let them [priests] take note that in their parishes there be no excommunicated, usurers, keepers of concubines, gamblers, rebels, blasphemers, sorcerers, or superstitious, such as, for example those who lay the invalid on the ground so that he may die more quickly, and those who remove the roof so that the soul may exit, as if the soul could be kept in by the roof, which is madness and faithlessness to believe.'

The same condemnation is found in a booklet printed in 1673 by a canon of Toulouse (*Mélusine*, I [1878], coll. 526, 528.)

12

58 ASM, *Inquisizione*, b. 2, libro 5, f. 93 v.

59 The principal texts that deal with it (which go to the beginning of the sixteenth century) have been collected or cited by J. Hansen, in *Quellen*, and analysed in *Zauberwahn*. For the following period, with special reference to Italy, see G. Bonomo, *Caccia alle streghe* (most inadequate)

60 See M. Del Rio, *Disquisitionum*, p. 551: 'Ipsae quoque striges cum idem quod dicunt in Hispania, dicant in Italia, et quod in Germania, totidem factis, et verbis referunt in Gallia, et quod uno anno, id alio semper iam ab annis plusquam octoginta continuis in eculeo, et extra quaestiones libere profiteantur, idque tam apposite, ut mulierculae, et pueri litterarum alioquin rudes videantur legisse, intellexisse, et memoriae mandasse, quaecumque viri docti de his rebus scripto per Europam totam variis linguis tradiderunt, nonne hic consensus universalis plus satis convincit haec iis non accidisse in somniis? nam si haec somniarunt, quo pacto sic semper omnes idem somniarunt eodem sibi evenisse modo, eodem loco, eodem tempore, die, hora? Ut medici docent ciborum quantitas et qualitas, diversa aetas, et varia corporis humorum temperatio generant diversa somnia, hic idem somniant omnino, divites splendidi, et Iro pauperiores egentioresque, famelici, et dapsiliter habiti: viri feminaeque, anus et pueri, biliosi et flegmatici, sanguinei et melancholici. Ergone omnes istos tam diversae aetatis, nationis, conditionis, tempore alio atque alio, simili semper ciborum usos quantitate, et qualitate, aequali temperamento corporum fuisse dicent, quia eadem semper somnia fuerunt?'

61 See Samuel de Cassinis, *Question de le strie* (1505), republished in J. Hansen, *Quellen*, p. 270. Regarding Alciato, see *Parergon iuris*, 1. 8, f. 22, cited by J. Hansen, *Quellen*, pp. 310–12. On the *Canon Episcopi*, see Hansen's *Zauberwahn*, pp. 78ff.

13

62 ACAU, *S. Uffizio*, 'Ab anno 1574 . . .', trial n. 64, f. 9 v: 'Cum prius in principio per aliquantulum ploraret et fleret lacrimas autem numquam visa est emittere.' On this point, see, for example, ASM, *Inquisizione*, b. 8, trial against Grana of Villa Marzana, interrogation of 7 May 1601. unnumbered leaves; ASL, *Cause Delegate*, n. 29, f. 40 v (year 1605).

63 See R. Pettazzoni, *Le superstizioni. Relazione tenuta al Primo Congresso di etnografia italiana* (Rome, 1911), p. 11 of the reprint.

64 That the isolation of many villages of the Friuli abetted the persistence of superstitious practices, as well as the spread of witchery and diabolical possessions, was lamented by representatives of two comunes in the Carnia, Ligosullo and Tausia, to Monsignor Carlo Francesco Airoldo, archbishop of Edessa, an apostolic nuncio to the Venetian Republic. The late date of the document (15 August 1674) renders it even more significant. Many possessed women had been found at Ligosullo, and the village was in an uproar. But there was nothing surprising about it: Ligosullo 'situated 4 miles, along a difficult road, from the Church of S. Daniele above the Villa di Paluzza, with steep hills, stretches of water, which with any hard rain become uncrossable, especially in winter, since the Villa is high in the mountains, where the snow falls to inordinate depths, and for 6 months prevents going to Holy Mass and divine services, not only to children and the decrepit, but also robust people; and also those without money have to pass up making the journey because, by the time

the devotions are over it is noon, and the people, exhausted, can not start home without taking nourishment. Thus, because of these obstacles the young people grow up deprived of Christian doctrine, and there are some older folk who do not know the Lord's Prayer, and occasionally some die without receiving the last rites of the Church.' Diabolical possession entered into this miserable situation: 'Our Common Enemy soon found the way to take possession of those bodies . . .' (L. Da Pozzo, 'Due documenti inediti del 1674 riferentisi a casi di stregoneria,' *Pagine friulane*, 15 [1903], n. 11, pp. 163–4).

65 The origin of the Ember Days in the Roman agriculture calendar (*Feriae messis* in June, *vindemiales* in September, *sementiciae* in December) has been argued by G. Morin, 'L'origine des Quatre-Temps', *Revue Bénédictine*, 14 (1897) pp. 337–46. This hypothesis is not accepted by L. Fischer, *Die Kirchlichen Quatember. Ihre Enstehung, Entwicklung, und Bedeutung* (Munich, 1914), see especially, pp. 24–42. For the beliefs associated with the Ember Days, see J. Baur, 'Quatember in Kirche and Volk', *Der Schlern*, 26 (1952) pp. 223–33.

66 That the Ember Days were connected to fertility in the popular mind emerges from a passage in a sermon, attributed to Abraham a Sancta Clara (*Der Narrenspiegel* [*Centifolium stultorum von Abraham a Sancta Clara, neu herausgegeben mit 46 abbildungen aus der Nurnberger ausgabe von 1709 durch . . . Karl Bertsche*, [M. Gladbach, 1925] pp. 25–6). E von Schwartz ('Die Fronleichnamsfeier in den Ofner Bergen [Ungarn]', *Zeitschrift für Volkskunde*, n.s., 2 [1931] pp. 45–6) observes that in south Germany processions intended to secure prosperous harvests from God take place during the Ember Days. See also J. Baur, 'Quatember', p. 230.

67 See, V. Ostermann, *La vita in Friuli*, I, p. 129.

68 See, F. di Manzano, *Annali del Friuli, ossia raccolta delle cose storiche appartenenti a questa regione* (Udine, 1879), VII, pp. 177–8. cf. also A. Battistella, *Udine nel secolo XVI* (Udine, 1932) p. 267.

69 ACAU, 'Sententiarum . . . liber primus', f. 95 r. ('Domestics' could naturally also signify family members). Ostermann found traces in the Friuli of the belief that witches can be injured simply by striking them with branches of viburnum (*paugne*): 'Usancis e superstizions del popul furlan', *Società Alpina Friulana, Cronaca del 1885–86, anno V and VI*, (Udine, 1888) p. 125, also partially cited in *Il Nuovo Pirona*, article 'paugne'. For the same belief in the area of Belluno, see G. Bastanzi, *Le superstizioni delle Alpi venete* (Treviso, 1888) p. 14, n. 1 (based on a study by A. Cibele Nardo on the superstitions in the zones of Belluno and Cadore).

70 ACAU, 'Sententiarum contra reos S. Officii liber tertius', f. 133 v. For Pellizzaro's trial, see ACAU, *S. Uffizio*, 'Ab anno 1593 usque ad annum 1594 incl. a n. 226 usque ad 249 incl.', trial n. 228. A Sicilian proverb with a sense similar to the statement cited ('Manure works more miracles than saints') was copied by Nietzsche in a note book (see 'Aurora e frammenti postumi [1879–1881]', in *Opere*, ed. Colli-Montinari, (Milan, 1864) V^1, 468. After all, it was only a blasphemous common-place. See an English example from 1655 cited in *The Oxford English Dictionary*, I, 533 (under 'atheistically').

71 ACAU, *S. Uffizio*, 'Ab anno 1574 . . .', trial n. 64, f. 1 v. The belief was still in existence at the beginning of this century among Slovenian peasants that staffs, used as weapons by witches, had to be buried to prevent the latter from fighting with the *Kerstniki* (individuals corresponding to the Friulian benandanti): see F.S. Krauss, *Slavische Volkforschungen* (Leipzig, 1908) pp. 41–2.

72 ACAU, *S. Uffizio*, 'Ab anno 1574 . . .', trial n. 64, f. 6 r. For the use of fennel in Friulian popular medicine, see V. Ostermann, *Là vita in Friuli*, I, p. 149. Fennel was employed against spells in eastern Prussia (see A. Wuttke, *Der deutsche Volksaberglaube der Gegenwart*, 3rd rev. ed. by E.H. Meyer [Berlin, 1900] pp. 101, 435). See also O. von Hovorka and A. Kronfeld, *Vergleichende Volksmedizin* (Stuttgart, 1908) I, pp. 132–3. For the same belief in Béarn, see H. Barthéty, *La sorcellerie en Béarn et dans le pays*

basque, (Pau, 1879) p. 62. In Lucca in the sixteenth century a healer used a brew composed of fennel and of rue to treat a person 'crushed by the dead', that is, victim of a spell: see ASL, *Cause Delegate*, n. 125, f. 170 v (for the expression 'crushed by the dead' ['pesta dai morti'] see Chapter II).

73 On the basis of the evidence offered in the benandanti trials we shall have to re-examine the complex problem of the relationship between witchcraft and secret youth associations (it should be noted that benandanti enter their 'company' – and the term itself is significant – at a precise age, corresponding approximately to the onset of virility, and abandon it after a set period; moreover, we should remember the military character of this sort of association, fitted out with a captain, etc.): on this question, see especially O. Höfler, *Kultische Geheimbünde der Germanen*, vol. I (Frankfort a. M., 1934); see also A. Runeberg, 'Witches, Demons and Fertility Magic', *Societas Scientiarum Fennica: Commentationes humanarum litterarum*, 14, 4, (Helsingfors, 1947) pp. 59 ff. J. Baur, in particular, ('Quatember', p. 228) recalls that in Bressanone various *Brüderschaften* met to march in procession on the Ember Days. We should note that the two elements cited recur, in varying measure but at any rate occasionally, in the witches' confessions. In these accounts it is frequently asserted that the initiation takes place at a youthful age: with a special twist the Lucchese witch Margherita of San Rocco declared that she had begun to go to the sabbat 'at age thirty, because before one cannot go' (ASL, *Cause Delegate*, n. 175, f. 195 v). Extremely rare, instead, are references to military style organization for witches and warlocks: they only seem to crop up with any frequency in Hungarian trials, in which mention is made of captains, corporals, and companies of witches, who go off to the conventicles to the sound of trumpets, carrying flags of black silk (see the anonymous article, 'Das Hexenwesen in Ungarn', *Das Ausland*. LII, n. 41, 13 October 1879, pp. 815–18, also cited by W. Schwartz, 'Zwei Hexengeschichten aus Waltershausen in 'Thüringen nebst einem mythologischen Excurs über Hexen-und ähnliche Versammlungen,' *Zeitschrift für Volkerpsychologie und Sprachwissenschaft*, 18 [1888] pp. 414–15; see also H. von Wlislocki, *Aus dem Volksleben der Magyaren. Ethnologischen Mitteilungen* [Munich, 1893], p. 112).

74 On the beating upon the sides and other parts of the body of a man or of an animal, conceived as fertility rite, see W. Mannhardt, *Wald-und Feldkulte*, I, pp. 251–303 ('Der Schlag mit der Lebensrute'), and especially pp. 548–52, on the feigned ritual battles designed to produce fertility. Mannhardt collected a great deal of evidence, most of it German, on the custom, at the beginning of spring or the end of winter, of beating men or animals with plants or tree branches, a rite which he interpreted as a chasing away of the malignant spirits hostile to vegetation. Later, this interpretation was refuted, and these beatings were seen as a magical rite intended to communicate to men and animals the powers of the tree used as a whip: see S. Reinach, *Cultes, mythes et religions* (Paris, 1905) I. pp. 173–83; G. Dumézil, *Le problème des Centaures* (Paris, 1929), pp. 217–18, etc.

75 We can suppose a rite similar to one practised by the Eskimo, as described by Frazer (*The Golden Bough*; Italian edition, II, p. 99): at the approach of winter, two ranks, respectively formed of people born in winter and in summer, conduct a test of strength. If the latter win, a good season can be hoped for (the significance of this evidence has frequently been stressed, for example by M.P. Nilsson, 'Die volkstümlichen Feste des Jahres', *Religionsgeschichtliche Volksbücher für die deutsche christliche Gegenwart* (Tübingen, 1914), ser. 3, fasc. 17–18, 29. Needless to say, for our problem a rapprochement of this type proves nothing.

76 See W. Liungman, 'Der Kampf zwischen Sommer und Winter', *Academia Scientiarum Fennica, FF Communications*, n. 130 (Helsinki, 1941) (with rich documentation). Liungman supposes ancient origins for the rite (no less than the battles between the Mesopotamian divinities, Tiamat and Marduk); of a different opinion is W. Lynge, 'Die Grundlagen des Sommer – und Winterstreitspieles', *Oesterreichische Zeitschrift*

für Volkskunde, 51 (1948), fasc. 1–2, 113–46.

77 Frazer connected these rites to the 'spirit of vegetation' postulated by Mannhardt (see *The Golden Bough*; Italian ed., II, pp. 96–7).

78 An exception to this is the variant practised on the Isle of Man, in which the battle between the Queen of May and the Queen of Winter is a real struggle, and the conclusion not foregone (see W. Liungman 'Der Kampf,' pp. 70–1). Also of interest is the evidence discovered by E. Hoffmann-Krayer ('Fruchtbarkeitsriten im schweizerischen Volksbrauch', in *Kleine Schriften zur Volkskunde*, ed. P. Geiger [Basel, 1946] p. 166): in certain Swiss areas the ceremony of the driving away of Winter, which takes place on the first of March and includes a ritual battle between two formations of youths, is performed 'to make the grass grow' – an embryonically magical element in which a residue of more ancient rites is perhaps to be seen.

79 'This year would have been one of great shortages and the poor would have starved if divine providence had not opened the granaries of Germany, from which so much wheat, rye, barley and corn flowed that it sufficed to fill up the hungry. It is reported, however, that two women from a village below Udine were found dead from hunger with their mouths stuffed with wild grasses' (Cristoforo di Prampero, *Cronaca del Friuli dal 1615 al 1631* [Udine, 1884] [per nozze Marangoni – Masolini – Micoli], pp. 26–7 [year 1618]). Reading Friulian chronicles of the period we continually encounter similar declarations, which eloquently describe the precarious, in fact, miserable conditions of the peasants of the zone. See also the deliberations of the Great Council of Udine, in which the threat of famine is constantly present (BCU, *Annalium libri*, Ms.). A Battistella (*Udine*, p. 302) refers to an interesting piece of evidence from the late sixteenth century.

14

80 We do not possess a satisfactory study on youth associations in Italy. See, with extreme caution, the muddled and amateurish hotchpotch by G.C. Pola Falletti di Villafalletto, *Associazioni giovanili e feste antiche. Loro origini*, 4 vols, (Milan, 1939–43).

15

81 ACAU, *S. Uffizio*, 'Ab anno 1574 . . .,' trial n. 64, ff. 10 v, 6 r.

82 *Ibid.*, ff. 11 v, 12 v.

83 I use Modena for purposes of comparison because of the wealth of inquisitorial material preserved in that archive. Unfortunately, as is well known, the runs of inquisitorial trials available in Italian archives are very few.

84 See E. Verga, 'Intorno a due inediti documenti di stregheria milanese del secolo XIV', *Rendiconti del R. Istituto lombardo di scienze e lettere*, ser. II, 32 (1899) pp. 165–88, and G. Bonomo, *Caccia*, passim.

85 ASM, *Inquisizione*, b. 2, libro 3, f. 14 v.

86 *Ibid.*, libro 5, ff. 44 r – 46 v, Domenica Barbarelli of Novi, tried in 1532, declared that she went *'ad cursum Diane'*, where she profaned the cross and danced with devils, at the order of the *'domina ludi'*; *ibid.*, ff. 87 v – 89 r, Orsolina la Rossa, of Gaiato, tried in 1539, confessed under torture having gone to the sabbat where she renounced her faith and baptism and saw, besides men and women absorbed in dancing and feasting, *'quedam mulier'* – undoubtedly the *'domina ludi'* – who commanded her to eat nothing if she wanted to remain.

87 On this point I should like to defer the discussion to a forthcoming work. Here I have suppressed a passage in the original edition which referred briefly to the Toulouse trials of 1335; N. Cohn has demonstrated brilliantly that, in fact, they were nothing

but nineteenth-century forgeries (*Europe's Inner Demons: An Enquiry Inspired by the Great Witchhunt* [London, 1975] pp. 126–38).

16

88 See H. von Bruiningk, 'Der Werwolf in Livland and das letzte im Wendeschen Landgericht und Dörptschen Hofgericht i. J. 1692 deshalb stattgehabte Strafverfahren,' *Mitteilungen aus der livländischen Geschichte*, 22 (1924), 163–220. The credit for having brought this document, appearing in such an out-of-the-way organ, into the light of day, belongs to O. Höfler who reprinted it in part, with commentary, in the appendix to *Kultische Geheimbünde*, pp. 345–57.

89 O. Höfler (*Kultische Geheimbünde*, p. 352), in addition to recalling, a propos this trial, the ritual battles between Winter and Spring (see above, pp. 24–5), inserts the beliefs documented there into the mythical-cultic complex of Balder – Attis – Demeter – Persephone – Adonis. For the interpretation in an archetypal key of the 'ritual battles' between Summer and Winter, see M. Eliade, *Patterns in Comparative Religion* (Cleveland & New York, 1970) pp. 319 ff., who accepts Liungman's conclusions in this regard.

90 The observation is by von Bruiningk, in the introduction to the document, p. 190. He observes that the details in the account of the old man appear in no other source known to him (*Der Werwolf in Livland*, pp. 190–1).

91 C. Peucer, *Commentarius de praecipuis generibus divinationum* (Wittenberg, 1580), ff. 133 v – 134 r. This passage had already been cited by Von Bruiningk. One should note that Peucer introduces his discussion of the problem of the werewolves in a section devoted to 'ecstatics' (about whom, see above, pp. 40–1).

II THE PROCESSIONS OF THE DEAD

1

1 ACAU, *S. Uffizio*, 'Ab anno 1581 usque ad annum 1582: incl. a n. 93 ad 106 incl.', trial n. 98, f. 1 v.

2 *Ibid.*, f. 2 r.

3 *Ibid.*, ff. 3 r–v.

4 *Ibid.*, f. 4 r.

5 *Ibid.*, f. 5 r.

6 *Ibid.*, ff. 7 r–v.

7 In trial n. 64, in response to a question from the inquisitor, Moduco had said: 'There are no women among us, but it is true that there are women benandanti, and women go against women' (f. 6 r; see above, p. 154).

8 See above, p. 180, n. 44.

9 ACAU, *S. Uffizio*, Ab anno 1581 . . .', trial n. 98, ff. 5 r – 6 r. In 1582, Easter fell on 15 April.

10 *Ibid.*, unnumbered leaf.

11 *Ibid.*, f. 6 r.

2

12 ACAU, *S. Uffizio*, 'Ab anno 1581 . . .', trial n. 100, unnumbered leaves. For mention of Aquilina's activity, see the trial against Moduco and Gasparutto, ff. 1 r, 3 v.

13 *Ibid.*, ff. 2 r–v, 3 v.

14 *Ibid.*, ff. 7 r–v, 10 v.
15 *Ibid.*, ff. 14 r–v.

3

16 ACAU, *S. Uffizio*, 'Ab anno 1581 . . .', trial n. 106, f. 1 r.
17 *Ibid.*, ff. 2 r–v.
18 ASL, *Cause Delegate*, n. 175, f. 215 r.
19 ACAU, *S. Uffizio*, 'Ab anno 1574 . . .', trial n. 64, ff. 5 v, 9 r.

4

20 See *Reginonis abbatis Prumiensis libri duo de synodalibus causis et disciplinis ecclesiasticis*, ed. F.G.A. Wasserschleben (Leipzig, 1840) p. 355. The work was written in 906, or slightly later (*Ibid.*, p. VIII).
21 See, on the entire problem, 'Perchta', in the *Handwörterbuch des deutschen Aberglaubens*; J. Grimm, *Deutsche Mythologie*, 4 th ed., by E.H. Meyer (Berlin, 1875), I, pp. 220 ff.; II, pp. 765 ff.; V. Waschnitius, 'Perth, Holda und verwandte Gestalten. Ein Beitrag zur deutschen Religionsgeschichte', in *Sitzungsberichte der Kaiserlichen Akademie der Wissenschaften in Wien, Philosophisch-Historische Klasse*, vol. 174, dissertation 2 (Vienna, 1914) (with full bibliography); O. Höfler, *Kultische Geheimbünde*; W. Liungman, 'Traditionswanderungen: Euphrat – Rhein: Studien zur Geschichte der Volksbräuche', II, *Academia Scientiarum Fennica, FF Communications*, n. 19 (Helsinki, 1938) pp. 569–704; W.E. Peuckert, *Deutscher Volksglaube des Spätmittelalters* (Stuttgart, 1942) pp. 86–96 (somewhat hasty discussion, arguable on some points); L. Kretzenbacher, *'Berchten* in der Hochdichtung', *Zeitschrift für Volkskunde*, 54 (1958) pp. 186–7 (adds to the bibliography in Waschnitius).
22 There is a disagreement among scholars about the relationship between Diana and Perchta-Holda. Among those who adhere to the hypothesis of the *interpretatio romana* is A. Runeberg, 'Witches, Demons', p. 18. Liungman, ('Traditionswanderungen', II, pp. 694–6) supposes confusedly that the Graeco-Roman tradition of Diana-Hecate was preserved in Illyria, later to be diffused in the Germanic world by the Baiuwarii (Bavarians) after the seventh century. This second hypothesis (which seems to have slight basis) is accepted, among others, by W.E. Peuckert, *Geheimkulte*, p. 272 and R. Bernheimer, *Wild Men in the Middle Ages* (Cambridge, Mass., 1952) pp. 79–80, 132.
23 Guillaume d' Auvergne, *Opera Omnia*, (Paris, 1674), I, p. 1036. See also the similar references at pp. 948, 1066.
24 Guillaume de Lorris and Jean de Meun, *Le Roman de la Rose*, ed. E. Langlois (Paris, 1922), IV, vv. 18425–60. Langlois ('Origines et sources du Roman de la Rose', *Bibliothèque des Ecoles d' Athènes et de Rome*, fasc. 58, [Paris, 1891] p. 167) interprets the expression 'li tiers enfant de nacion' as 'le tiers du monde'. Correctly, instead, A. Mary offers this translation in her modern French version of the *Roman de la Rose* (Paris, 1928) p, 314: 'ils recontent que les troisièmes enfants ont cette faculté' [of going out with dame Abonde].' F.S. Krauss (*Slavische Volkforschungen*, p. 42) observes that Slovenes have the belief that the last of twelve brothers is a *Kerstnik* – that is, translated into Friulian, a benandante. See also the magical properties popularly attributed to seventh sons (M. Bloch, *Les rois thaumaturges* [Strasbourg, 1924] pp. 293 ff.).
25 ACAU, *S. Uffizio*, 'Ab anno 1574 . . .', trial n. 64, ff. 1 v, 11 r. For a recurrence of the same theme, see the 'Errores Gazariorum, seu illorum, qui scobam, vel baculum equitare probantur' (Savoy, ca. 1450), cited by J. Hansen, *Quellen*, p. 119; M. Sanuto,

I diarii (Venice, 1889), XXV, col. 642.

26 ACAU, *S. Uffizio*, 'Ab anno 1581 . . .', trial n. 98.

27 For the Friuli, see R.M. Cossàr, in *Ce Fastu?* 5(1929), 14; M. Romàn Ros, *Ibid.*, 16 (1940) pp. 222–3; 17 (1941) p. 44; P. Memis, *Ibid*, pp. 61–4; for the Biellese area and Sardinia, see V. Maioli Faccio, *Lares*, 22 (1956) pp. 202–5; for the Abruzzi, see G. Finamore, *Credenze, usi e costumi abruzzesi* (Palermo, 1890) pp. 181–2; for French evidence (Neuville-Chant-d'Oisel), see F. Baudry, *Mélusine*, 1 (1878), col. 14; etc., etc. In the Tyrol, food was left for the dead during the Ember Days: see J. Baur, 'Quatember', p. 232. Very superficial is the attempt at a general interpretation by G. Bellucci, 'Sul bisogno di dissetarsi attribuito ai morti ed al loro spirito', *Archivio per l'antropologia e la Etnologia*, 39 (1909), fasc. 3–4, 213–29.

28 ACAU, *S. Uffizio*, 'Ab anno 1574 . . .', trial n. 64, f. 9 v; for Lucchese evidence, see above, p. 19.

29 ASCM, *Sentenze del podestà*, vol. II (Cimeli, n. 147), f. 53 r: 'illa domina [Diana] cum sotietate vadunt per diversas domos diversarum personarum et maxime divitum, et ibi comedunt et bibunt et multum letantur quando inveniunt domos bene spaciatas et ordinatas, et tunc dat illa domina benedictiones dicte domui' (trial of Pierina de' Bugatis, 1390). This trial, and another slightly posterior which resembles it, was published and summarized by E. Verga, in 'Intorno a due inediti documenti'.

30 See V. Waschnitius, 'Perht', pp. 62–3 and A.E. Schönbach, 'Zeugnisse zur deutschen Volkskunde des Mittelalters', *Zeitschrift des Vereins für Volkskunde*, 12 (1902) pp. 5–6. In Italy, as we know, Perchta became the *Befana* (Epiphany), represented as a witch mounted on a broom, who leaves gifts of sweets or coal to children: See W. Liungman, 'Traditionswanderungen', II, pp. 673–4.

5

31 Waschnitius ('Perht', p. 62), observes, in underlining the similarities between these figures, that the connections and relations of dependence among them are not clear (and see also W.E. Peuckert, *Geheimkulte*, pp. 277–8). But from our point of view what counts is the fact that from the fifteenth century on they were felt as interchangeable (to the examples mentioned we can add one cited by W. Liungman, 'Traditionswanderungen', II, p. 658).

32 See J. Nider, *Praeceptorium divinae legis* (Basel, 1481), preceptum I, ch. X and XI (q.X). References to these passages are made by Martin d'Arles, *Tractatus de superstitionibus* (Rome, 1559) p. 10. Even the mention by B. Basin, canon of Saragossa, to 'quibusdam vetulis, quae se in raptu dicunt videre animas purgatorii, et plura alia, ut furta et res perditas: quarum pedes pro tunc adusti non sentiunt ignem' ('De artibus magicis ac magorum maleficiis', in *Malleus maleficarum, maleficas et earum haeresim framea conterens, ex variis Auctoribus compilatus* [Lyons, 1669], II[1], 10) is lifted bodily from Nider, who is not even cited.

33 Matthias von Kemnat, 'Chronik Fiedrich I des Siegreichen', ed. C. Hofmann, in *Quellen und Erörterungen zur bayerischen und deutschen Geschichte* (Munich, 1862), II, pp. 117–18. The passage is used also by S. Riezler, *Geschichte der Hexenprozesse in Bayern*, pp. 73–5, who underscores the importance of the distinction between the two types of witchcraft, one presumably more ancient, the other more recent, and he supposes that the second was diffused through the stimulus of the inquisitors.

34 See Jacopo da Varazze [Jacopo da Voragine], *Legenda aurea vulgo historia Lombardica dicta*, rec. Th. Graesse, 2nd ed., (Leipzig, 1850) p. 449.

35 J. Schacher von Inwil, *Das Hexenwesen im Kanton Luzern nach den Prozessen von Luzern und Sursee (1400–1675)* (Lucerne, 1947) p. 16; L. Rapp, *Die Hexenprozesse und ihre Gegner aus Tirol* (Innsbruck, 1874) pp. 147, 154, 159, 162; A. Panizza 'I processi contro le streghe nel Trentino', *Archivio Trentino*, 7 (1888) pp. 208–9, 212–14, 224, etc. See

also F. Röder von Diersburg, 'Verhöre und Verurtheilung in einem Hexenprozesse zu Tiersperg im Jahre 1486', *Mittheilungen aus dem Freiherrl. v. Röder'schen Archive* [n.p., n.d.] pp. 96, 98; W. Krämer, *Kurtrierische Hexenprozesse im 16. und 17. Jahrhundert vornehmlich an der unteren Mosel* (Munich, 1959) pp. 16–17, 31–2.

6

36 *Die Emeis, Dis ist das Büch von der Omeissen . . . von dem Hochgelerten doctor Ioannes Geiler von Kaisersperg* (Strasbourg, 1516) ff. XLII v- XLIII r. The passages from Geiler concerning popular superstitions have been collected and annotated in *Zur Geschichte des Volks-Aberglaubens im Anfange des XVI. Jahrhunderts. Aus der Emeis von Dr. Joh. Geiler von Kaisersberg*, ed. A. Stöbwer, 2nd ed., (Basel, 1875).

37 *Die Emeis*, f. XXXVII r. The passage is also cited by O. Höfler, *Kultische Geheimbünde*, pp. 19–20.

38 ACAU, *S. Uffizio*, 'Ab anno 1574 . . .,' trial n. 64, f. 7 r.

39 The anonymous illustrator of the *Emeis* borrowed engravings from other texts in other cases too and especially from the Virgil edited by Brant (*Publii Virgilii Maronis opera cum quinque vulgatis commentariis: expolitissimisque figuris atque imaginibus nuper per Sebastianum Brant superadditis* [Strasbourg, 1502]). They involve extremely general representations (see, for example, the bucolic scene at f. VIII r, taken from the Virgil of Brant, f. XXXXI r), or engravings from which all specific allusions had been eliminated; thus, in the frontispiece of *Her der Künig* (another work of Geiler's published with the *Emeis*), it too taken from Brant's Virgil, f. CCCLXXVIII r, the names of Drances, Latinus and Turnus, above the heads of the personages represented, have been removed, although incompletely. In addition, see also, by way of contrast, the assurance with which Geiler's illustrator went back to iconographic models which were traditional (or about to become such) to depict witches at the sabbat (f. XXXVI v), devils (f. LV v), werewolves (f. XLI r).

40 S. Brant, *Stultifera navis. Narragonice profectionis nunquam satis laudata navis*. Colophon: In . . . urbe Basiliensi 1497 kalendis Augusti (*Gesamtkatalog der Wiegendrucke*, 5061), f. CXLV r. The figure with the wagon-load of fools inserted for the first time in this edition (see also W. Weisbach, *Die Baseler Buchillustration des XV. Jahrhunderts* [Strasbourg, 1896] p. 55) served as model for an illustration in another work of Geiler's, *Navicula sive speculum fatuorum* (Strasbourg, 1510) (a collection of sermons on the theme of Brant's book). This illustration was used again in the second edition of the *Emeis*. The identification of the two images of the 'Furious Horde' was accomplished by L. Dacheux (*Les plus anciens écrits de Geiler de Kaysersberg*) [Colmar, 1882] pp. CXLVIII f.).

41 See instead, by way of contrast, the humanistic interpretation of the 'Furious Horde' in the so-called 'sabbat' attributed to Agostino Veneziano, or to an artist in the circle of Marc' Antonio Raimondi: see E. Tietze-Conrat, 'Der *stregozzo* (Ein Deutungsversuch)', *Die Graphischen Künste*, n.s., 1 (1936) pp. 57–9.

7

42 For a comprehensive picture of the areas in which the 'Furious Horde' led by Perchta, Holda, etc., appeared during the Ember Days, see the chart prepared by W. Liungman, 'Traditionswanderungen,' II, pp. 632–3. This connection finds expression, frequently, in the names attributed popularly to the divinity which leads the host of the dead, the 'Furious Horde': in south Austria, in Carinthia, among the Slovenes, 'Quatembermann' (the man of the four Ember Days) or 'Kwaternik'; in Baden, in Swabia, in Switzerland, and with the Slovenes again, 'Frau Faste' (the lady

of the Ember Days) or similar names such as 'Posterli', 'Quatemberca', 'Fronfastenweiber', (see *Ibid.*). On 'Frau Faste' and 'Posterli', in particular, see E. Hoffmann-Krayer, 'Die Frau Faste', *Schweizerisches Archiv für Volkskunde*, 14 (1910) pp. 170–1; *Idem.*, 'Winterdämonen in der Schweiz', *Schweizer Volkskunde – Folk-Lore Suisse*, 1 (1911) pp. 89–95. For the Tyrol, see J. Thaler, 'Können auch in Tyrol Spuren vom Germanischen Heidenthume vorkommen?', *Zeitschrift für deutsche Mythologie und Sittenkunde*, 1 (1853) p. 292; I.V. Zingerle, 'Sagen aus Tirol', *Ibid.*, 2 (1855) p. 181; *Idem.*, *Sagen, Märchen und Gebräuche aus Tirol* (Innsbruck, 1859) pp. 8–9; J. Baur, 'Quatember', p. 231.

43 Ordericus Vitalis, *Historiae Ecclesiasticae libri tredecim*, ed. A. Le Prévost, 5 vols, (Paris, 1838–55), III, pp. 367–77. See now, *The Ecclesiastical History of Orderic Vitalis: edited and translated with introduction and notes by Marjorie Chibnall*, 6 vols, (Oxford, 1969–80).

44 For a different interpretation of the passage, see R. Bernheimer, *Wild Men*, pp. 78–9. Actually, even contemporaries discerned in the processions of the dead a myth which could be incorporated in a Christian framework and directed towards pious ends. This emerges clearly from a passage in Guillaume d' Auvergne, *Opera*, I, pp. 1065–70, in which the appearance of armies (a theme which unquestionably should be traced to the groups of dead described by Orderic Vitalis: see *Ibid.*, p. 948, and [Alfonso Spina] *Fortalicium fidei contra Iudeos, Saracenos, aliosque christiane fidei imimicos* [Nuremberg, 1494], f. CCLXXXIII r) are viewed not as the ranks of the souls of the unplacated dead, but rather as purged souls, whose wandering is ordained by God.

45 On this argument, see O. Driesen, *Der Ursprung des Harlekin. Ein Kultur-Geschichtliches Problem* (Berlin, 1904).

46 Ordericus Vitalis, *Historiae*, III, p. 367 n. 5.

47 ASM, *Inquisizione*, b 2, libro 3, f. 105 v, 109 v–110 r.

48 *Ibid.*, f. 106 r.

49 *Ibid.*, ff. 107 r, 106 r.

50 *Ibid.*, f. 107 v. Evidently, the gathering to discuss the crusade summoned thirty years earlier by Pius II to no avail, had left lively echoes in the popular mind.

51 *Ibid.*, f. 107 r–v.

52 *Ibid.*, ff. 106 v, 110 r.

8

53 I.V. Zingerle, 'Frau Saelde' *Germania, Vierteljahrschrift für deutsche Alterthumskunde*, 2 (1857) pp. 436–9. For scholars who have dealt with this trial, but from other points of view, see: L. Laistner, *Das Rätsel der Sphinx. Grundzüge einer Mythengeschichte* (Berlin, 1889), II, pp. 352–4 and V. Waschnitius, 'Perht', pp. 86–7. On Frau Selga, besides Laistner, *loc. cit.*, with bibliography, see W. Liungman, 'Traditionswanderungen', II, p. 670 (in Switzerland, 'Frau Saelde', called 'Frau Zälti' or 'Frau Selten', guides the procession of children who died before baptism, which goes forth, incidentally, on Wednesday night of the Ember Days of winter).

54 See, in addition to the already cited trial of Giuliano Verdena, W. Crecelius, 'Frau Holda und der Venusberg (aus hessischen Hexenprocessacten)', *Zeitschrift für deutsche Mythologie und Sittenkunde*, 1 (1853) p. 273 (on which, see above, pp. 56–7). The interpretation of the passage suggested by Laistner (*Das Rätsel*, II, p. 353) is mistaken.

9

55 On the *Seelenmutter* see A. Dettling, *Die Hexenprozesse im Kanton Schwyz* (Schwyz, 1907) pp. 16–22 (it reproduces the essential portion of an essay which I have not

been able to consult: T. von Liebenau, 'Die Seelenmutter zu Küssnacht und der starke Bopfahrt', which appeared in *Kath. – Schweizer Blätter*, 1899). Other references to the *Seelenmutter* are in A. Lütolf, *Sagen, Bräuche, Legenden aus den fünf Orten. Lucern, Uri, Schwyz, Unterwalden und Zug* (Lucerne, 1865), II. pp. 236–8 (on p. 236 she is called 'Hexenmutter') and in J. Schacher von Inwil, *Das Hexenwesen im Kanton Luzern*, pp. 75–6.

56 A. Dettling, *Die Hexenprozesse im Kanton Schwyz*, pp. 18–19.

57 R. Brandstetter, 'Die Wuotansage im alten Luzern', *Der Geschichtsfreund. Mitteilungen des historischen Vereins der fünf Orte*, 62 (1907) pp. 101–60, especially pp. 134–5, 137–8. Brandstetter, who uses principally the *Chronica Collectanea* (in manuscript) by R. Cysat (1545–1614), previously utilized by Lütolf (*Sagen, Bräuche*), criticizes the textual criteria of the latter (pp. 118–19).

58 See A. Lütolf, *Sagen, Bräuche*, II, p. 237. Beliefs that people born during the Ember Days could see spirits were widely diffused in this period. We find them mentioned and refuted as foolish ('merae nugae sunt') by L. Lavater, *De spectris, lemuribus et magnis atque insolitis fragoribus, variisque praesagitionibus quae plerunque obitum hominum, magnas clades, mutationesque Imperiorum praecedunt* (Geneva, 1575) p. 107. See also E. Hoffmann-Krayer, *Feste und Bräuche des Schweizervolkes*, new ed. by P. Geiger, (Zürich, 1940) p. 156; N. Curti, *Volksbrauch und Volksfrömmigkeit im katholischen Kirchenjahr* (Basel, 1947) p. 77; G. Gugitz, *Fest – und Brauchtums – Kalender für Oesterreich, Süddeutschland und die Schweiz*, (Vienna, 1955) p. 150. The same belief appears in the folklore of the Tyrol; see I.V. Zingerle, *Sitten, Bräuche und Meinungen des Tiroler Volkes*, 2nd enlarged ed., (Innsbruck, 1871) p. 3, paragraph 4; J. Baur, 'Quatember', p. 232.

59 See K. Hofmann, 'Oberstdorfer "Hexen" auf dem Schaiterhaufen', in *Oberstdorfer Gemeinde – und Fremdenblatt* (Oberstdorf, 1931), especially pp. 27–39 of the reprint. The editor was not aware of the importance of these documents and published them in an unsatisfactory manner. To the best of my knowledge they have not been analysed, or even cited by other scholars. On the 'nocturnal host' (*Nachtschar*) as synonymous with the 'Furious Horde', (*Wuotisheer*) testified to in ancient Swiss popular traditions, see W. Liungman, 'Traditionswanderungen', II, p. 670.

10

60 ASV, *S. Uffizio*, b. 72, f. 5 v. See above, pp. 99–106.

61 On Holda, see J. Grimm, *Deutsche Mythologie.*, I, pp. 220–5; V. Waschnitius, 'Perht'; W.E. Peuckert, *Deutschen Volksglaube*, pp. 100 ff. On the connection to fertility, see, for example, J. Grimm, *Deutsche Mythologie*, I, p. 222; O. von Reinsberg-Düringsfeld, *Das festliche Jahr, in Sitten, Gebräuchen, Aberglauben und Festen der Germanischen Völker*, 2nd ed., (Leipzig, 1898) p. 23; W. Junk, *Tannhäuser in Sage und Dichtung* (Munich, 1911) p. 10. On the various characteristics assumed by Holda with the passing of time, see E.A. List, 'Frau Holda as the Personification of Reason', *Philological Quarterly*, 32 (1953) pp. 446–8; *Idem.*, 'Holda and the Venusberg', *Journal of American Folklore*, 73 (1960) pp. 307 ff. On Venus as the learned equivalent of Holda, see W. Junk, *Tannhäuser*, p. 15. In general, on the associations between *Wild Heer* and fertility, see O. Höfler, *Kultische Geheimbünde*, pp. 286–96.

11

62 M. Crusius, *Annales Svevici sive chronica rerum gestarum antiquissimae et inclytae Svevicae gentis*, (Frankfort, 1596), II, pp. 653–4 (already partially cited by J. Janssen, *Geschichte des deutschen Volkes* (Freiburg i. Br., 1893), VI, 476, n. 4; F. Kluge [and G. Baist],

'Der Venusberg', *Beilagen Allgemeinen Zeitung*, nos 66–7, 23–24 March 1898, p. 6; P.S. Barto, *Tannhäuser and the Mountain of Venus: A Study in the Legend of the Germanic Paradise* (New York, 1916) pp. 30, 127, n. 29; O. Höfler, *Kultische Geheimbünde*, p. 240. Crusius (*Annales*, p. 654) declared that he took his account from G. Widman. There is no trace of it, however, in *Widman's Chronica*, ed. C. Kolb, (Stuttgart, 1904) [Geschichtsquellen der Stadt Hall, Zw. Bd., Württembergische Geschichtsquellen, sechster Bd.] It may be that the passage which interests us was part of Widman's *Murshardter Chronik*, written on the basis of local traditions, and now largely lost (see *Widman's Chronica*, pp. 33–4).

63 W.A. Scribonius (*De sagarum natura et potestate, deque his recte cognoscendis et puniendis physiologia* [Marburg, 1588] pp. 59 r-v, 61 r) writes about 'ecstatics', distinguishing them from witches. Vague as the following allusion in Scribonius may be (p. 61 r: the 'ecstatics' describe 'gaudio exulantes in coelis angelos, igne crematos in inferno impios: item quae observarint in hortis, campis, et aliis in locis amoenissimis . . .') it leads us back to the beliefs we are examining. See also the reference to J. Weyer in A. Tenenti ('Una nuova ricerca sulla stregoneria', *Studi storici*, 8 [1967] p. 389) concerning the belief, widespread in mid-sixteenth century Bavaria, in the *'vagabundi spiritus'*, who, four times yearly, leaving the lifeless body, participated at meetings, banquets and dances, at which the emperor himself was present.

64 See A. Lütolf, *Sagen, Bräuche*, II, p. 89.

65 See F. Byloff, *Hexenglaube und Hexenverfolgung*, pp. 137–8 (unfortunately an extremely hurried reference). It should be noted that in Bressanone the *Johannesbruderschaft* gathered on the Ember Days (J. Baur, 'Quatember', p. 228).

12

66 W. Crecelius, 'Frau Holda und der Venusberg'. This trial has been frequently studied, especially in connection with the Venusberg and the saga of Tannhäuser.

67 See I. Lupo, *Nova lux in edictum S. Inquisitionis* (Bergamo, 1603) pp. 386–7. Research conducted in the archives of the Curia Vescovile in Bergamo (thanks to the courtesy of Cardinal Testa and of the archivist Father Pesenti) intended to uncover documentary support of this fact, has been fruitless.

13

68 See Hansen, *Zauberwahn*, p. 85.

69 On the *Perchtenlaufen* see M. Andree-Eysn, *Volkskundliches aus dem bayrisch-österreischen Alpengebiet* (Braunschweig, 1910) pp. 156–84 (with bibliography). W.E. Peuckert (*Geheimkulte*, pp. 281 ff.) makes some acute suppositions on the subject, partially confirmed by Friulian sources; but the conclusions which he reaches, because of his racist presuppositions, are clearly absurd. For the aspect of the *Perchtenlaufen* as fertility rite, see I.V. Zingerle, *Sitten, Bräuche*, p. 139, and M. Andree-Eysn, *Volkskundliches*, pp. 179, 182–3. On the connections between 'Furious Horde' and ritual battles, see O. Höfler, *Kultische Geheimbünde*, pp. 154–63, especially pp. 154–6.

70 See W. Liungman, 'Traditionswanderungen', II, pp. 885–1013; at p. 897, in particular, the author matches the battle between the 'beautiful' and 'ugly' Perchte to the contest between the powers of creation and those of chaos which took place in Babylonia at the start of each year during the festivities in honour of the god Marduk. At p. 990 the *Perchtenlaufen* are seen as a prototype of the driving away of winter (see also F. Liebrecht, *La Mesnie furieuse, ou la Chasse sauvage*, in appendix [pp. 173–211] to Gervasius of Tilbury's *Otia Imperialia*, edited by Liebrecht himself [Hanover, 1856]).

14

71 ACAU, *S. Uffizio*, 'Ab anno 1574 . . .', trial n. 64, ff. 3 v, 7 r, 4 r.

72 See above, pp. 3, 6.

73 Lucca: ASL, *Cause delegate*, n. 25, f. 172 r; Bergamo: ACVB, *Visite Pastorali*, n. 4 ('1536–37. Lippomani Petri visitatio'), f. 157 v.

74 ASM, *Inquisizione*, b. 8, trial 1592–9, unnumbered leaves. After having been recognized as possessed (and as such exorcised), and subjected to torture in order to obtain a fuller confession, Grana had to make an abjuration as one who was found to be 'lightly' suspect in matters of the faith.

75 A. Runeberg ('Witches, Demons', pp. 89, 94 and *passim*) makes correct, if excessive, observations on the matter.

76 See T.R. Forbes, 'The Social History of the Caul', p. 499 (who also mentions the custom of tying the membrane around the child's neck as an amulet). See, in addition, H.F. Feilberg, 'Totenfetische im Glauben nordgermanischer Völker,' *Am Ur-quell, Monatschrift für Volkskunde*, 3 (1892) p. 116; E. Sidney-Hartland, in *Encyclopaedia of Religion and Ethics*, II, p. 639; *Handwörterbuch des deutschen Aberglaubens*, III, coll. 890 ff., VI, coll. 760 ff.

77 ACAU, *S. Uffizio*, 'Ab anno 1574 . . .', trial n. 64, f. 10 r.

15

78 ACAU, *S. Uffizio*, 'Anno integro 1599, a n. 341 usque ad 404 incl.', trial n. 397 (now in a miscellaneous folder with dark green cover, lacking indications of any sort), unnumbered leaves. G. Marcotti (*Donne e monache*, p. 291) mentioned this trial on the basis of the inventory of the cases held before the tribunal of the Holy Office of Aquileia (BCU, MS. 916). Marcotti erroneously interpreted a notation in the inventory, 'aliud non apparet,' as a formula of reticence.

79 ACAU, *S. Uffizio*, 'Ab anno 1601 usque ad annum 1603 incl. a n. 449 usque ad 546 incl.', trial n. 465.

17

80 ASV, *S. Uffizio*, b. 72, f. 38 v.

81 ACAU, *S. Uffizio*, 'Ab anno 1621 usque ad annum 1629 incl. a n. 805 usque ad 848 incl.', trial n. 806 (in the manuscript inventory it is incorrectly indicated as n. 805), unnumbered leaves.

82 The old one may be an echo of the faithful Eckhart, who appeared in the 'Furious Horde', as well as in the sagas about the Venusberg, where he had characteristics resembling those mentioned in the trial (see O. Höfler, *Kultische Geheimbünde*, pp. 72–5). In the trial against Anna la Rossa cited before, it was asserted that the accused had said that her dead husband had appeared to her, and had led her 'to his piece of land and showed her the markers of his property, because when he was alive he had moved them so as to add a little land, and so he told her that they should be restored to the proper place, and as long as this was not done he would be in great pain . . .' (ACAU, *S. Uffizio*, 'Ab anno 1581 usque ad annum 1582 . . .', trial n. 98, f. 7 v).

83 ACAU, *S. Uffizio*, 'Ab anno 1621 . . .', deposition inserted in trial n. 810, on another subject.

84 ACAU, *S. Uffizio*, 'Ab anno 1621 . . .', trial n. 832, unnumbered leaves.

85 ACAU, *S. Uffizio*, 'Ab anno 1643 usque ad annum 1646 incl. a n. 931 usque ad 982 incl.,' trial n. 957, f. 4 r.

86 See P. Zorutti, *Poesie edite ed inedite* (Udine, 1881), II, p. 613.

III THE BENANDANTI BETWEEN INQUISITORS AND WITCHES

1

1 ACAU, *S. Uffizio*, 'Anno integro 1583 a n. 107 usque ad 128 incl.', trial n. 113, f. l r.
2 *Ibid.*, ff. l r–v.
3 *Ibid.*, f. 2 v.
4 *Ibid.*, f. 2 r.
5 *Ibid.*, f. 2 v.
6 *Ibid.*, ff. 3 r, 4 r.
7 *Ibid.*, ff. 5 r–v.
8 Cited by F. Odorici, *Le streghe di Valtellina e la Santa Inquisizione* (Milan, 1862) p. 145 (the transcription of the document is clearly defective). On this point see A. Battistella, *Il Sant' Officio*, pp. 47–50. See also the instructions that the doge Leonardo Loredan gave to the *podestà* of Brescia, Marco Loredan, and to the captain, Nicolò Giorgio, on the subject of witchcraft trials (May 24, 1521: ASCB, *Privilegi*, t. 29, 1552, f. lv).
9 BCAU, MS. 105, *'Bisanzio-Lettere . . .'*, ff. 174 r–v. In the manuscript (an eighteenth-century copy, as we have said,) the letter is dated, mistakenly, 1585 instead of 1582.
10 The mildness of the Friulian inquisitors in prosecuting these widespread superstitions may be due, to some extent, to the fact that they belonged to the Franciscan order. It was a Franciscan, Fra Samuele de Cassinis, at the beginning of the sixteenth century, who was the first to speak out against the recently initiated persecution of witches. And it was a Dominican, Fra Vincenzo Dodo, who replied to his accusations, thereby setting in motion a long and bitter polemic. It was, primarily, a dispute between monks belonging to antagonistic orders and theological schools. But it is also possible that these motifs themselves later gave way, in Franciscan circles, to a tradition of greater scepticism, and consequently one that was less rigorous towards witchcraft suspects. On the polemic between Cassinis and Dodo, see J. Hansen, *Zauberwahn*, pp. 510–11 and *Quellen*, pp. 262–78. In addition to the texts cited by Hansen, see *Contra fratrem Vincentium or. predicatorum qui inepte et falso impugnare nititur libellum de lamiis editum a f. Samuele ordi. minorum* ([n.p.], but Papie, per Bernardinum de Garaldis, 1507. British Library: 8630. c. 32), and Dodo's second reply: *Elogium in materia maleficarum ad morsus fugas et errores fra. Samuelis Cassinensis contra apologiam Dodi* (1507 . . . Impressum Papie per magistrum Bernardinum de Garaldis. British Library: 8630 dd. 20). On the other hand, even a Dominican such as Silvestro Mazzolini da Prierio urged that people should be considered only 'lightly' suspect who 'in angulis conventicula celebrant, aut in temporibus anni sacratioribus, in campis vel sylvis, nocte vel die': a brief reference in A. Tenenti ('Una nuova ricerca', p. 390) who connects it with the beliefs studied here.
11 BCAU, MS. 105, *'Bisanzio. Lettere . . .'*, ff. 71 r, 112 v, 114 v.
12 *Ibid.*, f. 131 r. [It was the witch of Endor who summoned Samuel to Saul's presence (1 Samuel 28). A Pythoness is a priestess of Apollo, endowed with prophetic powers. Translators' note].

2

13 ACAU, *S. Uffizio*, 'Ab anno 1587 usque ad annum 1588 incl. a n. 158 usque ad 177 incl.', trial n. 167, unnumbered leaves. Fra Felice da Montefalco was succeeded, in 1584, by Fra Evangelista Peleo (1584–7), and he, in turn, by Fra G.B. Angelucci da Perugia (1587–98). See A. Battistella, *Il Sant' Officio*, p. 127.
14 For survivals or similarities in popular traditions, see R.M. Cossàr, 'Usanze, riti, e

superstizioni del popolo di Montona nell' Istria,' pp. 62–63; G. Finamore, 'Tradizioni popolari abruzzesi. Streghe-stregherie,' *Archivio per lo studio delle tradizioni popolari* 3 (1884), 219; *Idem.*, *Credenze, usi e costumi*, pp. 57, 76–78. See, in genèral, T.R. Forbes, 'Midwifery and Witchcraft,' *Journal of the History of Medicine and Allied Sciences*, 17 (1962), 264–83.

15 ACAU, *S. Uffizio*, 'Ab anno 1587 . . .,' trial n. 167, unnumbered leaves: 'in duobus diebus dominicis in ecclesia divi Ambrosii ante fores ipsius ecclesiae dum missa celebratur stet ipsa Catherina genibus flexis cum candella accensa in manu . . .'

3

16 ASV, *S. Uffizio*, b. 68 (trials of Latisana), unnumbered leaves.

17 For the beliefs associated with the valley of Josaphat, see W.E. Peuckert, *Handwörterbuch des deutschen Aberglaubens*, IV, coll. 770–4, where there is a reference also to the Tyrol.

18 As we can see, here we depart from the tradition, shared by the other benandanti, of gathering four times a year, during the Ember Days. Note also that the *Kerstniki*, the Slovenian equivalents of the benandanti, battle the witches on St John's eve (F.S. Krauss, *Volksglaube*, p. 128).

19 See K. Hofmann, 'Oberstdorfer "Hexen" ', p. 46; K.H. Spielmann, *Die Hexenprozesse in Kurhessen*, p. 48.

20 See above, p. 17.

4

21 ASM, *Inquisizione*, b. 2, libro 3, f. 72 v. See also ASL, *Cause delegate*, n. 175, f. 218 r: 'And since the lord *podestà* knows that who treats and cures spells also knows how to cast them.'

22 See, for example, ASL, *Cause delegate*, n. 175, f. 196 v (Margherita of San Rocco): 'And all these children whom I bewitched I also cured, since I was given something by everybody for my labours.' See also, *Ibid.*, ff. 202 r–v.

5

23 ACAU, *S. Uffizio*, 'Anno integro 1600 a.n. 405 usque ad 448 incl.', trial n. 409, unnumbered leaves. From the frequently cited manuscript inventory it emerges that even Caterina, the wife of Domenico and daughter of Taddeo of Mortegliano, tried on 12 December 1595, was a benandante. However, despite all my searching in the archive of the Curia Arcivescovile in Udine, this trial, numbered 277, did not come to light.

24 For the trial against Antonia la Cappona, see ACAU, *S. Uffizio*, 'Anno integro 1599 . . .', trial n. 363. More than a trial it is actually a spontaneous appearance, preceded, however, by a series of denunciations: la Cappona admitted that with various superstitious means she had treated 'several sick people and also that she had looked into a crystal'; 'and this,' she said, 'was to earn something, because I was poor.' She was ordered not to leave Udine, and to remain at the disposal of the Holy Office; but shortly after the order was revoked.

25 In other words, Grado.

6

26 ACAU, *S. Uffizio*, 'Anno integro 1600 . . .', trial n. 418, unnumbered leaves. See also the similar depositions made against a peasant of the Carnia, Giovanni della Picciola, benandante ('Ab anno 1606 usque ad annum 1607 incl. a n. 618 usque ad 675 incl.', trial n. 632, dated 16 March 1606), and against a boy, servant of a certain doctor Locadello of Udine, who had told the nephews of his previous proprietress, 'that he is a *belandante*, rides a lamb and beats himself with fennel' ('Ab anno 1621 usque ad annum 1629 incl. a n. 805 usque ad 848 incl.', trial n. 811, mistakenly numbered 807 in the manuscript inventory preserved in the Biblioteca Comunale, Udine).

27 ACAU, *S. Uffizio*, 'Ab anno 1608 usque ad annum 1611 incl. a n. 676 usque ad 742 incl.', trial n. 705, unnumbered leaves.

28 ACAU, *S. Uffizio*, 'Ab anno 1612 usque ad annum 1620 incl. a n. 743 usque ad 804 incl.', trial n. 758.

29 ACAU, *S. Uffizio*, 'Ab anno 1630 usque ad annum 1641 incl. a n. 849 usque ad 916 incl.', trial n. 850.

30 ACAU, *S. Uffizio*, 'Ab anno 1612 . . .', trial n. 777. In Modena, in 1540, a don Ludovico was denounced 'who knows witches from their faces' (ASM, *Inquisizione*, b. 2, libro 5, unnumbered fascicle).

7

31 ACAU, *S. Uffizio*, 'Ab anno 1606 . . .', trial n. 634, unnumbered leaves.

32 On Gerolamo Asteo, born in Pordenone of a noble family, inquisitor of Aquileia from 1598 or 1599 to 1608, bishop of Veroli from 1611, died in 1626, see: *Dictionnaire d'histoire et de géographie ecclésiastiques*, IV, coll. 1156–7, with bibliography; G.-G. Liruti, *Notizie delle vite ed opere scritte da' letterati del Friuli* (Udine, 1780), III, pp. 325–30; *Annales Minorum*, XXV, pp. 101, 264; XXVI, p. 484. He wrote various works, especially on legal subjects.

8

33 ACAU, *S. Uffizio*, 'Ab anno 1621 . . .', trial n. 806, unnumbered leaves.

34 See above, p. 67.

35 For an exact duplication of this belief, see E. Fabris Bellavitis in *Giornale di Udine e del Veneto Orientale* a. XXIV, 2 August 1890.

36 It was the custom (especially in Germany) to shave the hair of those accused of witchcraft as a precaution against charms.

9

37 ACAU, *S. Uffizio*, 'Ab anno 1621 . . . ,' n. 814, unnumbered leaves. For the period of activity of Fra Domenico Vico, see A. Battistella, *Il Sant' Officio*, p. 127.

38 See D. Merlini, *Saggio di ricerche sulla satira contro il villano* (Turin, 1894) pp. 182, 184, 185. The burlesque cited here was widely diffused: see *Le malitie de Vilani con alquanti Stramotti* [sic] *alla Bergamascha. Et uno contrasto de uno Fiorentino et uno Bergamascho* [n.p.n.d.] (British Library c. 57.1 7 [3]); and *Santa Croce de' Villani* cited by E. Battisti, *L'antirinascimento* (Milan, 1962) p. 473 (with some variants). See also the *Dialogo de gli incantamenti e strigarie con le altre malefiche opre, quale tutta via tra le donne e huomini se esercitano . . . Composto dal Eccellentissimo Dottor de le arte et medico Aureato* [sic] *messer Angelo de Forte* (Venice, 1533). In the middle of a long list of popular superstitions

which are minutely described, it is said: 'Oh my lords [it is Prudence speaking before the gods of Olympus] who isn't moved to laughter after hearing about the follies of the blind and beastly populace . . .'

39 ACAU, S. *Uffizio*, 'Ab anno 1621 . . .', trial n. 815, ff. 1 r–2 v.

40 *Ibid.*, f. 7 v.

41 *Ibid.*, ff. 1 v–7 r.

42 *Ibid.*, f. 4 r.

43 *Ibid.*, ff. 9 v–10 r.

44 *Ibid.*, ff. 5 v, 4 r 8 r–v.

45 *Ibid.*, ff. 8 v, 7 v–8 r, etc.

10

46 ACAU, S. *Uffizio*, 'Ab anno 1621 . . .', trial n. 820, f. 1 r.

47 *Ibid.*, f. 2 r. For a similar authorization by a confessor permitting treatment by a sorceress with superstitious means, see ASL, *Cause delegate*, n. 175, f. 146 r.

48 ACAU, S. *Uffizio*, 'Ab anno 1621 . . .', trial n. 820, ff. 2 v–3 r.

49 *Ibid.*, ff. 4 r–5 r.

50 *Ibid.*, trial n. 844, unnumbered leaves.

51 Such boasting is frequent in witchcraft trials. See, for example, ASL, *Cause delegate*, n. 29, trial against Francesca of Marignano, nicknamed Cecchina (year 1605), unnumbered leaves. Among other things, Francesca was accused of having said, repeatedly, that 'the illness which her husband has, on whom spirits have been discovered . . . besides God *and herself no one can* free him from this evil, no matter how many monks and priests may try, and that for her *to free her husband would be no more difficult than lifting a spindle off the ground* (the italics are in the manuscript).

11

52 This last piece of information comes from a benandante, Toffolo di Buri, but it is confirmed by popular traditions which are still alive in that zone. See R.M. Cossàr, 'Costumanze, superstizioni e leggende dell' agro parentino,' *Il Folklore italiano* 8 (1933) pp. 176–7; *Idem.*, 'Usanze, riti e superstizioni del popolo di Montona nell' Istria', pp. 62–3; *Idem.*, 'Tradizioni popolari di Momiano d'Istria', p. 179.

53 ACAU, S. *Uffizio*, 'Ab anno 1621 . . .', trial n. 848, unnumbered leaves.

54 ASP, sez. VI, 119, Ms. 38, f. 63 r (and f. 65 r).

55 As we saw in chapter II, while we can identify numerous parallels to the tradition of the processions of the dead (which is probably of Germanic provenance), the other crucial element in the myth of the benandanti, namely, the nocturnal battles, appears isolated – at best we can speak of survivals in the folklore, such as the *Perchtenlaufen*. The single exception, apart from the trial of the Livonian werewolf, is a passage from a popular account noted by W. Schwartz, ('Zwei Hexengeschichten aus Waltershausen', p. 396) in which battles, presumably of a ritual character, among witches at the sabbat, are described. At p. 414 Schwartz recalls a reasonably similar passage in Burchard of Worms (mentioned above, p. 57). Pale and insignificant is the comparable allusion by B. Spina, *Quaestio de strigibus*, p. 49.

IV THE BENANDANTI AT THE SABBAT

1

1 ASV, *S. Uffizio*, b. 72 (Panzona, Maria, etc.) ff. 3 r–v.

2 *Ibid.*, ff. 5 r–v. In one of the Milanese trials from the end of the fourteenth century discovered and summarized by E. Verga, ('Intorno a due inediti documenti', we read that the defendant 'confessa fuit se a iuventute sua semper usque tunc ivisse ad ludum Diane quam appellant Herodiadem et eidem semper reverentiam fecisse inclinando sibi caput et dicens "Bene stage Madona Horiente" et ipsa sibi respondebat "Bene veivatis filie mee".' (ASCM, *Sentenze del podestà*, vol. II, Cimeli n. 147, ff. 52 r–v).

3 ASV, *S. Uffizio*, b. 72, trial (Panzona, Maria) ff. 5 v–7 r.

4 *Ibid.*, ff. 13 v–14 r.

2

5 ASV, *S. Uffizio*, b. 72, trial (Panzona, Maria).

6 Italian: *furion del forno*, fork-shaped pokers, elsewhere called *soboradori* or *saboradori*. It is interesting that in a woodcut illustrating one of the oldest witchcraft treatises (Ulrich Molitoris, *De laniis et phitonicis mulieribus. Teutonice unholden vel hexen*, Ex Constantia, 1489, table III; Hain 11536), we see two witches flying, mounted not on a broom handle, as the later tradition prescribes, but on a forked stick.

7 ASV, *S. Uffizio*, b. 72, trial (Panzona, Maria) ff. 38 r–39 v.

8 *Ibid.*, f. 41 v.

9 Certain supporters of the thesis of the unreality of the sabbat, in fact, did not exclude the guilt of witches. More than a century earlier, at the conclusion of his treatise in the form of a dialogue on witchcraft, Molitoris wrote: 'quod quamvis effectualiter huiusmodi maledicte mulieres nihil efficere possunt, nihilominus tamen, quare instigante dyabolo tales mulieres vel ob desperationem, vel paupertatem, vel odia vicinorum, vel alias temptationes per dyabolum immissas quibus non resistunt, a vero et piissimo deo recedentes sese dyabolo holocaustomata et oblationes offerendo apostatant, hereticam pravitatem sectantes. Et propterea succedit . . . quod propter huiusmodi apostasiam et corruptam voluntatem de iure civili tales scelerate mulieres . . . morte plecti debent.' (U. Molitoris, *De laniis et phitonicis mulieribus*, f. 26 v.)

10 ASV, *S. Uffizio*, b. 72, trial (Panzona, Maria) ff. 43 v–44 v.

11 *Ibid.*, ff. 45 v–47 r.

3

12 ACAU, *S. Uffizio*, 'Ab anno 1630 usque ad annum 1641 incl. a n. 849 usque ad 916 incl.', trial n. 859, leaves only partially numbered. The words 'outside confession' (*extra confessionem*) are an addition, clumsily intended to conceal the violation of the secret of the confessional; thus, a few lines later 'he confessed me' was later corrected to 'he told me.'

13 The term *Picenale*, that is, barrel, recalls the *Barlotto* or cask of the conventicles of the Fraticelli (see, for example, the 1466 trial published by F. Ehrle, 'Die Spiritualen, ihr Verhältniss zum Franziskanerorden und zu den Fraticellen', *Archiv für Litteratur-und Kirchengeschichte des Mittelalters*, 4 [1888] pp. 117–18) which later came to indicate the gathering place of the witches of Como and of other, especially Lombard, localities. See C. Cantú, *Storia della città e della diocesi di Como* (Florence, 1856), I. p. 423; TCLD, MS. 1225, ser. II, vol. 2, f. 33 v, etc.

14 ACAU, *S. Uffizio*, 'Ab anno 1630 . . .', trial n. 859, ff. 1 r–3 r.

4

15 ACAU, *S. Uffizio*, 'Ab anno 1630 . . .', trial n. 859, f. 5 v. There is an allusion to a 'backward Pater Noster' (*Pater Noster alla roversa*) in ASM, *Inquisizione*, b. 2, libro 3, f. 26 v.

5

16 ACAU, *S. Uffizio*, 'Ab anno 1630 . . . ,' trial n. 859, ff. 24 v–25 v (note that when the inquisitor begins the interrogation of witnesses, the numbering of the trial records also begins anew).

17 *Ibid.*, f. 45 v.

18 See above, p. 177, n. 31.

19 See above, p. 71.

6

20 ACAU, *S. Uffizio*, 'Anno integro 1642 a n. 917 usque ad n. 930 incl.', trial n. 918, ff. 1 r–3 v.

21 *Ibid.*, ff. 14 v–15 r.

22 On Menghi, besides the brief mention in L. Thorndike, *A History of Magic and Experimental Science* (New York, 1941), VI, p. 556, see also the uninteresting work by Massimo Petrocchi, *Esorcismi e magia nell'Italia del Cinquecento e del Seicento* (Naples, 1957) pp. 13–27.

23 ACAU, *S. Uffizio*, 'Anno integro 1642 . . .', trial n. 918, f. 17 v.

24 *Ibid.*, ff. 10 r, 29 v.

25 *Ibid.*, f. 33 r. 'ut evitaret tumultus et pericula possibilia ratione dictarum nundinarum si dictus Michael conduceretur ex Castro Utinensi in aedes Sancti Officii.'

7

26 ACAU, *S. Uffizio*, 'Anno integro 1642 . . .', trial n. 918, ff. 33 v–34 r.

27 See above, p. 130.

28 ASCM, *Sentenze del podestà*, vol. II, Cimeli n. 147, f. 51 r; see also G. Bonomo, *Caccia*, pp. 102–4.

29 ACAU, *S. Uffizio*, 'Anno integro 1642 . . .', trial n. 918, f. 35 r.

8

30 See S.R. Burstein, 'Demonology and Medicine in the Sixteenth and Seventeenth Centuries', *Folk-Lore*, vol. 67, March 1956, pp. 16–33. Naturally, from the beginning, the persecution had provoked more or less sporadic opposition. But in the second half of the sixteenth century in certain areas scepticism towards the witchcraft trials must have been fairly widespread, to judge from an abjuration pronounced on 18 March 1581 by an inhabitant of Challant: 'I abjure, reject and detest the error and heresy, or rather the infidelity, which falsely and deceitfully holds and believes that on earth there are not any heretics, witches, sorceresses, and states and affirms that

no one must believe that there are heretics, witches and sorceresses who can do any injury to either rational or irrational beings, with the assistance of the devil. Such infidelity expressly militates against the teaching of the Holy Roman Mother Church and of the holy Fathers, in fact against imperial laws, which prescribe that such offenders be burned (TCLD, MS. 1226, ser. II, vol. 3, f. 454 r). The trial had taken place in the presence of Fra Daniele de Bonifacio, O.P., vicar of the renowned Cipriano Uberti, inquisitor of Vercelli, Ivrea and Aosta.

31 ACAU, *S. Uffizio*, 'Anno integro 1642 . . .', trial n. 918, ff. 37 r–v.

32 *Ibid.*, ff. 39 r–40 r.

9

33 ACAU, *S. Uffizio*, 'Anno integro 1642 . . .', trial n. 918, ff. 41 r–42 r.

34 *Ibid.*, ff. 44 r, 52 v.

35 *Ibid.*, ff. 52 v–53 r, 49 v.

10

36 ACAU, *S. Uffizio*, 'Anno integro 1642 . . .', trial n. 918, ff. 64 r–65 v. The problem of suggestive interrogations was underscored, I believe for the first time, with particular clarity and on the basis of an extremely interesting documentation, by W.G. Soldan, *Geschichte der Hexenprozesse*, new ed. by H. Heppe (Stuttgart, 1880), I, pp. 384–93.

37 See above, p. 23.

11

38 ACAU, *S. Uffizio*, 'Anno integro 1642 . . .', trial n. 918, ff. 66 v, 70 r–v.

39 ACAU, *S. Uffizio*, 'Epistolae Sac. Cong. S. Officii ab anno 1647 incl. usque ad 1659 incl.', ff. 72 r–v.

40 On the *Instructio*, see N. Paulus, *Hexenwahn und Hexenprozess vornehmlich im 16. Jahrhundert* (Freiburg i. Br., 1910) pp. 273–5. More recently, G. Bonomo (*Caccia*, pp. 294–8) has appropriately emphasized its importance, in the footsteps of Girolamo Tartarotti, and has provided summary information about its diffusion. An abridged and modified Italian version of the *Instructio* was inserted by E. Masini in the 1639 edition of the *Sacro Arsenale* and, in a complete version of the original text, by C. Carena as an appendix to the 1655 edition of his *Tractatus de officio sanctissimae Inquisitionis*, pp. 536–52 (see also the later editions of the *Sacro Arsenale* and of Carena's *Tractatus*). Carena, who asserted that 'in nostris Inquisitionibus Italiae per Reverendissimorum Inquisitorum manus circumferri Scripturarum quandam brevem huiusce argumenti' (p. 536) entitled the *Instructio*, *Tractatus de strigibus*. For evidence of its circulation in manuscript, see Bibl. Apost. Vaticana, Vat. lat. 8193, ff. 730 r–749 v; a partial echo in Bibl. Vallicelliana, MS. G. 62, ff. 462 v, ff: 'Prattica per procedere nelle cause del Sant' Offizio', ch. 8, entitled 'De i Sortilegi'. The *Instructio* was published separately with its true title in 1657 (see A. Panizza, 'I processi contro le streghe', *Archivio Trentino* 7 [1888], 84; a copy of this rare pamphlet is preserved at the Cornell University Library). It was translated into German in 1661 but only published by A. Dettling, *Die Hexenprozesse im Kanton Schwyz*, pp. 42–54. (For a fuller, recent discussion, see also J. Tedeschi, 'Appunti sulla *Instructio pro Formandis Processibus in Causis Strigum, Sortilegiorum et Maleficiorum*', forthcoming in the proceedings of a 1981 *convegno* entitled 'L'Inquisizione nei secoli XVI–XVII . . .', spon-

sored by the Istituto storico italiano per l'età Moderna e contemporanea in Rome, under the presidency of Armando Saitta).

41 But see also G. Bonomo, *Caccia*, pp. 299–300.

42 H.C. Lea, *A History of the Inquisition of Spain*, IV, pp. 206–41. See now also G. Henningsen, *The Witches' Advocate: Basque Witchcraft and the Spanish Inquisition (1609–1614)* (Reno, 1980).

43 L.M. Sinistrari d'Ameno, *De la demonialité et des animaux incubes et succubes . . .*, publié d' après le Manuscrit original découvert à Londres en 1872 et traduit du Latin par I. Liseux, 2nd ed., (Paris, 1876) p. 258.

44 ACAU, *S. Uffizio*, 'Epistolae Sac. Cong. S. Officii', f. 73 v.

45 ACAU, *S. Uffizio*, 'Anno integro 1642 . . .', trial n. 918, ff. 89 v–90 r.

46 From this point the leaves of the trial are not numbered.

47 ACAU, *S. Uffizio*, 'Epistolae Sac. Cong. S. Officii', f. 75 v.

13

48 ACAU, *S. Uffizio*, 'Anno integro 1647 . . .', trial n. 983, unnumbered leaves.

49 ACAU, *S. Uffizio*,' Anno integro 1642 . . .', trial n. 918, ff. 58 r–v.

50 *Ibid.*, ff. 67 v–68 v.

51 ACAU, *S. Uffizio*, 'Anno integro 1647 . . .', trial n. 986.

52 ACAU, *S. Uffizio*, 'Ab anno 1662 usque ad 1669 incl. a num. 382 usque ad 462 incl.', trial n. 456 *bis*.

53 The girl had told the Sochietti woman that to get to the described gatherings she and her mother went out 'by way of the chimney', and, upon reaching the roof, found 'a gentleman' who brought them to the 'tall gentleman': a ritual detail which I do not believe affects the interpretation of the document proposed here. Similarly, the fact that Angiola should affirm, when she was already in Gradisca, that her mother had come at night to wake her and had conducted her 'to the tall gentleman, whom she observed closely and who is well tied with iron chains' simply appears to be a symptom of the profound impression made on the girl by the conventicles she had attended.

54 For two approximately similar examples, from the beginning and the end of the persecution of witchcraft (from periods, therefore, when the complex of beliefs about the sabbat had not yet taken hold or had already dissolved, permitting the reality of the conventicles, so much less picturesque, to filter through) see the passage in the *Malleus Maleficarum* (pars II, quaestio I, cap. II), cited and interpreted in the above sense by W.E. Peuckert, *Geheimkulte*, p. 135 and W. Eschenröder, *Hexenwahn und Hexenprozess in Frankfurt am Main* (Gelnhausen, 1932), pp. 60–1 (a propos of the last witchcraft trial held in Frankfort; Eschenröder too interprets the evidence in a 'realistic' sense).

14

55 F. Byloff did not understand this point fully in his otherwise valuable work, *Hexenglaube und Hexenverfolgung* (for example, pp. 11–12).

56 ASM, *Inquisizione*, b. 2, libro 5, f. 46 r.

57 *Ibid.*, f. 93 v.

58 ACAU, *S. Uffizio*, 'Ab anno 1630 . . .', trial n. 888, ff. 16 v, 2 r. On the case of the Torsi woman, who admitted she was a frequent backslider, see also the letters sent to Udine by Cardinal Barberini (ACAU, *S. Uffizio*, 'Epistolae Sac. Cong. S. Officii . . .', ff. 64 r–65 v).

59 ACAU, *S. Uffizio*, 'Anno integro 1647 . . .', trial n. 997, unnumbered leaves. For a

fleeting reference to this trial, based on the above frequently cited manuscript index, see G. Marcotti, *Donne e monache*, p. 293.

60 Freud, in his analysis of the pact made with the devil by a seventeenth-century German painter, discerned a substitution of the father by the devil, which in some ways resembles the case of the Friulian girl. See S. Freud, *Eine Teufelsneurose im siebzehnten Jahrhundert* (Vienna, 1924). We should remember, however, that, as Byloff pointed out (*Hexenglaube*, pp. 121–2), Freud based himself on a passage interpreted erroneously.

15

61 ACAU, *S. Uffizio*, 'Ab anno 1643 usque ad annum 1646 incl. a n. 931 usque ad 982 incl.', trial n. 942.

62 In the transcription that follows, after a few leaves we have, instead, 'benandante'.

63 ACAU, *S. Uffizio*, 'Ab anno 1643 . . .', trial n. 942, ff. 1 r–4 r.

64 *Ibid.*, ff. 6 v–9 r.

65 *Ibid.*, f. 5 r.

66 In this second part of the trial the leaves are unnumbered.

16

67 ACAU, *S. Uffizio*, 'Ab anno 1630 . . .', trial n. 870, unnumbered leaves.

68 ACAU, *S. Uffizio*, 'Ab anno 1630 . . .', trial n. 889. Three years later Menigo was again denounced as a benandante; it emerged, among other things, that one freezing night, looking out 'at the weather and the fields from his balcony,' he had exclaimed to his wife: 'Ortenscia, sin has prescribed it so,' – that is, his wife had explained telling about the episode – 'the sin has to be of this husband of mine, because when he is out opposing the witches healing someone, he returns home crushed and his body aching, and I know this because I see him collapsed; but it can't be seen from outside, and he is not able to move or work, nor has he ever said anything to me, but I can just imagine it' (ACAU, *S. Uffizio*, 'Anno integro 1642 . . .', trial n. 922, unnumbered leaves).

69 ACAU, *S. Uffizio*, 'Ab anno 1630 . . .', trial n. 926, unnumbered leaves.

70 ACAU, *S. Uffizio*, 'Incipit secundum millenarium ab anno 1648 incl. a num. 1 usque ad numerum 26 inclusive', trial n. 18 *bis*, unnumbered leaves.

71 ACAU, *S. Uffizio*, 'Anno integro 1647 . . .', trial n. 987 (against Liph of Trivignano); 'Anno eodem 1648 completo a num. eodem 27 usque ad 40', trial n. 31 *bis* (against Paolo of Lavarian); 'Anno 1649 completo usque ad 1650 inclusive a num. 83 usque ad 135 inclusive', trial n. 88 *bis* (mention is made of Piero Fresco of Flumignano, benandante); 'Ab anno 1651 usque ad 1652 incl. a num. 136 usque ad 215 incl.', trial n. 165 *bis* (against Lonardo di Iuvaniti); 'Ab anno 1653 usque ad 1654 incl. a num. 216 usque ad 274 incl.', trial n. 224 *bis* (against a benendante called Crot of Villalta); 'Ab anno 1662 usque ad 1669 incl. a num. 382 usque ad 462 incl.', trial n. 389 *bis* (against Pietro Torrean); *Ibid.*, trial n. 410 *bis* (against Giovanni Percoti of Orsara); *Ibid.*, trial n. 411 *bis* (against Pietro Torrean); *Ibid.*, trial n. 431 *bis* (against the same); *Ibid.*, trial n. 432 *bis* (against Battista Titone); *Ibid.*, trial n. 433 *bis* (against the same); *Ibid.*, trial n. 434 *bis* (general mention of the benandanti); *Ibid.*, trial n. 449 *bis* (against Pietro Torrean); 'Ab anno 1701 usque ad annum 1709 a num. 607 usque ad 686', trial n. 697 *bis* (against Leonardo of Udine).

72 ACAU, *S. Uffizio*, 'Ab anno 1662 . . .', trial n. 410 *bis*; trial n. 411 *bis*; trial n. 432 *bis*.

73 ACAU, *S. Uffizio*, 'Ab anno 1662 . . .', trial n. 421 *bis*.

74 ASV, *S. Uffizio*, b. 109 (Nerizalca etc.) ff. 3 r–v. A witness declared that the witches

'had begun to crumble up the ears of grain, taking the oats and leaving the straw; they did the same in the vineyards with the bunches of grapes, and . . . thus successively they went throughout the island taking the proceeds; and . . . they took the above mentioned wines and grains to Puglia to certain deep and muddy places; the grains . . . they sold for ten *lire* the bushel, and the wine . . . they left since they could not dispose of it' (ff. 1 v–2 r).

75 See F.S. Krauss, *Volksglaube*, pp. 97–108, 110–28; *Idem., Slavische Volkforschungen*, pp. 41–3.

76 See K. Vojnovič, 'Crkva i država u dubrovačkoj republici', *Rad Jugoslavenske Akademije*, 121 (1895) pp. 64–7; HAD, *Diplomata et acta*, n. 1685.

17

77 ACAU, *S. Uffizio*, 'Ab anno 1630 . . .' trial n. 900, unnumbered leaves.

78 ACAU, *S. Uffizio*, 'Incipit secundum millenarium . . .', trial n. 26 *bis*, unnumbered leaves. Rome urged that mercy be used in this case too. On 6 February 1649 Cardinal Barberini wrote: 'Since Giovanna Summagotta's crime consisted of simple boasting, my most eminent colleagues have resolved that the case be closed with a simple warning and salutary penances. Your Reverence must not fail to carry this out' (ACAU, *S. Uffizio*, 'Epistolae Sac. Cong. S. Officii . . .', f. 79 v). Naturally, this was obeyed.

79 ACAU, *S. Uffizio*, 'Anno eodem 1648 . . .', trial n. 28 *bis* (it is the priest of Fanna, Domenico Segala, speaking, in a denunciation addressed to the inquisitor of Aquileia), unnumbered leaves.

80 For similar instances, see ACAU, *S. Uffizio*, 'Anno 1649 completo . . .', trial n. 101 *bis* (against Menico of Ponte di Palazzolo), and 'Ab anno 1662 . . .', trial n. 423 *bis* (against Giambattista of Paderno).

81 ACAU, *S. Uffizio*, 'Ab anno 1657 . . .', trial n. 381 *bis*, unnumbered leaves.

82 ACAU, *S. Uffizio*, 'Miscellaneo K. 1.2. Processi ab anno 1672 ad an. 1686,' unnumbered leaves. The ancient devotion for guardian angels intensified in the course of the seventeenth century. The special holy day dedicated to them established by Paul V (1608), limited to the imperial states, was extended by Clement X (1670) to the entire Church.

83 ACAU, *S. Uffizio*, 'Ab anno 1662 . . .', trial n. 452 *bis*, unnumbered leaves.

APPENDIX

1 In the manuscript 'and in their words benandanti' is written in the margin.

2 *Recte*(?): Tivarutio.

3 In the MS: Paduario.

4 In the MS: Romanutti.

5 In the MS: Romanutto.

INDEX OF NAMES

Abonde, 40–2, 44, 54, 187
Abraham a Sancta Clara, 183
Abundia, *see* Abonde
Adonis, 186
Agnabella of San Lorenzo, 83, 85
Agostino Veneziano, 189
Agrigolante, Pascutta, 79, 80
Airoldo, Carlo Francesco, 182
Alciato, Andrea, 21, 178, 182
Alexander IV, pope, 177, 178
Aloysia, called la Tabacca, 99, 101
Amorosi, Vincenzo, 73
Anastasia, called la Frappona, 178
Andrea of Orsaria, 38
Andree-Eysn, M., 192
Andres a Laguna, 180
Angelucci, Giovambattista, 73, 194
Anna, called la Rossa, *see* Artichi, Anna
Antonia, called la Cappona, 79, 195
Antonia of Nimis, 97
Apollo, 194
Apuleius, 174
Aquilina of Grazzano, 37, 38, 65, 70, 147, 150, 186
Arigoni, Pompeo, 178
Arrigoni, Vincenzo, 74–6
Artichi, Anna, called la Rossa, 33–7, 39, 41, 60, 72, 193
Artichi, Domenico, 33
Asteo, Gerolamo, 62, 82, 84, 85, 196
Attimis, Troiano de', 3, 150, 151
Attis, 186
Aurelia of Gemona, 33, 35
Avicenna, 127

Bacchus, 45, 46
Badau (or Badavin), Lunardo, 89–92
Baduario, Giovanni, 148, 157, 159, 162, 164, 167
Bächtold-Staubli, H., 174
Baist, G., 191
Baldassari, Francesco, 68
Balder, 186
Barb, A. A., xxii
Barbarelli, Domenica, 16, 185
Barbaro, Francesco, 64
Barberini, Francesco, 125–8, 201, 203
Barilli, A., 179
Barthéty, H., 183
Barto, P.S., 192
Bartolomeo of Cividale, 109
Basili, Alessandro, 62
Basili, Florida, 62–6, 78
Basilio, father, 142
Basin, Bernardo, 188
Bastanzi, G., 183
Battista, master, 34, 35
Battista Vicentino, 8, 156, 158, 159, 162
Battistella, A., 174, 175, 183, 185, 194, 196
Battisti, E., 196
Baudry, F., 188
Baur, J., 183, 184, 188, 190–2
Bellucci, G., 188
Berengo, M., xxii
Bergamasco, Mattia, 95
Bernardino da Genova, 91
Bernardino da Siena, Saint, 179
Bernardo da Como, 178
Bernardo of Santa Maria la Longa, 81
Bernheimer, R., 187, 190
Bertsche, K., 183
Bertuzzi, Giovanni, 179
Betta of Aquileia, 63
Bevilaqua, Zannuto, 91
Biasutti, G., xxii
Biat, Giacomo, 115, 119–21, 127
Biat, Giambattista, 115, 121
Bing, G., xxii
Bisanzio, Paolo, 36, 71, 72, 177
Bloch, M., xxi, 187
Bobbio, N., xxii
Bonomo, G., 180, 182, 185, 199–201
Borghese, Camillo, *see* Paul V, pope
Bortolotto, Sebastiano, 61
Brandis, Francesco, 96
Brandstetter, R., 191

Brant, Sebastian, 46, 189
Breull, Diel, 56, 57
Bruiningk, H. von, 186
Bugatis, Pierina de', 188
Burchard of Worms, 57, 197
Burke, P., xii, 173
Burlino, Giacomo, 90, 92, 94, 95
Burstein, S. R., 180, 199
Busetto, Antonio, 80
Busetto, Maddalena, 79, 80
Byloff, F., xviii, 174, 192, 201, 202

Caldo, Olivo, 138–41
Camillo of Minons, 136
Cancianis, Giovanni, 89, 91
Canobbio, Polissena, 181
Cantimori, D., xxii
Cantù, C., 198
Cao, Valentino, 134
Cappello, Benedetto, 138
Carena, Cesare, 126, 200
Casciano, Francesco, 127
Cassinis, Samuel de, 182, 194
Caterina, called la Guercia, 38
Caterina of Mortegliano, 195
Cattaro, Andrea, 144
Cecco of Zuz, 155
Centrino, Francesco, 116
Cervignan, Cappona de, 79
Chianton, Menega, 91
Chibnall, M., 190
Cibele Nardo, A., 183
Claudia of Correggio, 181
Clement VIII, pope, 23
Clement X, pope, 203
Cohn, N., xiv, 173, 185
Colloredo, Leonardo, 163
Cossàr, R. M., 179, 188, 194, 197
Crecelius, W., 190, 192
Crezia of Pieve San Paolo, 19
Crot of Villalta, 202
Crusius, Martin, 55, 56, 59, 191, 192
Cumana, Elena, 179
Cummo, Francesco, 64, 65, 79, 80
Curti, N., 191
Cut (or Cucchiul), Gerolamo, 92–95
Cysat, Rennward, 191

Dacheux, L., 189
Dahl, J., 180
Daniele de Bonifacio, 200
Da Pozzo, L., 183
De Biasio, L., 175
Delaiolo, Giulio, 167, 171
Della Porta, Giovanni Battista, 17, 180
Del Rio, Martin, 176, 182
DeMaio, R., xxii
De Martino, E., xxii, 181
Demeter, 186
DeNardis, L., 179
Dettling, A., 190, 191, 200
Diana, xv, xx, 16, 28, 40, 42–5, 50, 54, 118, 185, 187, 188, 198
Diana, Pietro, 127
Diedo, Antonio, 112
Dioscorides, 180
Dodo, Vincenzo, 194
Domenatta, Caterina, 73, 74, 195
Domenico d'Auxerre, 68
Domenico of Mortegliano, 195
Donato della Mora, 81, 82
Driesen, O., 190
Duerr, H.-P., 173
Dumézil, G., 184

Ebendorfer von Haselbach, Thomas, 42
Eckhart, 193
Ehrle, F., 198
Elena di Vincenzo (of Borgo San Pietro), 92, 93, 95
Eliade, M., xv, 173, 186
Endor, witch of, 194
Eschenröder, W., 201

Fabris Bellavitis, Elena, xxi, 174, 179, 196
Facile, M. R., 175
Feilberg, H. F., 193
Felice da Montefalco, 5–8, 10–13, 20, 22, 33, 34, 36–8, 67, 76, 107, 151, 157, 162, 163, 166, 167, 170, 194
Ferro, Bartolomeo del, 62
Finamore, G., 188, 195
Fiorelli, P., 181
Firpo, L., xxii
Fischer, L., 183
Forbes, T. R., 179, 193, 195
Foretić, V., xxii
Forte, Angelo de', 196
Francesca (or Cecchina) of Marignano, 197
Franceschina, from 'the village of Frattuzze', 81
Frattina, Ludovico, 141
Frazer, J. G., xix, 181, 184, 185
Fresco, Piero, 202
Freud, S., 202
Friedenwald, H., 180
Frugoni, A., xxii, 180
Fumi, L., 181
Furlano, Battista, 74
Furlano, Pasqua, 74

Galatini, Raimondo, 144
Galen, 127
Gallo, Cornelio, 151
Garaldi, Bernardino de', 194
Garosci, A., xxii
Garzoni, Andrea, 82
Gasparo, father, 159
Gasparo, the shop boy, 82–5
Gasparutto, Gerolamo, 151

Gasparutto, Maria, 159, 181
Gasparutto, Paolo, 1–6, 8–12, 14–17, 19–29, 31, 35, 39, 41, 44, 54, 56, 59, 60, 66, 71, 72, 77, 78, 84, 107, 124, 147–51, 155, 157, 159, 162, 163, 167, 169–71, 177–9, 181, 186
Gasperina of Grazzano, 65–7
Geiger, P., 185, 191
Geiler von Kaisersberg, Johann, 44–7, 66, 189
Germano, Saint, 43
Gerolamo of Villalta, 108, 109, 111
Gervasius of Tilbury, 192
Giacoma of Faedis, 136
Giacomo of Camino, 141
Giacomo of Gemona, 141
Giacomo, priest, 153
Giambattista da Perugia, 73
Giambattista of Manzano, 93
Giambattista of Paderno, 203
Gianna, a witch, 19
Giberti, Gian Matteo, 20, 181
Gioannina of Cendre, 177
Giorgio, Nicolò, 194
Giovambattista da Perugia, *see* Angelucci, Giovambattista
Giovanni, the shepherd, 67
Girardi, Giovan Francesco, 86
Giuliano, Giambattista, 114
Giulio d'Assisi, 1, 3, 147, 148
Giuseppe of Moimacco, 111
Godelmann, Johann, 119
Golizza, Bartolomea, 141
Gombrich, E. H., xxii
Gradenigo, Marco, 115
Graesse, T., 188
Grana of Villa Marzana, 59, 60, 182, 193
Gratian, 40
Grillando, Paolo, 179
Grimm, J., 187, 191
Grisola of Cividale, 109, 111, 112
Gritti, Pietro, 36
Gugitz, G., 191
Guillaume d'Auvergne, 40, 187, 190
Guillaume de Lorris, 187

Halliday, W. R., 174
Hansen, J., xviii, 174, 176, 177, 180, 182, 187, 192, 194
Harlequin, 49, 190
Henningsen, G., 201
Heppe, H., 200
Herodias, xx, 43, 50, 198
Heuschkel, W., 181
Höfler, O., 184, 186, 187, 189, 191–3
Hoffmann-Krayer, E., 174, 185, 190, 191
Hofmann, C., 188
Hofmann, K., 191, 195
Holda, xx, 40, 45, 55, 56, 187, 189, 190–2
Holle, *see* Holda
Holt, *see* Holda
Hovorka, O. von, 183

Innocent X, pope, 127

Jacopo da Voragine, 43, 188
Jacquier, Nicolas, 177
Janssen, J., 191
Jean de Meun, 187
Junk, W., 191

Kemnat, Matthias von, 43, 188
Kingdon, R. M., 173
Kluge, F., 191
Kolb, C., 192
Krämer, W., 189
Krauss, F. S., 181, 183, 187, 195, 203
Kretzenbacher, L., 187
Kronfeld, A., 183
Kurz, O., xxii

Laistner, L., 190
Lambaia, Minena, 68
Langlois, E., 187
Lavarello, Ettore, 151
Lavater, Ludwig, 191
Lazzarini, A., xxi, 174
Lea, H. C., 178, 201
Lena of Pescaglia, 19
Lenoir, Hugo, 177
Leonardo of Udine, 202
Le Prévost, A., 190
Liebenau, T. von, 191
Liebrecht, F., 192
Liph of Trivignano, 202
Lippomano, Pietro, 193
Liruti, G. G., 196
Liseux, I., 201
List, E. A., 191
Liungman, W., 184–92
Locadello, physician in Udine, 196
Lonardo di Iuvaniti, 202
Longhi, Giorgio de', 65, 66
Loredan, Leonardo, 194
Loredan, Marco, 194
Lucia of Cividale, 109
Lucia, 'the witch of Ghiai', 81
Ludovico da Gualdo, 108–11, 114, 135
Lütolf, A., 191, 192
Lupo, Ignazio, 57, 192
Lynge, W., 184

Maddalena of Gradisca, 151
Maddalena of Udine, 64
Magnassuto, 151
Magnossi, Bastian, 144
Maioli Faccio, V., 188
Maniaco, Francesco, 92
Mannhardt, W., 181, 184, 185
Mantovano, Giovanni, 86–9

Manzano, F. di, 183
Maracco, Jacopo, 1, 3, 147, 148, 152
Marchetto, Alessandro, 86–9
Marcotti, Giuseppe, xxi, 174, 175, 193, 202
Marduk, 184, 192
Margherita of San Rocco, 19, 39, 184, 195
Maria of Gonars, 153
Maroschino, Machor, 74, 75, 77
Martin d'Arles, 188
Martino, priest, 153
Marx, J., xx, 174
Mary, A., 187
Masetto, Antonio, 167, 170
Masini, Eliseo, 200
Mattia of Fanna, 143
Mayer, A., xx, 174
Mazzolini, Silvestro, 194
Memis, P., 188
Menega of Camillo of Minons, 136, 137
Menghi, Girolamo, 115, 199
Menica of Cremons, 18, 20
Menichino della Nota, 17, 74–7, 84, 100, 140
Menichino of Latisana, *see* Menichino della Nota
Menico of Ponte di Palazzola, 203
Menigo of Udine, 141, 202
Menis, Leonardo, 90–1
Menos, Bastiano, 129–33
Merlini, D., 196
Meyer, E. H., 183, 187
Michelet, J., xix, 174
Midelfort, H. C. Erik, xiv, 173
Mierlo, don, 130
Mintino, Belforte, 150, 151
Miol, Domenico, called Totolo, 130–3
Missini, Giulio, 115–17, 119, 123, 124, 126, 127, 136, 137
Moduco, Battista, 3, 6–10, 12–17, 22, 24–9, 31, 39, 41, 54, 56, 59–61, 66, 71, 72, 77, 84, 107, 147, 150, 151, 153, 160, 161, 163, 165–7, 177, 178, 186
Moduco, Giacomo, 153
Moduco, Maria, *see* Maria of Gonars
Molitoris, Ulrich, 198
Monter, E. W., xiii, 173
Morin, G., 183
Morosa of Prutars, 68
Mozza, named in an Udinese trial, 62
Murray, M., xiii, xix, xx, 173, 174
Musin, Wyprat, 50, 51

Nicholas V, pope, 177
Nider, Johann, 42–4, 47, 58, 66, 188
Nietzsche, F. W., 183
Nilsson, M. P., 184

Odorici, F., 194
Olivo della Notta (also della Nota), 75
Ordericus Vitalis, 48, 50, 59, 62, 67, 190
Orsolina, called la Rossa, 20, 135, 185
Ostermann, V., xxi, 174–6, 179, 183

Panfilo, Jacopo, 104
Panizza, A., 188, 200
Panzona, Maria, 18, 54, 67, 99–108, 112, 118, 180, 198
Paola, named in an Udinese trial, 33
Paolo of Lavariano, 202
Papino, 157
Paschini, P., xxii, 175–7
Passavin, Bortolo, 142
Patavino, Paolo, 157
Paul V, pope, 178, 203
Paulus, N., 200
Pegna, Francesco, 178
Peleo, Evangelista, 194
Pellizzaro, Niccolò, 23, 24, 183
Peloza, M., xxii
Peltrara, Lucia, 33, 34
Perchta (or Percht), xx, 40, 42, 44, 45, 54, 57, 187–91
Percoti, Giovanni, 202
Peresut, Narda, 79, 80
Persephone, 186
Petricci, Bastian, 80, 81
Petrocchi, M., 199
Pettazzoni, R., 182
Peucer, Caspar, 31, 186
Peuckert, W. E., xix, 174, 180, 187, 188, 191, 192, 195, 201
Picciola, Giovanni della, 196
Piero di Cecco of Zuz, 155
Piero, 'the sorcerer', 82
Pietro Martire da Verona, 106, 107, 110, 113, 129, 130
Pietro Veneto, 179
Pius II, pope, 190
Placucci, M., 179
Pola Falletti di Villafalletto, G. C., 185
Polissena of San Macario, 19, 35, 180
Pontenuto, Giovan Giacomo, 128
Ponzinibio, Giovan Francesco, 178
Porta, Pio, 119, 127
Pradiola, Paolo, 163
Prampero, Cristoforo di, 185
Prosperi, A., 181

Raimondi, Marc' Antonio, 189
Raimondi, Raimondo, 147, 150
Rapp, L., 188
Refort, L., 174
Regino of Prüm, 40, 187
Reinach, S., 184
Reinsberg-Düringsfeld, O. von, 191
Riegler, F., 180
Riezler, S., 174, 188
Rodaro, Domenico, 76, 77
Röder von Diersburg, F., 189
Romàn Ros, M., 188

Rosamani, E., 174
Rotaro, Pietro, 1–5, 19, 27, 147–9, 151, 152, 159, 181
Runciman, S., 174
Runeberg, A., 174, 184, 187, 193
Russell, J. B., xiv, 173

Sabbata of Faedis, 136
Saitta, A., xxii, 201
Sambin, P., xxii
Samuel, Hebrew prophet, 194
Sanuto, Marino, 187
Satia, 40, 42, 44, 54
Saul, king of Israel, 194
Savorgnano, Mario, 103
Schacher von Inwil, J., 188, 191
Schönbach, A. E., 188
Schwartz, E. von, 183
Schwartz, W., 184, 197
Scribonius, Wilhelm Adolf, 192
Seelenmutter of Küssnacht, 52, 56
Segala, Domenico, 203
Selga, 51, 54, 190
Serafino, named in a trial, 160
Sforza, Evangelista, 36
Sgabarizza, Bartolomeo, 1, 2, 4, 5, 14, 24, 147, 148, 150–3, 156–8
Sidney-Hartland, E., 193
Silenus, 45, 46
Simon di Natale, 149
Sinistrari d'Ameno, L. M., 127, 201
Sion, Giovanni, 107–14, 118
Skeistan, peasant of Lemburg, 29
Snell, O., 180
Sochietti, Caterina, 133, 134, 201
Soldan, W. G., 200
Soppe, Michele, 114–33, 137, 199
Spee, Friedrich von, 119
Spielmann, K. H., 181, 195
Spina, Alfonso, 190
Spina, Bartolomeo, 177, 178, 180, 197
Spizzica, Martino, 157
Stefano of Gorizia, 157
Stiglmayr, E., 174
Stöbwer, A., 189
Stöcklin, Chonradt, 52–4, 56
Strömback, D., 174
Summagotta, Giovanna, 143, 203

Taddeo of Mortegliano, 195
Tamborra, A., xxii
Tamburlino, Giambattista, 75–7
Tartarotti, Girolamo, xviii, 174, 200
Tazotta, Ursula, 101
Tech, Giacomo, 96
Tedeschi, J., 200
Tejado Fernandez, M., 174
Tenenti, A., 192, 194
Terencano, Giovanni, 115
Terenzia, named in an Udinese trial, 34
Testa, cardinal, 192
Thaler, J., 190
Thiess, the werewolf, 29–31
Thorndike, L., 199
Tiamat, 184
Tietze-Conrat, E., 189
Tin of San Lorenzo, 83
Tirlicher, Paolo, 155
Titone, Battista, 202
Tivarutio, Bonaventura, 151, 167, 171, 203
Tobia, Domenico, 120, 121
Toffolo di Buri, 69–71, 73, 78, 197
Torrean, Pietro, 202
Torsi, Sestilia, 135, 201
Tostado, Alfonso, 17, 180
Tranquille, Giovanni Battista delle, called Titone, 143
Trevisana, Marietta, 81
Trevor-Roper, H. R., xiv, 173

Uberti, Cipriano, 200

Valento, Giambattista, 82
Valento, Maria, 82, 83
Vendramin, Francesco, 101
Ventura, A., 177
Venturi, F., xxii
Venus, 43–5, 51, 55, 56, 191, 192
Verdena, Giuliano, 49–51, 190
Verga, E., 185, 188, 198
Vico, Domenico, 89, 196
Vidossi, G., xxi, 174, 175
Vignazio, Giandomenico, 102
Vincenzo da Brescia, *see* Arrigoni, Vincenzo
Vincenzo dal Bosco del Merlo, 101, 103
Violante, C., xxii
Virgil, 46, 189
Vivaruccio, Bonaventura, *see* Tivarutio, Bonaventura
Vojnovic, K., 203

Walch, Jakob, 52, 53
Waschnitius, V., 187, 188, 190, 191
Wasserschleben, F. G. A., 187
Weisbach, W., 189
Weiser-Aall, L., xx, 174
Weyer, Johann, 21, 119, 192
Widman, Georg, 192
Wlislocki, H. von, 184
Wuttke, A., 183

Zachariae, T., 179
Zamparia, Domenica, 93
Zan de Micon, 160
Zanetin, 50, 63
Zanutti, Valentin, 62
Zingerle, I. V., 190–2
Zorutti, Pietro, 68, 193
Zorzi, Alessandro, 143
Zorzi, Antonio, 71